Tayeb Salih

Middle East Literature in Translation
Michael Beard and Adnan Haydar, *Series Editors*

Tayeb Salih

Ideology and the Craft of Fiction

Waïl S. Hassan

Syracuse University Press

First Edition 2003
03 04 05 06 07 08   6 5 4 3 2 1

Mohamad El-Hindi Books on Arab Culture and Islamic Civilization are published
with the assistance of a grant from Ahmad El-Hindi.

The paper used in this publication meets the minimum requirements of
American National Standard for Information Sciences—Permanence of
Paper for Printed Library Materials, ANSI Z39.48–1984.∞™

Library of Congress Cataloging-in-Publication Data
Hassan, Waïl S.
Tayeb Salih : ideology and the craft of fiction / Waïl S. Hassan.—
1st ed.
p. cm.—(Middle East literature in translation)
Includes bibliographical references (p.) and index.
ISBN 0–8156–3013–1 (alk. paper)—ISBN 0–8156–3037–9 (alk. paper :
pbk.)
1. Salih, al-Tayyib—Criticism and interpretation. I. Title. II.
Series.
PJ7862.A564 Z69 2003
892.7'36—dc22   2003017681

To My Parents

Waïl S. Hassan is an assistant professor of English at Illinois State University, teaching courses in comparative literature, postcolonial studies, and literary and cultural theory. He holds advanced degrees in English and comparative literature from the American University in Cairo and in French and comparative literature from the University of Illinois.

Contents

Preface

MORE THAN A QUARTER-CENTURY AGO, the prominent Egyptian critic Ali al-Ra'i wrote: "Tayeb Salih is one of those writers who come upon us stealthily while the books are arranged on the shelves, the paintings hang on the walls, and each statue is in its place . . . We welcome those visitors cheerfully and rejoice in them, but discover, after they leave, that they have stolen something precious from us. They have taken away our peace of mind and made it imperative for us to reconsider everything and to rearrange the books, paintings, and statues. That is because Tayeb Salih is not only a new writer; he is also a new dimension" (1976, 101–2). Normally, it would not have been easy for a new Sudanese writer who had published two slender volumes in Beirut while living in England to capture the spotlight in Cairo, the Arab world's cultural center, where the literary scene was crowded with such towering figures as Tawfiq al-Hakim, Yahya Haqqi, and Naguib Mahfouz, and talented younger writers like Salwa Bakr, Seham Bayumi, Fathi Ghanim, Gamal al-Ghitani, Sun'allah Ibrahim, Yusuf Idris, Ihsan Abd al-Quddus, Nawal al-Saadawi, Yusuf al-Siba'i, Yusuf al-Qa'id, Latifa al-Zayyat, and others. Salih, however, rapidly rose to prominence on that scene: a seminal collection of essays by leading Arab critics hailed him, in 1976, as "'abqari al-riwayya al-'arabiyya" (genius of the Arabic novel).

Salih's marginality was one reason for the originality of the "new dimension" he added to modern Arabic literature. As a Sudanese, he came from a liminal place where the Arab world merges with black Africa, and he wrote as an immigrant in London. His fictional village of Wad Hamid in northern Sudan represents the complexities of such a location: situated between the fertile Nile valley and the desert, inhabited by peasants and nomads, and crisscrossed by blacks, whites, and browns. Its religion, "popular Islam," is a mixture of orthodox Islamic, Sufi (mystical), and animist beliefs. The village is beset by tensions that have defined Arab modernity since the nineteenth century: between old and new, science and superstition, tradition and modernity. As an Arab African immigrant in England, Salih could write about the colonial metropolis from a vantage point inaccessible to Levantine Arab intellectuals, since he understood English society better than his Arab peers who returned home (often dazzled) after studying in Europe, and he also felt the predicament of the native there more intensely than they did, both as an African and as an Arab. Such a unique perspective ensured that his enormous talent would produce the most powerful representation yet of colonial relations, at a time when the contradictions of Arab discourse on modernity were reaching a crisis point. Commenting on his success, Salih said, "I have redefined the so-called East/West relationship as essentially one of conflict, while it had previously been treated [by Arab writers] in romantic terms" (LAUB 1980a, 16). Those writers' "fascination with the West," as Salih calls it elsewhere (IM 1976b, 129), is one aspect of the deep ambivalence of Arab attitudes toward Europe during the past two centuries. And despite the potentially polarizing view he himself expresses, Salih's novels and short stories not only debunk Western stereotypes about Arabs and Africans, but also undermine the dominant Arab ideologies of modernity and discourses on cultural identity.

This is, then, a book about the ideologies of Arab resistance to colonialism and imperialism in the nineteenth and twentieth centuries, focusing specifically on the 1950s, 1960s, and 1970s, the decades when Salih, who was born in 1929, wrote the majority of his fiction. This period witnessed the decolonization of Arab states, the rise of pan-Arabism, and the escalation of the Arab-Israeli conflict. It also witnessed the modernist movement in Arabic literature at the hands of a new generation of writers, Salih being an outstanding figure among them. Those writers were driven not only by the anxiety of influence vis-à-vis the generation of literary giants preceding them, but also were nourished by the euphoric triumphalism of Arab nationalism, only to see it collapse in the June war of 1967. Throughout that period and until now, Salih has lived in England but always maintained close contacts with the Arab world. Born to a family of Muslim religious teachers and a graduate of colonial schools, he has a firm grounding in both Arab Islamic and European cultures, and his work explores the consequences of their renewed contact in modern times.

In another respect, this is also a study of the development of one of the most gifted artists of his generation and of the fictional world he creates. Most of Salih's texts are episodes in a continuous narrative that I have called the Wad Hamid Cycle (after the fictional village of Wad Hamid which is the principal setting). Although critics have studied them as self-contained texts, the continuities among these novels and short stories run deeper than the circumstances of identical setting and characters suggest, and are rooted equally in the development of Salih's craft and in the unfolding of contemporary Arab history and intellectual discourse. Salih published a number of short stories during the 1950s, which were collected and republished in one volume with the novella "The Wedding of Zein" ("'Urs al-Zayn") in 1962. *Season of Migration to the North* (*Mawsim al-hijrah ila al-shamal*) followed in 1966, and the two parts of *Bandarshah* (*Bandar Shah: Dau al-Bayt* and *Maryud: al-juz' al-thani min Bandar Shah*) first appeared in 1971 and 1976 respectively. Two more short stories followed: "The Cypriot Man" ("Al-rajul al-qubrusi") in 1973 (revised and republished in 1976), and "A Blessed Day on the Coast of Umm Bab" ("Yawm mubarak 'ala shati' Umm Bab") in 1993. In tackling the questions of cultural memory and identity, the impact of the West on Arab societies, the relationship between modernization and traditional belief systems, social reform, legitimate political authority, and the status of women, these texts address the social, cultural, and political upheavals of their times. In studying the evolution of Salih's narrative art, my intention is ultimately to elucidate and to assess the ideological project of the Wad Hamid Cycle.

That project is rooted in the discourse of the Arab *Nahda* that sought, in the early nineteenth century, to rebuild Arab civilization after centuries of decay under the Ottoman Empire and to confront the threat of European imperialism. The *Nahda* attempted to weld together two elements: Arab Islamic heritage on the one hand, and modern European civilization, especially its scientific and technological achievements, on the other. Far from conceiving the two as contradictory or incompatible, *Nahda* intellectuals regarded the second as the natural extension, if not the proper offspring, of the first, particularly in view of the scientific advances that medieval Arab civilization had produced. Therefore, the project of the *Nahda* consisted in selectively synthesizing the material advances of Europe and the spiritual and moral worldview of Islam.

However, this conciliatory vision became more difficult to sustain when Europe eventually began to colonize parts of the Arab world in the late nineteenth century, and especially after the defeat of the Ottoman Empire in World War I and the betrayal by the European powers of the Arab revolutionaries who had assisted Europe in the war in exchange for the promise of independence. Arab resentment deepened in the face of the Balfour Declaration of 1917, which promised the establishment of a Jewish national home on Arab land, and of Western support for the State of Israel after its establishment in 1948. At this juncture, the progressive discourse of the *Nahda* fostered the ideology of nationalism, and the pluralistic vision of cultural and civilizational regeneration came to be embodied in the ideology of pan-Arabism and its antagonistic stance toward the West. The collapse of this ideology in 1967 spelled a profound identity crisis that resonated at all levels of Arab consciousness and called for new ways of conceptualizing the past, present, and future—even while it further solidified essentialized notions of Self and Other, East and West.

Thus in a more general way this is also a book about boundaries and identities. In the turbulent decades that give the Wad Hamid Cycle its temporal frame, the contours of personal, cultural, and civilizational identity shift, sometimes violently, within a complex matrix of social values, traditions, institutions, power relations, personal choices, new ideas, and outside pressures. Colonization and decolonization involve the drawing and redrawing of cultural and geopolitical boundaries, mobilizing in the process an array of national and religious feelings.

But within those sweeping historical movements individual lives unfold. Human beings suffer the traumas and pressures of continuity and discontinuity, both within and across social and cultural boundaries. Salih's fiction vividly portrays such dislocations, lending a human face to otherwise abstract historical processes, and allowing a vision of human community based on greater justice, peace, and understanding, rather than on rigid boundaries jealously guarded by antagonistic communities.

The introduction maps the dominant Arab ideologies of modernity and outlines the critical methodology used in analyzing Salih's fiction. Chapter 1 focuses on Salih's early short stories of the 1950s, which present the major themes and techniques (some in embryonic form) of the Wad Hamid Cycle as a whole. In chapter 2, I argue that the novella "The Wedding of Zein" is a utopian text whose idyllic vision of harmony and social progress, unanimously celebrated by critics, hardly disguises the tensions of modernity inherent to the project of the *Nahda*. Those tensions deepen and explode in *Season of Migration to the North,* a text that to my mind prefigures the crisis of consciousness of 1967. Here, the happy marriage of Western and Arab civilization that the *Nahda* envisioned gives way to the brutality of colonial violence and the nightmare of social disintegration. Chapter 3 analyzes the novel as an anticolonial text that undermines the authority of colonial discourse in the work of European writers; as a critique of the perceptions of East/West relations in Arabic narrative discourse; and as an interrogation of the discourse of the *Nahda* and its recent ideological manifestation. In chapter 4, I read the unfinished novel *Bandarshah* and the short story "The Cypriot Man" as paradigmatic of what Elias Khoury calls the "new writing"—the avant-garde's attempt to forge a new historical consciousness in the aftermath of the collapse of the nationalist project. In *Bandarshah,* Salih engages the seminal texts of classical Arabic literature in an attempt to create a new style that gives full expression to the state of dissolution experienced throughout Arab societies. In the conclusion, I discuss the short story "A Blessed Day on the Coast of Umm Bab" and consider Salih's abandonment of *Bandarshah* in favor of literary journalism.

I could not have completed this book without the contributions of a great many people. I am grateful for the invaluable insights of all those who have read, in part or in whole, commented on, or discussed the book with me over the years: Evelyne Accad, Charles Batson, Nancy Blake, Christopher Breu, Chester J. Fontenot, Elnour Hamad, Mustapha Hamil, Lahoucine Ouzgane, Michael Palencia-Roth, Tayeb Salih, and Zohreh Sullivan. I also wish to thank Mary Selden Evans of Syracuse University Press for her strong and unflagging support; my wife, Stephanie Hilger, for her patience, companionship, and textual support; and my parents for much else. The generosity of those who have contributed to this book is not an endorsement on their part of the views I express here, the responsibility for which, as well as for all error, rests solely with me.

An earlier version of part of chapter 3 appeared in *Men and Masculinities* 5, no. 3 (January 2003):311–26. Permission to reprint selected passages from *The Wedding of Zein and Other Stories* (copyright © 1968 by Tayeb Salih and Denys Johnson-Davies) and from *Season of Migration to the North* (copyright © 1969 by Tayeb Salih and Denys Johnson-Davies), both by Tayeb Salih, has been granted by Lynne Rienner Publishers, www.rienner.com; all rights reserved. Permission to reprint selected passages from *Bandarshah* (copyright © 1996 by UNESCO Publishing), by Tayeb Salih, has been granted by Kegan Paul International, www.demon.co.uk/keganpaul; all rights reserved.

A Note on Translation and Transliteration

SINCE THIS BOOK IS INTENDED primarily for an English-speaking audience, I have, for the most part, used English translations of the titles of Salih's works in discussing those works. However, I have included the original Arabic title of each on first reference, and the original editions in Arabic are listed in the References. Parenthetical text citations refer to the English-language translations of Salih's works except where no published translations exist. The two parts of *Bandarshah* (*Bandar Shah: Dau al-Bayt* and *Maryud*), which were originally published as separate volumes in Arabic, are combined in one volume in the English translation. Abbreviations of *Dau al-Bayt* and *Maryud* are used in text citations, but page numbers refer to the published translation, *Bandarshah*. Where no published translation is listed in the References, translations from Arabic and French are mine.

Names are rendered in the form used by those who bear them. In the case of Salih's first name (Tayeb, al-Tayyib), I have chosen the form appearing on the cover of his books in English. Names of characters in Salih's fiction are rendered as they appear in the published translations, except for names where an apostrophe incorrectly indicates a glottal stop rather than an 'ayn (e.g., Sa'eed is changed to Sa'eed). In all other cases, I have used a simplified version of the transliteration system of the *International Journal of Middle East Studies*, without diacritical marks.

Abbreviations Used in Referencing Salih's Works

B	*Bandarshah* (English translation)
"BDCUB"	"A Blessed Day on the Coast of Umm Bab" (Arabic original; see "Yawm mubarak 'ala shati' Umm Bab")
"CM"	"The Cypriot Man" (English translation)
DB	*Bandar Shah: Dau al-Bayt* (Arabic original)
"DPS"	"A Date Palm by the Stream" (English translation)
"DTWH"	"The Doum Tree of Wad Hamid" (English translation)
"HD"	"A Handful of Dates" (English translation)
IM	Interviews in *Al-Tayyib Salih: 'abqari al-riwaya al-'arabiyya*, edited by Muhammadiyya et al.
"ISC"	"If She Comes" (Arabic original; see "Idha ja'at")
LAUB	Lecture at the American University in Beirut
"LE"	"A Letter to Eileen" (English translation)
M	*Maryud* (Arabic original)
"P"	"Preliminaries" (Arabic original; see "Muqaddimat")
RTS	*On the Road with Tayeb Salih: Outline of an Autobiography* (Arabic original; see *'Ala al-darb ma'a al-Tayyib Salih: Malamih min sira dhatiyya*)

"SIWG"   "So It Was, Gentlemen" (Arabic original; see "Hakadha ya sadati")

SMN   *Season of Migration to the North* (English translation)

TSS   *Tayeb Salih Speaks: Four Interviews with the Sudanese Novelist* (English translation)

"UIWH"   Unpublished interview by author, July 2002

WZOS   *The Wedding of Zein and Other Stories* (English translation)

Tayeb Salih

Introduction

CUSTOMARILY, 1798 is cited as the beginning of the modern era in the Arab world. That year, in a remarkably pristine instance of imperial harnessing of power and knowledge, Napoleon Bonaparte arrived in Egypt at the head of an army of occupation that included a legion of scientists who were to compose the monumental *Description de l'Égypte*. It has since become an intellectual habit, both in Europe and in the Arab world, to divorce the colonial from the scientific mission, recasting the latter in terms of advantages or gifts compensating for the naked aggression of the former. The French government recently demonstrated this tendency through its nostalgic, year-long bicentennial celebration of the French Expedition, which included naming 1998 "L'année de l'Égypte," and presenting an exhibition bearing the innocuous title "Les savants en Égypte." [1]

This divorce has also marked Arab responses to modern Europe. The superior military power of the French made plain the need for modernization, which for Egypt's Ottoman ruler Muhammad Ali consisted mainly of rebuilding the army and acquiring modern European sciences. In 1826 he sent the first student mission to France—some forty Turkish, Georgian, Kurdish, Armenian, and Circassian young men, accompanied by a twenty-five-year-old Egyptian cleric who was to be their imam. One can say that the discourse of the *Nahda* began in 1834, the year this young graduate of al-Azhar, Cairo's ancient bastion of religious learning, published a monograph titled *Takhlis al-ibriz fi talkhis bariz*. [2]

---

1. Sponsored by the Muséum national d'histoire naturelle, March 11-July 6, 1998. Of course, imperialism has always depended, then and now, on suppressing the imbrications of power and knowledge from its discourse so that it can function efficiently, as evidenced today by the various expressions of colonial nostalgia in such cultural organizations as "Commonwealth" and "Francophonie."

2. Literally, "The extraction of gold in the description of Paris." The strangeness of the title reflects literary conventions that required not only titles but also prose to include rhyme, word play, and other rhetorical embellishments (*takhlis* and *talkhis, ibriz* and *bariz*)—something that has been recognized, even by Tahtawi himself, as a sign of decadence. Nevertheless, the editors of a recent edition of Tahtawi's book observe more than that in the title. Pointing out that the word *bariz* ("Paris"; since the Arabic alphabet contains no *p, b* serves as a substitute) had already been in use in Arabic before Tahtawi wrote it with a *z* rather than an *s*—*bariz* rather than *baris*—they see in

Rifa'a Rafi' al-Tahtawi (1801–73) was thus the first Arab intellectual to become acquainted with modern Europe through travel and study. During this first season of migration to the north (to identify the archetypal precedent of many real and fictional journeys, including Tayeb Salih's novel), Tahtawi studied the French language; observed French society, manners, and institutions; read Racine, Madame de Sevigné, Voltaire, Montesquieu, Rousseau, and other Enlightenment writers; conversed with many French intellectuals and Orientalists, including Sylvestre de Sacy and Edme-François Jomard; and returned home to write what was in effect his own *Description de France*. This journey made a powerful impression on Tahtawi and inspired him, on his return in 1831, to devote the rest of his life to translation, educational reform in his country, and teaching a generation of intellectuals who would later become the leaders of the *Nahda*. Yet, remarkably, Tahtawi underestimated the significance of the French occupation of Algeria in 1830, and failed to notice the links between the accomplishments of modern European civilization and Europe's imperial designs on not only the Arab world but the whole world. In other words, he failed to recognize the mutual imbrication of power and knowledge, which had crystallized merely three decades earlier in the French Expedition in Egypt.

Tahtawi's seminal book and the reform program it proposed were both "postcolonial" and "precolonial." Published three decades after the French were expelled from Egypt in 1801, and five decades before the British occupation in 1882, the book was addressed to readers for whom Europe was highly ambiguous. Europe was their old foe of the Crusades, certainly, but it was not an invincible one; indeed, Egyptians believed that they had defeated the French invaders in 1801. They were "free . . . of the inferiority complex which plagues those who are defeated vis-à-vis their enemy" (Abu Zayd 1995, 28). Nor was Europe perceived as the imperialist colonizer that France was to become for 'Abd al-Qadir al-Jaza'iri in Algeria in the 1840s, Britain for Ahmad 'Urabi in 1881–82 and Sa'd Zaghlul in 1919 in Egypt, or Italy for Omar al-Mukhtar during the 1910s and 1920s in Libya. For Tahtawi, Europe was only a rival with expansionist tendencies—which was nothing new, of course, in the long cultural memory of Arabs—a formidable rival that had recently acquired new strength through scientific discoveries and reformed social institutions. Tahtawi and his readers marveled that such properly "Islamic" things—for they hearkened back to the contributions their Arab Islamic civilization had made to the various natural and human sciences nearly a millennium before—were now the reserve of a

---

Tahtawi's deliberate modification of the word a clue to his attitude toward French culture and toward European civilization in general, an attitude that lies at the heart of his vision of reform: the ideas, institutions, culture, and civilization of Europe are not models to be blindly imitated, mimopted wholesale; instead they are to be adapted to the needs, condition, and ultimately ional worldview of Islamic society (Allam et al. 1993, 10).

"Christian" society (Tahtawi 1993, 65–73, 77–91). Thus Tahtawi saw no contradiction between his own religious heritage and the new sciences. Learning the new sciences was for Arabs not only a requirement for survival, but also tantamount to reclaiming what was theirs. After all, did not Renaissance Europe build on the discoveries of Muslim philosophers and scientists like Ibn Rushed (Averroës), Ibn Sina (Avicenna), al-Razi, al-Idrisi, and others? Indeed, it was from the secure ground of his solid religious training that Tahtawi was able to distinguish between what he perceived to be the virtues of modern European civilization and its evils, and more importantly—and this is the core of the *Nahda*'s program of reform—to see no difficulty in adopting only the former while rejecting the latter. From this point on, the discourse of the *Nahda* would seek to achieve this selective appropriation of European learning: reconciling or fitting together (*tawfiq*) the good things it had to offer with the culture, mores, and religious spirit of Arab society. In so doing, Arabs would be rebuilding their civilization in the way their ancestors in the early Abbasid period had built theirs—namely, by translating and learning from the Greeks, the Persians, and the Indians (Tahtawi 1993, 69–73).

Yet science and technology were not the only things Tahtawi found to admire in France. He also appreciated its city planning, its legal and education systems, the relative freedom it granted its women, and its constitution, which he translated in full and included in his book (Tahtawi 1993, 170–88). He also devoted several chapters to the revolution of 1830 (313–44), which he witnessed while living in Paris and which demonstrated to him (coming as he was from a country that had for centuries suffered under brutal and despotic foreign rulers) that a dissatisfied nation could depose its king. These themes—education, social and political reform, the status of women, the nature of legitimate authority—became the main preoccupations both of increasingly secularized *Nahda* intellectuals who looked to Europe for models, and also, by necessity, of their traditionalist adversaries, who were suspicious of change, especially that which resulted from European influence.

In the discourse of the *Nahda,* then, Europe in the middle decades of the nineteenth century did not constitute an imperial threat; rather, it was perceived as offering an opportunity for cultural and civilizational revival in the Arab world after centuries of isolation, decadence, and stagnation under Ottoman despotism. Sowing the seeds of Arab nationalism, Tahtawi actually found it possible to argue that "the French bore a closer resemblance to the Arabs than to the Turks" (Tahtawi 1993, 380). Thus, to revive their civilization, Arabs should look toward Europe and beyond the Ottomans, who had always derived the legitimacy of their rule from their posture as an Islamic state—a posture that secured the support of the traditional religious establishment within the Arab world. For Tahtawi, however, "civilized" (i.e., modern) Europe exhibited Islamic values in a way that the Ottomans did not. His student Muhammad

'Abduh would later famously say that in Europe he "found Islam without Muslims, while here Muslims live without Islam." By the time Taha Husayn published his landmark *Mustaqbal al-thaqafa fi misr* (The future of culture in Egypt, 1938), the tendency to idealize Europe was firmly established; not only that, but the colonialists' belief in the existence of an "Oriental mind" (which for Husayn meant Chinese and Japanese rather than Arab) that operated in a radically distinct manner from that of its presumed Western counterpart was no longer to be questioned. For Husayn, the issue was one of natural affinity and choice: To which "mind" did Egyptians feel a closer affinity, and which should they embrace as their own? (1938, 7). Husayn went on to argue that because of geographical proximity and the long history of cultural and commercial relations among Mediterranean peoples, Egyptians and Arabs had always been part of European, not Oriental, history, and that Kipling's dictum that "East is East, and West is West, and never the twain shall meet" should not be understood as referring to Egypt (24–26).

In all fairness to Tahtawi and his followers, one must point out that their society had for centuries been culturally besieged from without by foreign and despotic rulers, and from within by calcified, religious institutions of learning. This made it almost inevitable that they would perceive European culture as a revelation. Their eagerness to understand the secrets of Europe's strength and their enthusiasm for reform blinded them to the dual character of modern Europe. As the contemporary philosopher Nasr Abu Zayd observes,

> Europe of the mid-nineteenth and early twentieth century was colonialist and imperialist, while that Europe which Arabic thought wanted to reconcile to Islamic thought was that of the eighteenth century, Enlightenment Europe. And whereas Arabic thought believed itself to be facing one Europe that was unified by an ahistorical essence called "Progress," it could not interpret historically the contradiction between Europe's [imperialist] politics and its [Enlightenment] ideas. Indeed, Arabic thought itself became polarized: those who wanted to be assimilated into European culture and who had Enlightenment Europe in view, and those who sought to cast off the European Devil and to take refuge in Islamic identity, who saw colonialist Europe of the mid-nineteenth and early twentieth century prepare its armies and armadas to swallow up the Islamic world in general, and the Arab world in particular. (1995, 30–31)

The champions of Enlightenment Europe and the leading *Nahda* intellectuals include those whom Albert Hourani discusses in his important book, *Arabic Thought in the Liberal Age, 1798–1939*. These champions include Khayr al-Din (Tunisia), Butrus al-Bustani (Lebanon), Jamal al-Din al-Afghani (Afghanistan), Muhammad 'Abduh (Egypt), Qasim Amin (Egypt), Ahmad Lutfi al-Sayyid

(Egypt), 'Ali 'Abd al-Raziq (Egypt), Rashid Rida (Lebanon), Shibli Shumayyil (Syria), Farah Antun (Lebanon), Taha Husayn (Egypt), and many less-known others. The traditionalists are represented by the mainstream 'ulama' of the religious establishment, as well as by reformers who have advocated varieties of fundamentalism. They include the Mahdis (followers of Muhammad Ahmad al-Mahdi) in Sudan, the Wahabis (followers of Muhammad Ibn 'Abd al-Wahab) in Saudi Arabia (both these religious revival movements adopted a powerful national-liberationist political agenda), and the Muslim Brotherhood organization (founded by Hassan al-Banna) in Egypt and later in Sudan. Within each of the two main tendencies, Hisham Sharabi identifies three ideological orientations: secularism is "expressed in liberalism, nationalism, and socialism," while traditionalism is "articulated in reformist, conservative, and militant Islam" (1988, 10).

The two camps mobilized two contrasting kinds of memory with regard to Europe: the *Nahda* pointed to Europe's progression from the Dark Ages to the Enlightenment; traditionalism pointed to Europe's hostility to Islam, the Crusaders' aggression, and modern imperialism. According to Abu Zayd, this polarization in Arab discourse produced a false conception of both Arab identity and of Europe (1995, 26). In the case of the *Nahda*, the "selective," "utilitarian" approach (25) to modern European civilization on which the notions of *tawfiq* (reconciling, fitting together, synthesizing), *tajdid* (renewal), and *islah* (reform) depended was bound to bring about change on a superficial level—change that would leave social, political, and belief structures intact. Abu Zayd contends that such an approach was to some extent dictated by the circumstances of Arab society under colonialism on the one hand, and by traditionalist opposition to the *Nahda*'s project on the other; the end result in any case was that the project produced *talfiq* (fabrication) rather than *tawfiq* (35). In Sharabi's harsher assessment of contemporary Arab reality, this fabrication has taken the form of "neopatriarchy," the particular form of "modernized" Arab patriarchy that developed under the conditions of "dependent capitalism" imposed by colonialism. Sharabi dates the beginning of neopatriarchal society with the beginning of the *Nahda* (1988, 6), arguing that this kind of "distorted development" was the outcome of an alliance between imperialism as a capitalist project and traditional patriarchy, which sought to adapt itself to the modern age without losing its basic structure. In this way, traditional patriarchal institutions have been modernized and given new life instead of being destroyed. (Patriarchy is broadly understood here as a hierarchical system of subordination: at the domestic level, it involves the absolute rule of the father over the women and children in the home; at the level of states, it involves absolutist rule and the total subordination of citizens and institutions to the head of state). For Sharabi, neop neither entirely traditional nor truly modern; it is the product of change" in the Arab world.

The demise of the project of the *Nahda* in its socialist, pan-Arabist form in 1967 led, in the words of the Lebanese novelist and critic Elias Khoury, to a state of cultural "amnesia." Secular intellectuals who attempted to grapple with the crisis of ideology after 1967 include Zaki Najib Mahmoud (Egypt), Hassan Hanafy (Egypt), 'Abd Allah al-'Arawi (or Laroui, Morocco), Nawal al-Saadawi (Egypt), Farag Foda (Egypt), Hisham Sharabi (Palestine), and Nasr Abu Zayd (Egypt). Since the failure of the *Nahda*'s project, however, traditionalism has become the dominant orientation, albeit a quite diverse one that encompasses the liberal reformism of Mahmoud Muhammad Taha (Sudan) as well as the radical fundamentalism that has emerged since the mid-1970s, as exemplified by al-Jama'a al-Islamiyya (Egypt), the National Islamic Front (Sudan), and the Islamic Salvation Front (Algeria). These movements are the products of historical processes whereby Western imperialism and oppressive, dictatorial Arab governments have combined to leave the Arab people in utter frustration and despair.

What all of these ideologies—socialist, nationalist, liberal, reformist, conservative, fundamentalist—have shared since the nineteenth century is a belief in the need for social and political change. All would agree today that Arab societies have suffered grievously under Western imperialism as well as corruption and political repression at home, and that ideologies across the spectrum are fueled by this plain fact. All would also agree that resistance can only succeed if it offers comprehensive reforms. However, they disagree about both the degree and the direction of change. With the independence of Arab states in the 1950s and 1960s came state-sponsored programs of secular reform along socialist lines in countries such as Egypt, Algeria, Syria, and Iraq. In other Arab states, monarchies, and principalities—those which remained conservative or fundamentalist—modernization (i.e., development) was offered instead. As Saree Makdisi points out, those official modernization programs have been articulated in the terms originally devised by the advocates of *Nahda* (1995, 92)—that is to say, according to the principle of *tawfiq*: selective synthesis and accommodation of technology and modern institutions to essentially traditional societies, belief systems, and social structures. Those programs have been able, with varying degrees of success, to build modern roads, hospitals, schools, and so forth; but they have failed to engage the sympathies of the masses, who have been excluded from political participation by the ruling elites.

In the case of Egypt, for example, in the era between the world wars, the forces of secularism and fundamentalism worked in alliance toward the goal of national liberation; Egypt had been formally independent since 1922, but the British effectively ruled through a puppet monarchy. In 1952 the military seized power and adopted a secular socialist nationalist agenda (Nasserism). Unwilling to share authority through the parliamentary democracy that had been established in the previous decades, the regime repressed all political opposition. But so long as Nasserism carried out its aggressive socioeconomic reform program, worked toward pan-Arab unity, and maintained a tough stance toward Western imperialism and Zionism, it was seen by the masses as legitimate. Then, when it failed to deliver on all three counts, the contradictions of its own policies (socially progressive, politically repressive) were laid bare; this left an open field for the fundamentalists to rally the disillusioned masses around their cause. Nasserism's collapse at the time of the 1967 war, however, did not lead to any fundamental change in the political system—on the contrary, Sadat's policies in the 1970s actually strengthened the system by turning Egypt into a client regime of the United States. This led to Sadat's assassination; it also helped fundamentalism become a grassroots movement by the mid-1970s. Since then, fundamentalism has grown more and more militant and intolerant of opposition. This is one example of how, across the Arab world, imperialist interests have overlapped with the interests of ruling elites and helped polarize public and intellectual life. Fundamentalism has emerged as the only outlet for the disillusioned, the economically depressed, or the politically disenfranchised.

In Sudan, the democratic process began in 1953, three years before independence, when the first Parliament was formed. That country has been embroiled ever since in religious sectarian politics—in particular, of the Mahdis and the Khatamiyya. Largely, this is a product of nineteenth-century colonialism (Sidahmed 1996, 23–30). The Muslim Brotherhood emerged in Egypt in the 1930s and by 1945 was exerting influence in Sudan. In 1949 a Sudanese branch of the Brotherhood was formed (45–47). Secular forces, in the form of labor activists and Marxist ideologues among the British-educated elites, formed a party along the lines of Marxist-Leninist parties elsewhere (44–45); however, that party never took root as a social movement and remained "an exotic cult." When it was dissolved, "secularism . . . lost its position as an acceptable form of Sudanese politics" (94), so much so that efforts were made to write a constitution banning communism altogether. Nimeiri's military dictatorship (1969–85) adopted socialist and then fundamentalist policies, but these were merely strategies to consolidate his rule. The National Islamic Front, an outgrowth of the Sudanese branch of the Muslim Brotherhood, has ruled Sudan since the military coup of 1989 and has established a theocracy.[3]

Thus the debate between fundamentalists and what is now no more than a small number of marginalized secular intellectuals has become more polarized than at any time in the past on the question of social and political reform. The simple synthesis (*tawfiq*) between Western modernity and Arab Islamic heritage that the *Nahda* discourse sought to achieve seems in hindsight to have been a flawed vision. Tahtawi's heirs are now advocating a critical reevaluation of the

---

3. Abdel Salam Sidahmed's *Politics and Islam in Contemporary Sudan* offers a comprehensive account of the role of Islam in Sudanese politics in general, and of the emergence of the NIF in particular.

Arab heritage that does not sacrifice Arab identity. Traditionalism (from moderate to radical varieties) offers a simple diagnosis and a miracle cure: "return" to an idealized vision of the past in which an Islamic society flourished under an Islamic government that ruled through Islamic law (*shari'a*). From the fundamentalist discourse of Hassan al-Banna and Sayyid Qutb to the mainstream 'ulama', to political mavericks like Hassan al-Turabi and radical militants such as Omar 'Abd al-Rahman, this is the simple, irreducible truth. It is the "Islamic solution"—a political slogan in the guise of religious revivalism. Questioning it draws charges of apostasy from the religious establishment, earns the indignation of the masses, and quite possibly leads to assassination (as in the case of Foda) or harassment either by the Azhar clerics (as in the case of Muhammad Sa'eed al-'Ashmawi), or by radical fundamentalists (in the case of Abu Zayd and Nawal al-Saadawi), or even by the state and its institutions, which occasionally resort to censorship so as to appease public opinion in the name of Islam. By the same token, the same charge of apostasy provided Nimeiri's regime, in its fundamentalist phase, with an excuse to execute the progressive religious reformer Mahmoud Muhammad Taha, whom it saw as a political threat.

Such are the political, cultural, and personal stakes of progressive Arab critical discourse. Yet it is precisely this kind of critical evaluation of Arab history, heritage, and memory that gives progressive Arab intellectuals their greatest potential. However marginalized by the regime, by the religious establishment, and by the masses, those intellectuals offer a critique of Arab reality that emphasizes the values of liberty, democracy, and equality and that presents viable long-term solutions to the cultural and civilizational crisis of Arab societies, rather than short-sighted, self-interested political maneuvers and metaphysical evasions. Moreover, many of those intellectuals are capable of critically evaluating the West without the idealizing admiration of the *Nahda* or the reactionary hostility of fundamentalism—and without mimicking Western critical discourse either. Thus, for example, Abdallah Laroui does not hesitate to advocate the usefulness, in the Arab context, of the concept of historicism, even though he is fully aware of its demise in the West (1976). In the same vein, Hisham Sharabi reinterprets Marxism and patriarchy in the light of the specificity of Arab history; thus, he discards the category of class, since ideas of class, nation, and citizenship do not apply to societies organized around kinship and tribal relations (1988). For his part, Nasr Abu Zayd displaces the techniques of semiotics and deconstruction from their structuralist and poststructuralist framework in the West, and redeploys them in what is fundamentally a hermeneutical project to reinterpret the sources of Islamic law in a way that reintroduces the values of democracy, equality, women's rights, and pluralism (all goals set by the *Nahda*) into contemporary religious and political discourse (1990, 1994, 1995). And Abdelwahab Elmessiri critiques the very paradigm of secularism, which has often been uncritically borrowed from Western intellectual history and applied to Arab thought in an attempt to define a progressive kind of Islamism (1994, 1998, 2002). These critiques of fundamentalism lead neither to a wholesale appropriation of Western interpretive paradigms, nor to a postmodern sublation of difference. Instead, they pursue a dialogic investigation that moves beyond the essentialized and calcified conceptions of Self and Other that have paralyzed Arab thought in the twentieth century. Taken together, the work of these and other theoreticians constitutes a far more sophisticated version of the *Nahda*'s project of revitalizing Arab thought and culture through contact with the West—one that may ultimately prove to be the right kind of beginning, should the political climate somehow become more favorable for planting its seed.

In this book I investigate the crisis of modern Arab culture and ideology through an analysis of Salih's fiction. The notions of culture and ideology I deploy are drawn, very broadly, from materialist philosophy, although my mode of literary analysis, which is inspired by Mikhail Bakhtin's theory of the novel, does not yield a Marxist reading of Salih's text in any strict sense. The term *culture* refers to the totality of beliefs (religious and otherwise) and practices (social, political, economic) that together constitute a society's way of life. In that sense, culture includes but is not limited to Matthew Arnold's notion of it as high art, refinement, the best that has been though and wrought. Culture, broadly speaking, extends to social, political, and religious institutions as well as to what Raymond Williams calls "the practice of everyday life," and furthermore, it constitutes an arena for competing ideologies. The term *ideology* has been subject to many, sometimes conflicting, definitions, of which Terry Eagleton lists no fewer than sixteen (1991, 1–2). Slavoj Žižek usefully maps the concept "around these three axes: ideology as a complex of ideas (theories, convictions, beliefs, argumentative procedures); ideology in its externality, that is the materiality of ideology, Ideological State Apparatuses; and finally, the most elusive domain, the 'spontaneous' ideology at work at the heart of social 'reality' itself" (1994, 9).

In this study I am concerned with the first and third of those domains, rather than with the second (which is not as fully encompassed by Salih's text as the other two); at the same time, I gravitate toward the more fluid notion of "discourse." As Aijaz Ahmad points out, "[Louis] Althusser's conception of ideology simultaneously as an 'unconscious,' as a system . . . of representations,' as 'the lived relation between men and the world,' and as something which saturates virtually all conceivable 'apparatuses' in political society (the state), makes it remarkably homologous with the concept of 'discourse' as it was developed . . . [by] Michel Foucault" (1992, 38–39). I retain the concept of discourse here because it is central both in postcolonial studies (we speak of Orientalist discourse, not Orientalist ideology) and in Bakhtin's theory of the novel. As a set of assumptions and procedures that organize and generate knowledge, discourse allows us to discern heterogeneity in the cultural field in a way that ideology as an analytic lens does not. In fact—and this leads to the heart of Bakhtin's use of these terms—*discourse* is a field within which different *ideologies* compete for primacy.

This flexible framework allows the deployment both of Bakhtin's theoretical insights into novelistic discourse and of psychoanalytical categories (which are central to Fredric Jameson's and Žižek's Marxist critical practice) for the purpose of analyzing how the ideologies of modernity are represented in Salih's fiction. I will elucidate those categories and insights as the study unfolds, but some unifying assumptions are worth noting here. My use of psychoanalysis is grounded not only in the kind of materialist approach I follow here, but also in Salih's own admission that during his work on *Season of Migration to the North* he was rereading Freud (IM 1976b, 215; LAUB 1980a, 15). Thus Freud's ideas, as well as those of his interpreters—especially Jacques Lacan and Julia Kristeva—are instrumental in understanding not only *Season* but also Salih's work as a whole. However, the psychoanalytic framework cannot by itself yield a sustained and satisfactory reading of Salih's œuvre. For example, although Freud's theories on "the return of the repressed" and Oedipal conflict are indispensable to analyses of *Season* and *Bandarshah*, his ideas on the interpretation of dreams are of limited value to understanding the many dreams recounted in "The Doum Tree of Wad Hamid" and *Bandarshah*, which play their role in the context of an Islamic belief system—a system with its own formidable tradition of dream interpretation. In other words, my approach to the various (Western) theories deployed in this work is to strive to use them critically and judiciously, while assessing the horizons of their applicability to the particular context at hand.[4]

No literary theorist has paid closer or more systematic attention to the working of ideology and discourse in the novel than Mikhail Bakhtin. For Bakhtin, the novel is the only artistic form that stages the multilayered, ideologically saturated registers that make up the totality of language at any given time and place. These strata, or idioms (*languages* in Bakhtin's sense of the different social dialects such as those of the various genres—oratory, journalism, poetry, fiction, and so forth—and the various professions—lawyers, bankers, priests, politicians, and so on), always voice their particular ideologies, each of which is specific to the historical period and location that gives it a significatory context and shapes its enunciative intention. These intentions are unidirectional and monologic, since they express "specific points of view on the world, forms for

---

4. I have addressed this theoretical issue at some length elsewhere (Hassan 2002).

conceptualizing the world in words, specific worldviews" (Bakhtin 1981, 291–92). In Bakhtin's theory of language,

> there are no "neutral" words and forms—words and forms that can belong to "no one"; language has been completely taken over, shot through with intentions and accents. For any individual consciousness living in it, language is not an abstract system of normative forms but rather a concrete heteroglot conception of the world. All words have the "taste" of a profession, a genre, a tendency, a party, a particular work, a particular person, a generation, an age group, the day and hour. Each word tastes of the context and contexts in which it has lived its socially charged life; all words and forms are populated by intentions. (293)

The special significance for Bakhtin of the novel as a genre derives from its ability to stage this "heteroglossia" of language in its totality. On the one hand, the poet, according to Bakhtin, strives toward unity of voice and generally aspires to the ideal of creating his or her own poetic language: "The poet is a poet insofar as he accepts the idea of a unitary and singular language, a unitary, monologically sealed-off utterance" (296). On the other hand, the novelist's task, by definition, is to create "images of languages," artistic representations of competing sociolinguistic strata that are constantly engaged in "dialogic" interaction. The novel, therefore, is a fertile, heteroglot ground for the writer to represent different ideologies, pitting them against one another, or "translating" the one into the idiom of the other, and thereby allowing each to "come to know" itself through the other's voice. In other words, the novel is, more than any other genre, the ideal ground for staging the encounter with the Other.

The intimate connection between form and ideology in Bakhtin's theory of the novel parallels the complex relationship between conscious and unconscious thoughts in Freudian psychoanalysis. Žižek explains that relationship in terms that closely parallel the Marxist rejection of the formalist polarization of form and content; simultaneously, he problematizes the poststructuralist erasure of the distinction between them altogether: "The theoretical intelligence of the form of dreams does not consist in penetrating from the manifest content to its 'hidden kernel,' to the latent dream-thoughts; it consists in the answer to the question: why have the latent dream-thoughts assumed such a form, why were they transposed into the form of a dream?" (Žižek 1989, 11). In other words, instead of asking separate questions about form and content, aesthetics and politics, styles and themes, literature and ideology, one should instead posit these categories in dialectical relationship to each other, and ask how they determine each other. Works of fiction, like dreams, not only represent ideology in the sense of consciously transmitting or delivering it, but also enact or embody ideology through their own modes of being: their forms, techniques, narrative points of view, characterizations, and so on. My discussion of the formal aspects of Salih's fiction proceeds from this assumption.

Bakhtin's dynamic conception of the novel as a hybrid, multilayered, and dialogic genre is especially pertinent to the Arabic novel, which is after all a form imported from Europe but that is also deeply rooted the Arabic literary tradition, in narrative genres such as Qur'anic narratives, *qissa, hikaya, riwaya, ustura, khurafa, sira* (both sacred and profane), and *muwashshah*. These classical Arabic narrative genres are themselves infused with narrative motifs and techniques borrowed from the literatures of Persia and India; such influences were cemented with the adaptation and translation into Arabic of the Indian *Panchatantra* by Ibn al-Muqaffa' in the eighth century C.E., and with the tremendous popularity over the following centuries of the tales of *The Thousand and One Nights,* which have Arabic, Persian, and Indian origins. The Arabic novel, in other words, carries within it resonances of discourses that span the entirety of Arabic literary and cultural history, which stretches back to the sixth century (something that Salih's *Bandarshah* exhibits to a higher degree than any other Arabic novel), as well as resonances of the ideologies of those European novels on which it consciously models itself [5]—and sometimes parodies (in Bakhtin's sense of parody as a "double-voiced" imitation), as in *Season.* Salih's fiction also lends voice to the popular imagination of the masses both in its sober pathos and in its "carnivalesque" modes of expression, as in "The Wedding of Zein." This immense hybridization of the Arabic novel is especially pronounced in Salih's fiction because it is deeply saturated with both Arabic and European cultural traditions.

Thus what the Bakhtinian conceptions of language and of the novel allow us to see in Salih's fiction is the author's staging of the process by which, in the decades of 1950s, 1960s, and 1970s, Arab ideologies of modernity contested one another. In another respect, Bakhtin's theory allows us to describe the development of Salih's art as the process of increasing integration of layers of cultural discourse: from early monological narrative sketches to increasingly polyphonic novels where form eventually explodes when it can no longer contain the immensely rich heteroglossia of Arabic cultural discourse, as well as its profound ideological crisis. Thus if for Bakhtin the novels of Rabelais and Dostoevsky best exemplify the genre's possibilities, Salih's fiction—especially his last

---

5. Naguib Mahfouz, for example, never tires of acknowledging his debt to Balzac, Dickens, Tolstoy, and Galsworthy, among others. See Roger Allen's discussion of the early development of the novel in the Arab world (1995, 11–51).

novel—in a sense illustrates the genre's limitations. Therefore, many of Bakhtin's ideas in his "Discourse in the Novel" and in his book-length studies of Rabelais and Dostoevsky are instrumental to my task of mapping the ideological project of Salih's fiction. My purpose, however, is not, like Bakhtin, to investigate the possibilities of genre, but the ways in which Salih's fiction both represents and embodies or enacts the ideologies of modernity in the Arab world.

The Early Short Stories

Seasons of Migration

IN THE WINTER OF 1953, when he was twenty-four, Tayeb Salih arrived in London to work in the Arabic section of the BBC. Some forty years later, he commented:

> When I came to London I felt an inner chill. Having lived the life of the tribe and the extended family of uncles, aunts, grandparents, among people you know and who know you, in spacious houses, under a clear star-studded sky, you come to London to live in an emotionless society, surrounded by the four walls of a small room. There was a small heater in that room and you had to lie under a heap of blankets to feel warm. Your neighbors don't know and don't care about you. It is quite possible that when you go out, only "Good morning" would be enough, and sometimes you even get no response to that. I had an overwhelming feeling that I had left good things behind. . . . When I began writing, nostalgia for the homeland and for a world which I felt was fast disappearing dominated my work. Nevertheless, I tried not to be carried away by that nostalgia so that what I wrote didn't turn into mere contemplation of abandoned campsites. (*RTS* 1997, 15–16)[1]

Striking about this passage is the close resemblance it bears to the much-quoted opening of *Season of Migration to the North*. The autobiographical experience of physical, emotional, and cultural dislocation links the writer to the troubled central character of his fictional world. Salih's experience has been a common one among the tens of thousands of Arab youths who have migrated to the north since Rifa'a al-Tahtawi. But underlying the trauma of alienation and the powerful expressions of nostalgia and rootedness is the conviction that dislocation is a condition for cross-fertilization, and that there is no simple way to adapt tradition (metonymically represented by the pre-Islamic poetic convention of weeping at the abandoned campsite of the beloved's tribe) to the conditions of the

---

1. A reference to the conventional beginning of the classical *qasida* (ode) in which the pre-Islamic Arab poet meditates on the abandoned campsite of his beloved's tribe.

present, as *Nahda* intellectuals envisioned. For Salih, tradition is part of a cultural memory that must constantly be reinterpreted, not nostalgically fetishized and jealously guarded. Salih chose the life of an immigrant over the "life of the tribe," but—to use Gertrude Stein's metaphor—he took his roots with him, rather than merely lamenting their uprooting from their native soil. Even at its most nostalgic, the immigrant's perspective afforded him the critical distance to realize—if only intuitively at first—that the vision of unproblematic *tawfiq* (synthesis) between tradition and modernity could only lead, as Nasr Abu Zayd puts it, to *talfiq* (fabrication). This is a central idea in most of Salih's early stories, collected in *The Doum Tree of Wad Hamid: Seven Short Stories. (Dawmat Wad Hamid: sabʿ qisas)*.[2] It is also the lesson that Meheimeed, the main narrator of the Wad Hamid Cycle (identified by name in *Bandarshah*), learns in *Season*, a novel that begins with the naïve euphoria of his triumphant return home after seven years of study in England and that ends with what seems, for all practical purposes, to be his attempted suicide.

What I have called the Wad Hamid Cycle comprises the majority of Tayeb Salih's works that focus on the fictional village of Wad Hamid in northern Sudan. This setting is animated by recurrent characters, themes, and motifs. Like William Faulkner's Yoknapatawpha County, Gabriel García Márquez's Macondo, and Naguib Mahfouz's Cairo, Wad Hamid is a constant, distinct setting. It allows the novelist to foreground the local culture and show how it is affected by the tides of history. To this end, Salih depicts successive generations inhabiting the same locale. The Wad Hamid Cycle also resembles another narrative cycle, Marcel Proust's *A la recherche du temps perdu,* in that a central character remembers, evaluates, and narrates his life story and in doing so paints the portrait of an age. Like Proust's protagonist Marcel, Salih's Meheimeed is constantly engaged in recollection, reorganization, and reinterpretation of the past. Naguib Mahfouz is widely reported to have said that time is the protagonist in his Cairo Trilogy and in many of his other novels as well. Salih, in contrast, always emphasizes his preoccupation with *place,* to the extent that he likens his endeavor in *Bandarshah* to that of an archaeologist (*TSS* 1982, 31; *RTS* 1997, 121–22; LAUB 1980a, 16). Of course, in the work of both writers time is the fourth dimension of space; much the greater part of Mahfouz's fiction is defined

---

2. Salih's seven early short stories were first collected in one volume in Arabic in 1962, together with the novella "The Wedding of Zein," as *The Wedding of Zein and Seven Short Stories.* Before 1966, some of the short stories were published in Sudanese and Lebanese magazines, as well as in English, German, French, and Italian translations. In 1968, two short stories, "The Doum Tree of Wad Hamid" ("Dawmat Wad Hamid") and "A Handful of Dates" ("Hafnat tamr"), were published with "Wedding" in an English translation as *The Wedding of Zein and Other Stories by Tayib Salih.* In subsequent editions, the short stories were published in Arabic by themselves under the title *The Doum Tree of Wad Hamid: Seven Short Stories.*

by its Cairene setting, and the Wad Hamid Cycle would have been inconceivable without the pivotal role of history and memory in it. Mona Takieddine Amyuni observes that "as the *place* is a constant focal point in the fiction of Tayeb Salih, the *out of place* is another constant of his imaginative world" (1985, 24). Salih's early short stories, written between 1953 and 1962 and collected in *Dawmat Wad Hamid: Sabʿ qisas* (The doum tree of Wad Hamid: seven short stories), fall roughly into two groups, which can be described as coming under the two rubrics of "place" (the village of Wad Hamid) and the "out of place," which is always the north (London, Cairo, Beirut, or Nicosia). Of course, "place" and "out of place" are also metaphorical ways of describing psychological, cultural, and historical dislocations.

The first group includes four stories—"Preliminaries" ("Muqaddimat"), "A Letter to Eileen" ("Risala ila Eileen"), "So It Was, Gentlemen" ("Hakadha ya sadati"), and "If She Comes" ("Idha ja'at")—and treats the relations between south and north. In these stories, Sudanese characters are displaced physically, socially, or psychologically. These stories are not part of the Wad Hamid Cycle since they are not set in the village and since none of their characters reappear in subsequent works; they are clearly experimental—drafts and sketches for the highly complex characters and situations of *Season*. Most importantly, they dramatize—however monologically in this early stage of Salih's development as an artist—one of the central notions that, according to Salih, mediate the relationship between south and north, namely, *wahm,* or illusion. Salih has said that while planning and writing *Season,* he

> was pondering the idea of the illusory relationship [*ʿalaqa wahmiyya*] between our Arab Islamic world and Western European civilization specifically. This relationship seems to me, from my readings and studies, to be based on illusions [*awham*] on our side and on theirs. Illusion colors our self-perception, what we think of our relationship with them, and their view of us as well. Western Europe has imposed itself and its civilization on us . . . for a long time and become part of our cultural and psychological makeup whether we like it or not. (IM 1976b, 125)

Readers with access to Salih's writing in Arabic will find that *wahm* (pl. *awham*) is a recurrent word-concept; readers of his works in translation will notice the frequency of words, images, and metaphors capturing the notion of *wahm,* such as "illusion," "mirage," "disguise," "lie," "fabrication," and "phantom." Such words undermine homogenized identities and pave the way for ones that are dialogically conceived—hybrid, interdependent, symbiotic, and mutually determining. Salih's characters are dramatizations of identitarian "illusions": they self-consciously stage themselves as role players in a historical and cross-cultural drama, one that each of them perceives from his or her own eccentric point of view.

These narratives also, like that of *Season,* cast the relationship between north and south in terms of sexual quests and metaphors. Desire for the north becomes desire for the European woman. Except for Baha' in "If She Comes" and Mustafa Sa'eed in *Season,* most of the southern male characters populating Salih's narratives are looking not simply for casual relationships, but for love and marriage. In the chapter on *Season* I will discuss at some length the central role of colonial power relations in sexualized and racialized perceptions of Europe. Suffice it here to point out that the romantic quest for love and acceptance by the Other in the shorter narratives bespeaks, on the one hand, the sexually mediated desire for assimilation into metropolitan culture, and on the other hand, the frustrations of young people in sexually conservative societies.

"If She Comes" is a satirical treatment of the fascination with the West and of some of the "illusions" associated with it. Three urban youths attempt to capture some of those illusions by establishing a travel agency that bears the ridiculously grandiose name The International Agency for the Arts of Tourism. The title phrase concludes the narrative without offering any closure. It expresses the hopes of Baha', one of the three, that the Swedish girl he has met earlier in the day and persuaded to see him that evening will actually show up. Everything for him seems to hinge on the phrase "if she comes." Upon that "if" also hinges the fate of Amin and Sana': if their tourist agency were to succeed (and they have not the slightest notion of how to ensure that), their bleak reality would be miraculously transformed into the fantasy world that each of them has fashioned for him/herself. They are helpless to realize their impossible dreams, and in a sense their failure results from the fact that, as Meheimeed puts it in *Season,* they are "lies of their own making"—but that is not all, of course, since those are also the lies of modernity.

Third-person narration is employed at every turn—even intrusively at times—to ridicule the vanity and preposterousness of the characters. The least sympathetic of Salih's third-person narrators, this one goes to great lengths to point out the discrepancy between the protagonists' pretentious dreams and their harsh socioeconomic conditions, and the fact that they remain trapped in their illusions even after their business venture fails. This is achieved monologically: by exaggerating that discrepancy, the narrative voice monopolizes the interpretation of the events in such a way as to banish all pathos from the story, never permitting the reader to sympathize with the characters. The narrator employs two devices to carry out this satiric intent. First is the somewhat heavy-handed use of direct commentary, which sometimes consists in the parenthetical use of Arabic proverbs for the purpose of derision. For example, take this description of a bookcase in the office:

a shiny book case with glass doors filled with books resembling abandoned children who have been gathered in an orphanage. For example, volume seven of the *Encyclopedia Britannica, Choice Selections from the Graceful Arts,* a book on international law by a writer called Lilienthall, *Learn Spanish in Seven Days Without an Instructor, Ibn Battuta's Travels.* And who would you think accompanied our venerable traveler? Lucretia Borgia. Volume one of the telephone directory, letters A to G. In a deserted corner, *A Woman from Rome* was alone with Mustafa Sadiq al-Rafi'i. More curiously, Sa'eed 'Aql's Rindala and Bernard Shaw's Mrs. Warren found no blame in lying side by side. (How neglected the orphans are at the tables of the miserly.) ("ISC" 1970e, 56)

A comparison of the volumes to orphans is implied in the parenthetical proverb. This is comical, although potentially pathetic, for the owners of such volumes could be said by extension to be metaphorical orphans, given their general state of cultural and historical disorientation. However, this interpretive possibility is foreclosed by direct questions—such as "And who would you think accompanied our venerable traveler?"—that force on the whole episode a sense of frivolity, and by the puerile gossipiness of the absurd insinuation that title characters are actual people performing lewd acts in public. The narration is laced with rhetorical maneuvers of this kind.

Second, all three characters are treated derisively even when their insights seem reasonable. For example, this is Amin explaining why he dislikes the preposterous name of the agency: " 'If we over-market a product, people automatically become suspicious of it. You could call it the immune system which the unconscious uses to protect the consumer.' Amin had read bits of Freud and liked to pepper his conversation with 'the unconscious' " ("ISC" 1970e, 54). Mixed metaphors of "immune system" and "unconscious" aside, Amin is right to criticize the name's pomposity; but the narrator, oblivious to the fact that an average university graduate such as Amin would ordinarily have read no more than "bits of Freud," if any at all, turns the character's utterance into another occasion for ridicule. Such is the aggressively monological force of narrative intentions in this early short story: to lay bare the extent to which this young generation is caught up in the illusions of modernity and what Salih calls the "fascination with the West" (IM 1976b, 129).

The ostentatious sign bearing the name of the agency and symbolizing the characters' *wahm* hangs "from the third floor of an old, dilapidated building" ("ISC" 1970e, 53); at the end of the story it comes crashing down into the street. The irony does not stop at the discrepancy between the pompous sign and the building sporting it, for the inside of the office is as run-down as the outside. The paint is old; insects are crawling on the walls; the rug has seen better days; the bathroom is out of order. Yet the entire budget of the agency has been spent on furnishing the office with the sign, an air conditioner, a telephone, and a bookcase. The haphazard collection of books randomly juxtaposes different discursive registers that are never dialogically engaged in the story: from the travel narrative of a fourteenth-century Arab explorer to a lone volume of the *Britannica,* a tourist word book, international law, modern Arabic poetry, and an incomplete telephone directory. The collection demonstrates the shallowness of the three youths. Contrast this with Mustafa Sa'eed's library, which, though absurd in its lack of "a single Arabic book" (*SMN* 1969c, 137), reveals his immense erudition. The motif of books and bookshelves in Salih points to a mimicking of the colonizers: both the learned Mustafa and the three superficially educated youths are equally benighted by illusory perceptions of themselves and of Europe. The difference between them is in the degree to which they have been (de)formed by colonial education.

Amin and Baha' are recent university graduates who apparently lack clear plans for the future or promising career opportunities. The idea of a travel agency unites their purposes, for besides being potentially lucrative, it exposes them to the outside world, which to them is really only the West. Moreover, the idea of tourism is itself an expression of their desire to mimic Western modes of life. Arab history tells of great travelers such as Ibn Battuta (whose famous travelogue is "orphaned" in the bookcase); "tourism" is a parody of that past, a modern phenomenon tied to the history of capitalism as well as to colonialism, which opened the doors of the "Orient" to European travelers in the nineteenth century. Tourism is, therefore, something of an absurdity in a newly independent country—a luxury that the vast majority of people cannot afford. Thus, the financial success of the agency depends on attracting tourists to the country rather than sending tourists abroad. In other words, tourism now involves an exoticizing and commodifying of postcolonial space by the natives themselves—what Edward Said calls the self-Orientalizing of Orientals. In much the same way, Mustafa Sa'eed participates in his own exoticization in London.

Although he lacks Mustafa's self-consciousness, Baha' would exploit Orientalist and Africanist stereotypes in order to fulfill an absurd fantasy in which eroticism is mixed with exotic scenes and religious imagery:

> endless groups of tourists, like pilgrims coming from the corners of the earth—languages, costumes, hats, fezzes, rifles, wild beasts baring their fangs in the jungle, currencies of every color and shape—dollars, sterling, francs, marcs, liras. He envisioned a respectable, elegant office like a mecca surrounded by white clouds of cotton-clad pilgrims—beautiful, smiling girls, women with well-rounded bodies, mouths, necks, buttocks, and breasts. Millions of blond women thirsty for love, circling around a shining star that moves in orbits outside the boundaries of the universe: Baha'. ("ISC" 1970e, 64–65)

Mustafa travels to the north to conquer its women by means of colonial "lies"; Baha', who has never left Sudan, wants to bring them to the south through another "lie," The International Agency for the Arts of Tourism. Salih's treatment of the sexualization of colonial relations is satirical here. In the other short stories, however, it becomes more psychologically complex, and in the case of Mustafa and his English lovers that treatment becomes a troubling investigation of political, historical, and psychosexual conditions arising from colonial and patriarchal hegemony. Note that Baha' perceives Western countries (the United States, Britain, France, Germany, Italy, to tell by the currencies he thinks of) merely as potential exporters of "pilgrims" (an ironic take on Conrad's "pilgrims" in *Heart of Darkness*), that is, of "blond women thirsty for love." Note also the self-exoticizing involved in marketing tourist images of safaris, jungles, and wild animals—images that grace the walls of Mustafa's London apartment. The failure of the business enterprise does not seem to disturb Baha', for true success for him still lies ahead in meeting the Swedish girl that evening—that is, of course, "if she comes."

For his part, Amin is obsessed less with European women than with capitalism and the consumption of Western goods: "Harrods. H-A-R-R-O-D-S. A store in London. How I long to go to London and to buy a sweater from Harrods" ("ISC" 1970e, 55). This obsession accompanies a properly colonial sense of awe at all things Western. He can only assess the travel agency—and all else, for that matter—by British standards. He believes that compared to simply "Harrods," "The International Agency for the Arts of Tourism" sounds "vulgar. I believe in dignified, intelligent advertising which respects the consumer's mind, such as advertising at Harrods" (60). It was his idea to start a travel agency; he dreams of traveling the world like Conrad's Marlow:

> He remembered how The International Agency for the Arts of Tourism was born. He was reading about Henry David Thoreau's solitary life in Walden, when suddenly, for some unknown reason, he felt that strange longing. The lines in the book under his eyes turned into large, polished maps, immense blue, green, and red worlds, and he heard the humming of thousands of airplanes landing and taking off in deserts of asphalt. He actually smelled, yes smelled, perfumes and potions and medications in shapely bottles, wrapped in colored paper. They grew, bore leaf and odoriferous bloom in pharmacies without number. From this rich and fragrant world grew at once a new, fully developed idea. "Let's form a travel agency." (63–64)

Marlow's color-coded colonial map shows European spheres of influence in Africa, with blank spaces designating the parts still to be captured by Europeans. In contrast, Amin's world has already been charted. His imaginary travels in it are not an exploration like Ibn Battuta's, nor are they a conquest; rather, they are a self-abandoned wandering in a vast, colorful, technologically advanced world. The fantasmic content of his daydreams contrasts sharply with his dreary surroundings and—especially in that it is associated with pharmacies and medications—with the villagers' suspicion of things modern, including modern medicine, in "The Doum Tree of Wad Hamid." Both of the modes of life he contemplates are Western—either Romantic retreat or immersion in a capitalist phantasmagoria; for him, there is no local alternative, and local existence can be legitimated only insofar as it strives toward one of the foreign models. Note that Thoreau's text is no more meaningfully engaged here than any of the "orphaned" books; these texts are all emblems of other discourses and other worlds that are literally beyond the reach of the characters, as well as beyond any fruitful dialogic interaction. The absurd comparison of chemical products and drugs to flowers, of drugstores to gardens, and the entire romance of technology exemplified by airports and airplanes, express a desire for an imaginary, ungraspable modernity that is the colonial promise of progress and civilization. In its mimicry of the sterile Baudelairian cityscapes of steel and glass that promise an escape from the "ennui" of nineteenth-century bourgeois European life, Amin's imaginary world is not only naïve; it is a glaring parody of modernity as envisioned in the discourse of the *Nahda*.

Sana' expresses her desire for Westernization chiefly through the use of heavy makeup, which denotes a rejection of her status as a woman in a conservative, patriarchal society. She is portrayed with a great deal of sarcasm, although other female characters in Salih's fiction who are trapped in the same situation are typically dignified and sometimes tragic figures: Ni'ma in "The Wedding of Zein" ("'Urs al-Zayn"), Hosna Bint Mahmoud in *Season,* and Maryam in *Bandarshah.* Unlike them, Sana' is superficial and shallow: "She exaggerates in her use of facial powders and lipstick, and her strong perfume is inescapable. Her silk dresses make a dry, provocative, rustling sound when she walks. . . . Somehow she borders on vulgarity" ("ISC" 1970e, 54). Her family is well off; "her father is a company manager." She has contributed two-thirds of the necessary funds to open the agency (65). Unlike Baha' and Amin, Sana' never graduated; she "failed three times in the second year examinations at the university, before deciding to leave it" (54). In economic terms the travel agency matters less to her than it does to her two partners; it is, however, for her, a means to escape the life of a housewife. When she feels depressed she can almost "hear a great din in a large household and smell the odor of garlic." At such moments, "if Death appeared to her . . . she would smile at him" (66). As a woman, Sana' is trapped in a narrower existential circle than the male characters, and consequently she is better equipped than they are to make a meaningful decision: "A farce. This agency is a farce. I won't come back tomorrow. I'll return to the university, and I'm sure that this time I'll succeed" (67).

The agency never conducts any business. The telephone rings only once in an entire month, and it turns out that the caller has dialed the wrong number while, ironically, trying to reach the airport. The scene is tragicomic, but the important thing in it is the lexical parallel between its language and that which expresses Meheimeed's optimism about his own and his country's future (*SMN* 1969c, 2, 5, 112–13). In both texts, almost the same phrases and images are used to express vast hopes quickly deflated:

> Suddenly something happened, something which, in a moment outside the boundaries of time, turned the office with faded walls, the dilapidated rug, the air conditioner, the sanctuary of abandoned books into a unified whole, into something with meaning and purpose. Suddenly, it seemed as if life was still good, that not all lightning is false, that some hopes flower and bear fruit. The phone rang. Sana' jumped, Amin's mouth opened even wider, and Baha' reached with his hand to pick up the phone with a power and resolve symbolizing the determination of a whole generation to pave its way to heights beyond reach. ("ISC" 1970e, 60–61)

The language describing the hopes of "a whole generation" and the magical moment "outside the boundaries of time," like so many of Mustafa Sa'eed's and Meheimeed's impressions, proves to be a deception, a "lie," a "shimmering mirage" that beckons and frustrates—*wahm*. While Amin gloats over the destruction of the sign bearing the "vulgar name" ("ISC" 1970e, 68), his self-deprecating colonial mentality simply reaffirms itself. Baha', for his part, cannot be dissuaded from following the "shimmering mirage" that promises him the world (only, of course, "if she comes"). Except perhaps for Sana', they are trapped in their illusions.

The other narratives in this group of stories depict characters who have actually traveled to Europe. In the five brief pieces gathered under the heading "Preliminaries," (1970; originally published as "Muqaddimat" in 1962) and in the epistle titled "A Letter to Eileen" (1980; originally published as "Risala ila Eileen" in 1960), Salih tries his hand at different possible scenarios for interracial, cross-cultural love. These early sketches are variations on a romantic theme already treated by other Arab novelists such as Tawfiq al-Hakim, Yahya Haqqi, and Suhayl Idris. Later on, in *Season*, Salih would develop this theme with far greater complexity. The main interest of these pieces lies precisely in their status as "preliminaries" to the writing of that novel.

"The Test" ("Al-ikhtibar") depicts the situation that develops when the entry of a Ghanaian student into liberal circles challenges its members' convictions. The student—a blueprint for the character of Mustafa Sa'eed in Salih's later novel, *Season*—is handsome, popular, and well-spoken. The narrator implies that such a character is hard to "domesticate"; once he is "let in" across the color line, there is no telling what might happen. Mustafa "built quite a legend of a sort round himself—the handsome black man courted in Bohemian circles," regarded as "a show-piece" exhibited by those "affecting liberalism" (*SMN* 1969c, 58). Like Mustafa, the Ghanaian student becomes irresistible to women. The hostess runs away with him, an act that destroys the liberalism of her husband, a lawyer from Durban. There is no suicide or murder here, just a failure of conviction; Salih develops the theme of colonial and sexual violence in later works.

The next three sketches in "Preliminaries"—"Love Song" ("Ughniyat hubb"), "Susan and Ali" ("Susan wa 'Ali"), and "Yours till Death" ("Laki hatta al-mamat")—feature star-crossed lovers. The African characters hesitate to marry their lovers because of cultural differences, and the relationships end. The last sketch of the "Preliminaries," "A Step Forward" ("Khutwa ila al-amam"), strikes a different note from the other four, which makes it, together with "A Letter to Eileen," inconsistent with Salih's other cross-cultural narratives. In each of these two pieces, interracial lovers marry, but unlike the marriage of Jean Morris and Mustafa Sa'eed, these unions are successful. The lovers in "A Step Forward" (who get married at the same Registry Office on Fulham Road as Jean and Mustafa in *Season*), see themselves as bringing about a synthesis of north and south (what Mustafa promises Ann Hammond [*SMN* 1969c, 68]), a synthesis that produces a concrete symbol: a mulatto son who combines the facial features of his Sudanese father with those of his English mother. "This is good," opines the narrator regarding the child's hybrid features ("P" 1970f, 86). The parents name the child Sami, a name familiar in both cultures and easy to pronounce in Arabic and English. It is "a step forward," presumably, since the union undermines the north/south dichotomy.

In "A Letter to Eileen," Salih does not go so far as to envision a racial or cultural synthesis of Africa and Europe. The Sudanese character's anxiety anticipates Meheimeed's, even though there is a marked contrast between the scenes of their return. Eileen's marriage to this Sudanese takes place before he returns for the first time to his village on a month-long vacation. The letter is written on the day of his return. In the same frame of mind as the three who hesitate in the "Preliminaries," he muses:

> For eight months I'd been shirking it [marriage], expatiating at length, lecturing you on the differences which separate us. Religion, homeland and race. You're from Aberdeen in Scotland and I'm from Khartoum. You're a Christian and I'm a Muslim. You're young, cheerful and optimistic. I'm a mass of hangups. What made me fall in love with you? . . . What made you fall in love with me? I'm a strange lost wretch. In my heart I carry all the cares of my generation.

. . . You got married to . . . a disorganized turbulent East at the crossroads with
its pitilessly scorching sun. ("LE" 1980b, 76–77)

Strong notions of monolithic identities make it seem impossible to bridge cultural and religious differences. Yet even though the narrator, like Meheimeed,
feels the burden of his generation, he no longer belongs at home. His return
both prefigures Meheimeed's return to Wad Hamid at the beginning of *Season*
and contrasts with its imagery of rootedness: Eileen's husband is like "a date
palm on the bank of a river uprooted by the current and swept away far from
where it grew up." Returning to his people is endless torture: "The first night
without you. And after it thirty more nights in a row like a desert which knows
no end" (78). He experiences a profound sense of alienation when his relatives
and friends arrive to welcome him and he suddenly feels that "they were
strangers to him, and he was a stranger to them" (79). For Meheimeed, that is
the time of the greatest bliss in the entire novel, and he represses a great deal in
order to savor the "extraordinary moment when I at last found myself standing
amongst them" (*SMN* 1969c, 1). Conversely, Eileen's husband finds "horror"
in that moment. They ask him questions that he does not wish to answer. One
issue they, unlike the Wad Hamidians, certainly must have avoided is his marriage to an Englishwoman. In *Season*, after freely questioning Meheimeed about
European women, Bint Majzoub says bluntly: "We were afraid you'd bring back
with you an uncircumcised [Christian] for a wife" (*SMN* 1969c, 4).[3] Eileen's
husband would not have been addressed so casually, since by marrying a
stranger he has become a stranger himself. Meheimeed, of course, is a far more
complex character, since he is initially unaware of, and unwilling to acknowledge, his alienation.

The protagonist in "A Letter to Eileen" is a blueprint for Meheimeed in *Season*;
in the same vein, the first-person narrator of "So It Was, Gentlemen" foreshad-
ows Mustafa Sa'eed's figuration of the psychosexual dimension of racial and cultural stereotypes, as well as Meheimeed's identity crisis. As with Mustafa, this
protagonist's awareness of prejudice sharpens his perception in a way that renders him highly obsessive and paranoid. But whereas Mustafa casts himself in the
role of the conqueror and invader, this protagonist feels isolated and persecuted.
In both cases the psychic anxiety plays itself out in terms of gender relations:
Mustafa wages a sexual war against Europe, whereas his prototype desires ro-

---

3. The published translation inaccurately renders the Arabic word *"nasraniyya"* (Christian) as
"infidel." In Arabic, "infidel" (*kafir*, pl. *kuffar*) is never used to refer to Christians or Jews, who are
regarded as "People of the Book" who worship the same God of the Muslims; rather, it refers to
those who worship other gods.

mantic and sexual union with it. In fact, "So It Was, Gentlemen" is the story of how he met the woman to whom he is now happily married.

The most complex dramatization of Salih's notion of *wahm* thus far, "So It Was, Gentlemen" offers subtle insights into the dynamics of personal interaction in the context of racial, cultural, and sexual difference. The use of the unreliable narrator who betrays his own prejudices and insecurities—a technique perfected in the characterization of Meheimeed in later works—is introduced in this short story about an African dignitary at a reception in an unidentified European city. Things go awry between his anxiety at being a conspicuous stranger in a crowd he perceives to be made up of undifferentiated faces, and their self-congratulatory eagerness, which makes him increasingly uncomfortable. Misconceptions and ethnocentric biases on both sides eventually cause a violent scene. Nevertheless, an awkward *modus vivendi* is achieved at the end, one, however, that does not resolve the conflict between ethnocentric biases and monolithic notions of identity.

The journey north in this short story becomes a parody of the genre of the quest romance. The story traces the trajectory of the protagonist's journey through the crowded reception hall, where he arrives in the opening scene. He moves toward a woman he notices immediately and who is standing on the other side of the room. He has already formed a few general impressions about "people in this country," and his attraction to the young woman across the room is partly based on his mistaken assumption that she is, like him, a foreigner: "Why does this girl smile at me? Is it because I am a foreigner? Or is it because she has a large nose, big mouth, and blue eyes? People in this country like a woman with a small nose, tiny mouth, and black eyes; that is obvious from their attentions to those two girls over there" ("SIWG" 1970d, 69). Those who do not fit the stereotype belong by default to an imaginary minority of "foreigners" with whom he can identify. This imaginary solidarity encourages him to face a crowd that he likens to a "herd of sheep" (80) because they seem to look, think, and act alike, and who above all single him out as the outsider. The desired psychosexual union with Europe becomes possible when its catalyst, the girl across the room, turns out to be a semioutsider herself; but she must also— as the embodiment of desire and a figure of *wahm*—remain shadowy and insubstantial.

To reach her the protagonist must overcome a number of imaginary obstacles: "The girl stood on the other shore, a sea of trivial things separating us" ("SIWG" 1970d, 69). The "sea" and the "other shore" resonate with psychological and cross-cultural symbolism, and the trajectory of his movement across the room follows the allegorical pattern of medieval European quest romances, where the traveler (knight or pilgrim) undertakes a perilous journey in which he must overcome a number of obstacles in order to accomplish a difficult mission. As a symbol of the unconscious, the sea comes to represent hidden fears of, and anxieties toward, the Other, even though the protagonist dismisses those fears and anxieties as "trivial things." On the "other shore" is salvation and redemption. But to reach the safety of the "other shore," he must first confront those anxieties and fears. Note that Meheimeed almost drowns while crossing the river in *Season* and *Bandarshah*; both he and our protagonist undergo symbolic death in the process of crossing to the other shore; but rebirth remains abortive for both of them. Their crises, like the crisis of Arab societies in general, which these characters represent metonymically, are never completely resolved. The protagonist in "So It Was, Gentlemen" eventually reaches "the other shore" but only at the moment when he completely fails to overcome his anxieties and prejudices. Like Meheimeed, who is never able to reconcile himself to the past, this protagonist remains trapped in his *wahm*, in spite of the deceptively happy ending of the story.

Geographically, the sea separates Europe from its African colonies. Crossing the sea gives the privileged, educated native access to the colonizer's culture. Allegorically, the "sea" can be interpreted as racial and cultural prejudice (or *wahm*), which hinders cross-cultural understanding. Crossing the sea in this sense would mean attaining an understanding of others beyond cultural, racial, religious, or gender stereotypes. The "sea of trivial things" is a projection of the protagonist's own *wahm* as much as that of the people surrounding him. Like the medieval knight who must overcome monsters, evil sorcerers, enchanted castles and forests, and other formidable obstacles in order to free a maiden in distress or a captive princess, the protagonist of "So It Was, Gentlemen" must negotiate the crowd in order to reach the beautiful maiden. However, since he is an anti-hero, there is a reversal of roles here: he believes that the maiden (the safe shore) will save him from "the herd" if he can reach her. This reversal is consistent with the protagonist's fear and paranoia vis-à-vis the "herd," experienced as infantile dependence on the mother. Such dependence speaks to a problematic conception of femininity that anticipates Mustafa Sa'eed's estrangement from his own mother and his highly vexed conceptualization of gender and colonial relations in *Season*.

Five stages or obstacles face the protagonist of "So It Was, Gentlemen." He encounters the first of these as soon as he arrives at the reception:

> It was as though they had been expecting my arrival for a long while, as though they had rehearsed and prepared to meet me the way an actor prepares to meet the audience for the first time. If I was the audience, who were they? "Our country welcomes you." "Welcome, we're honored." "All of us are at your disposal." "Much obliged." "Don't you think that our country is the most beautiful one on earth?" How would I answer a question like that? I had no choice but to move my eyes from her chest to the mountain. True, the country is not

without charm—the foot of the mountain glows like fire where the calm, crystal-clear sea caresses it in the early evening hour. That is true, but to say that this is the most beautiful country on earth! "You are right, my lady. Your country is marvelous. I couldn't believe my eyes when the airplane hovered over this blaze of light! I thought, and still think, I'm in a dream." She understood what I meant, for she blushed slightly in embarrassment. I could have sworn she deliberately forced the blood into her cheeks, as if she could control the blood coursing in her veins. ("SIWG" 1970d, 69–70)

The image of the stage establishes the play of subjectivities as a performance of cultural and racial identities. Since he seems to be a prominent personality, he senses that they are putting on a show of some sort, which is also what he himself is doing. He also feels that, therefore, they must be hiding something or are themselves something other than what they pretend to be. His impressions are reinforced by their welcoming words, which clearly mark him as a stranger to "our country." Then immediately comes the ultimate implication of this sort of othering: on the hierarchy of things, "our country" (therefore also "we") is (are) best; not only do "we" deem it better than all others (yours included, of course), but "we" want "you" to confirm that. Consciously, they probably mean no offense, but they are too insensitive to hide their ethnocentricity. His diplomatic answer succeeds in conveying the gentle irony, to the embarrassment of his interlocutor.

The final observation in that passage is clearly delusional: these people—especially the women among them—seem to possess the superhuman capacity to control the flow of blood in their veins so that an involuntary reflex such as a blush must be, he thinks, a stage effect. This xenophobic fear is coupled with a masculinist attitude, which appears in his reaction to the woman's question. His gaze is fixed on her chest until she asks the naïve question, in reaction to which he turns his eyes to the sexually charged landscape scene of the mountain and the sea submissively caressing its foot. The phantasmic content of the "natural" scene defines for him the beauty of the country; it also reveals his androcentric stance. In *Season*, the scene recurs but without the symbolic veiling; the phantasmic content translates itself more directly in Mustafa's repeated description of his sexual "victories" in metaphors of reaching a mountaintop and planting a banner (which later on becomes the dagger he plunges in Jean Morris's chest); and Ann Hammond, playing what she imagines to be the part of a slave girl from *The Thousand and One Nights*, submissively kisses Mustafa's feet.

The symbolic landscape, which the protagonist finds "charming," must also be reassuring, for coupled with his fear of strangers is his fear of the feminine. He sees the hostess as a *femme fatale*, the enemy in "a silent battle . . . in which she will defeat me if I do not escape. Yet he is aware that another battle is raging inside him, that there is an "enemy" within—"the clock" ticking in his brain and "the little voice censoring his actions, without which he would "enjoy the evening, be able to laugh, flirt, and dissimulate" ("SIWG" 1970d, 71). Is the hostess then no more than a screen onto which he projects his anxiety, or is she a co-conspirator with that "little voice?" Unlike the hostess, who blushes at will, he has no control over his facial expressions, and his involuntary reflexes can betray him. The "mocking phantom" around his eyes will undermine his efforts to "laugh, flirt, and dissimulate." He is weak and divided, whereas "they"—and especially "she"—are endowed with superhuman powers.

He encounters the second obstacle when the majority's terrorizing pressure on him to conform to their ways confirms his paranoid delusions. He thinks that a drink might release some of his tension ("SIWG" 1970d, 71), yet when the host offers him a glass of whisky, he refuses. He will drink on his own initiative, not when tempted to do so by one of them. Yet this defensiveness seems justified in light of the deliberately exaggerated show of astonishment and dismay on the part of the host, who "looked at me from head to foot in amazement. 'You've lived in England for a long time, haven't you? . . . And in spite of that you don't drink?' 'Not out of piety, really. I tasted alcohol and didn't like it. I'll drink tonight if I have to' " (71–72).

That pressure takes on civilizational overtones when the point of contention is something that Christian Europe allows and Islam forbids. Accepting or refusing a drink suddenly becomes a declaration of allegiance to one camp or the other and a measure of civilizability. The host's rhetorical question implies that the guest's life in England should have cured him of his religious inhibitions, civilized him, and made him more like "one of us." Yet interestingly, the guest is less concerned about these insulting nuances than he is anxious to behave appropriately around strangers. The host calls on his wife, who threatens the guest that she will "gather the people around [him]" ("SIWG" 1970d, 72) if he does not drink—obviously a humorous threat, but in very bad taste. He gives in quickly to this pressure from the hostess.

He is as fascinated by this hostess as he is afraid of her: "I took the glass from her hand, her eyes having tempted me" ("SIWG" 1970d, 72). She reminds him of other women, or rather of a "type" of woman who combines several attributes of femininity. She is the unscrupulous seductress whose eyes encompass the sea and whose body evokes "primitive" instincts:

> Her eyes were green circled with blue like the shallow areas in the sea. . . . In my adolescent dreams, a woman like her ignited the fires of passion in my heart. In my early youth, a woman like her taught me love. A woman around forty. What a woman! A lively face, a firm, ferocious chest, and large, protruding buttocks. This woman is a primitive scream. No doubt she cheats on her husband,

then sleeps by his side at night undisturbed by guilt. If I drop my guard she'd defeat me without any great effort. ("SIWG" 1970d, 72–73)

She is an indomitable, unpredictable enemy, and she throws the third challenge in his face without warning when she says, "Your tongue is like a crimson sunset." He is stunned:

> At that, gentlemen, I swear to you, I was almost defeated by one surprise attack which came from I know not where. I had prepared myself for everything, sealed all the cracks, made my plans, and reinforced my defenses—my tawny brow, my kinky hair, my long eyelashes. But my tongue had never occurred to me, not to mention the sunset in my mouth! I staggered backwards from the force of the blow, and my interlocutor laughed, deliberately showing her even, pearly teeth, and stuck her tongue out at me. (73–74)

The elaborate compliment, which evokes exotic landscapes, is of a kind with the way Mustafa Sa'eed represents himself, and is so perceived by his English mistresses, who see him as "symbol of all [their] hearkenings" (*SMN* 1969c, 30). But the protagonist of this short story, who feels vulnerable especially to women, understands the remark not just as a violation of his dignity, but as a military attack; his African features are, for him, fortifications the enemy is attempting to breach. At that moment, however, he recalls another woman from the past—his own Jean Morris, as it were (the two women's facial features are rather similar: large nose, wide mouth, and haughty expression [*SMN* 1969c, 155; "SIWG" 1970d, 74])—who left him two years before, and whose memory still follows him at "every turn in the road" ("SIWG" 1970d, 74). The memory "rescues" him from the renewed attack by the hostess, since he, unlike Mustafa Sa'eed, understands the human cost of such exoticism (74).

Observing his vulnerability, the hostess pities him. Her relative strength and perceived ability to read his thoughts ("SIWG" 1970d, 73) qualify her for the role of mother and protector: the hostess "turned her face away from me, closed her mouth, and hid her smile somewhere. . . . At that moment, she had a mother's face" (74). As the hostess abandons the role of the *femme fatale*—or, rather, merges more completely with the archetype of the mother-prostitute— the guest's anxiety vis-à-vis the feminine is somewhat relieved (though not resolved, of course). He is now able to resume his journey toward what he perceives as salvation, the girl standing on "the other shore, [who] was watching me as if she were concerned for me" (75). However, a fourth obstacle hinders his progress:

[S]uddenly a man collided with me, a red-faced man of medium height and sturdy build. There was lewdness in his eyes and on his lips, as if he had been telling someone about a heinous act he had committed the night before. Has John Betjeman had sexual intercourse with this man?

> Business men with awkward hips,
> And dirty jokes upon their lips.

He looked at me as if he did not give a farthing about me. I had nothing to indicate my status to this man. At that moment, I was a lone foreigner. . . . It must have been out of vindictiveness that, with an arrogance I knew I possessed and tried to hide, an arrogance with which I shielded a weakness I knew was in me, I said to him, "You must be a bank or a company manager, or something like that."

Had he been like me, "something like that" would have struck him, but the first part of the question interested him more, and he said with pleasure, "Yes, how did you know?" Had I been generous, I would have humored his good spirits, but he had wronged me, and I don't forgive being wronged. "I have read John Betjeman." And while the sturdy, dull-witted man with lewd lips tried to understand, I stepped in her direction. (75–76)

This is the first time the narrator reacts aggressively, even though the offense is rather vague, if it can be called an offense at all. His aversion to and contempt for the man—whom he associates with "lewdness," "heinous acts," homosexuality, and business—prevail over the insecurity of a foreigner. To him, the red-faced man seems immoral and base, and this perception triggers the narrator's first self-assertive response. Feeling himself the object of scrutiny since his arrival at the reception, the protagonist now feels that he can fix someone else with his disdainful gaze, thereby uniting himself with the heterosexual majority. In so doing, the foreigner acquires a Self, a presence, a positivity. He can now assert his masculinity, which has so far been undermined by the scrutinizing, objectifying (or feminizing) gaze of the "people in this country" and by the real or imagined assaults of the *femme fatale*. Now somebody else can be the marginalized, despised, disreputable minority. If the guest has been the victim of racism, he is prepared to take refuge in other forms of prejudice. The guest's anxiety is heightened when the businessman unwittingly commits a "crime" by not acknowledging the stranger's "status," which may be his only concrete and incontestable (because officially documented) identity. Thus the latter's aggression is motivated not only by homophobia, intellectual snobbery, and moral superiority, but also by an outsider's anxiety and wounded pride. Not being recognized for his "status," the foreign dignitary is stripped naked of the only shield against the nonstatus of being a mere foreigner, a nonentity, someone who does not count.

At this point in the story, it becomes clear that the protagonist's reactions to the "people in this country" follow two distinct patterns according to their gender: fear and desire vis-à-vis women, and hostility toward men. With regard to women, he pursues an ideal of femininity in the figure of the girl standing "on the other shore"; yet at the same time he is ambivalent about the hostess, whom he sees in the role of the archetypal mother-prostitute. He finds the other women he meets along the way from the hostess to the presumably foreign girl (in effect, from a child's Oedipal attachment to the mother to the grown man's role as husband and father) to be a nuisance, annoying but not threatening. They all ask him the same question: Has he been to "our country" before and does he like it ("SIWG" 1970d, 76–77)? He humors their naïveté and moves on. However, confronted by men, he reacts more assertively and even aggressively. He refuses the drink from the host (the father figure) only to take it from the hostess, and is rude to the businessman, whom he considers to be a threat to his masculinity. When a third man throws the fifth challenge by asking the protagonist the same question women have been asking him, "Do you like our country?" he answers, "No" (77). By now the protagonist is drunk and lashes out against the crowd, at once exposing their self-delusions and betraying his own prejudices (78–81). For that he is punished with "a powerful punch in the jaw" from another man, an angry "blond youth" (81). Thus he drowns in the "sea of trivial things," undergoes a symbolic death, and is rescued by two women who rush to his aid: the hostess who now has a "mother's face" (82) and the prospective lover who turns out, conveniently, to be her younger sister. In this way, the romantic ideal merges with the Oedipal fantasy.

With that, the story comes to an end. The hostess blesses her younger sister's union with the narrator, and this leads to marriage. The character of the girl herself remains (in a story full of *awham*, or illusions) a shadowy confirmation of his ideal of femininity—one which lacks human substance. The protagonist's reconciliation with the female principle occurs as a regression into childhood fantasy, the reenactment of which requires the hostess to become a comforting mother and the girl (her substitute) to remain an abstract, romantic ideal. Not surprisingly, his reconciliation with the crowd must be based on "forgetfulness"—that is, on repression without resolution of conflict.

If the ending seems unconvincing, it is because it parodies happy endings—not least the happy marriage of Eastern traditions and Western science envisioned by the *Nahda*. The tensions running through the story are never resolved. The protagonist has not really crossed "the sea" of unconscious fears and cultural prejudice. If anything, he has drowned in it, much like Meheimeed at the end of *Season*, who screams for help. In this story with a violent climax, there is reconciliation at the end, but no resolution; a truce, not an end to the war of *awham*, the last word in the story. There has been a clash of stereotypes of every kind (racial, cultural, sexual, religious, professional), but no dialogue—

only forgetting, repressing, and moving on. The unsatisfactory ending acknowledges that prejudice is often repressed or hidden under a veneer of politeness (or "political correctness"), but not repudiated. In *Season,* Salih's increasingly subtle delineation of the psychology of colonialism, racism, and sexism pushes the conflict of stereotypes to its logical and devastating conclusion, while the mythical, allegorical, and archetypal overtones of "So It Was, Gentlemen" become defining features in *Bandarshah* and "The Cypriot Man."

The Wad Hamid Cycle

The stories in the second group—"A Date Palm by the Stream" ("Nakhla 'ala al-jadwal"), "A Handful of Dates," and "The Doum Tree of Wad Hamid"—are set in the village of Wad Hamid and introduce the concerns of the entire Cycle: spirituality, colonialism, resistance, tradition, modernization, patriarchy, and authority.

"A Date Palm by the Stream" is Salih's first published short story, written shortly after he arrived in London for the first time in 1953. It centers on the religious faith that helps simple villagers face adversity, and has strong echoes of the Old Testament Book of Job and its Qur'anic version (21: 83–84, 38: 42–45). "A Date Palm by the Stream" focuses on a poor peasant who finds himself forced into an exploitative business transaction with a greedy, wealthy merchant. Thus in this short story there is a battle between two very different worldviews: on the one hand is the religious or spiritual view embodied in the Qur'anic narrative; on the other hand is the cut-throat materialism represented by Hussein the merchant.

The symbolic function of the palm tree of the title is identical to that of the palm tree standing in the grandfather's courtyard in *Season*—it signifies the stability, rootedness, and strength of its owner, Sheikh Mahjoub. Furthermore, the palm has the same spiritual significance as the doum tree of Wad Hamid: it represents the soul of its owner in the same way that the doum tree represents the spiritual world of the entire village of Wad Hamid.[4] Sheikh Mahjoub would be selling his soul if he sold the palm tree to Hussein the merchant; in the same way, the Wad Hamidians would be selling the village's communal soul if they complied with the government's plans to cut down the doum tree.

The words *yiftah Allah* (may God open a way), often used to decline a business transaction, open and close the narrative. In between, these words take on a deeper, mystical meaning. The story reads like a straightforward parable: the elderly Sheikh Mahjoub has lost his wealth, as well as the companionship of two of his children—a loving, compassionate daughter who married and moved far away

---

4. This is not the same Mahjoub featured in "Wedding," *Season*, and *Bandarshah*.

with her husband, and Hassan, a son who went to Egypt five years earlier and severed his ties with his parents. The old man is reduced to penury on the eve of the Feast of Sacrifice, a time when people don new clothes and sacrifice an animal. He is tempted by a merchant (who is "a living picture of haughty arrogance" ["DPS" 1981b, 22]) to sell the palm tree, a token of God's blessing that once transformed Mahjoub's life as though by a "miracle" (22). His refusal to sell the date palm and his repeated prayers to God to "open a way" are rewarded with a letter and a gift of money and clothing from the long-absent son. The story draws a highly endearing portrait of a simple and humble man who has withstood great adversity, armed with little more than faith, courage, and dignity—qualities of the "fast-disappearing world" that Salih felt at the time that he had left behind in Sudan.

A similar situation is encountered in "A Handful of Dates," although here the spiritual victory of the religious parable gives way to profound doubt arising from an existential crisis and psychic division. Masood, like Sheikh Mahjoub, is a loving and kind-hearted man who is deeply attached to his palm trees; he believes they have a "heart" and "experience joy and suffering" and deserve to be treated with kindness ("HD" 1969b, 26–7). These values clash with those of the ruthless, materialistic merchants who take advantage of his financial need. The focus of "A Handful of Dates" shifts, however, to the effect on the little protagonist and first person narrator of a scene in which the ethic of social Darwinism clashes with the innocent idealism of his childhood. Thus the story is no longer about the metaphysics of faith, as in "A Date Palm by the Stream," but more squarely about the psycho-social world as experienced by Meheimeed in *Season*, "The Cypriot Man," and *Bandarshah*.

From a flashback in *Bandarshah* we learn that the child-protagonist in "A Handful of Dates" is Meheimeed and that his grandfather is Hajj Ahmad. The pattern of Meheimeed's narratives ("A Handful of Dates," *Season*, "The Cypriot Man," and *Bandarshah*) is always the same: progression from an initial state of peace and being at home in the world to one of profound estrangement or crisis. In the Wad Hamid Cycle, the recurrent theme of the grandfather-grandson relationship often frames concerns about the old and the new, tradition and modernity, conformity and dissent. The importance of this relationship is a function of the extended family household rather than the nuclear family as the basic social unit in rural Sudanese society. In such a household, the grandfather is the key figure of authority. In the Cycle, the grandfather-grandson relationship is ambivalent, ranging from idealization to rebellion and rejection. "A Handful of Dates" sets that process in motion for the first time.

The story is told by the adult Meheimeed, who reminisces about an incident of his early childhood. Up till then his existence has been defined by (and limited to) his grandfather's presence and the geographical fact of the village: "The strange thing was that I never used to go out with my father, rather it was my grandfather who would take me with him wherever he went, except for the mornings when I would go to the mosque to learn the Koran. The mosque, the river and the fields—these were the landmarks in our life" ("HD" 1969b, 23). By the end of the story it has become clear why the narrator's dislocating experience will eventually induce him to step outside the triangle of "landmarks" circumscribing his world. The conspicuous absence of the father as a shaping influence on the child and the powerful bond between grandfathers and grandchildren turn out to be important themes in "The Cypriot Man" and *Bandarshah*. I will discuss this at some length in chapter 4.

The three landmarks of village life cease to mark the frontiers of the boy's world. The beloved river in which he swims every morning after attending Qur'anic school is a recurring symbol in the Wad Hamid Cycle. In the opening chapter of *Meryoud,* at another crucial and traumatic childhood moment, Meheimeed will swim across the river. As a young man, the river will carry him to England and bring him back seven years later. In the final pages of *Season,* he almost drowns in the same river. At the end of "A Handful of Dates," by the river, he symbolically renounces his grandfather. The two other landmarks also become sites of psychic anxiety. The fields, "the arena for my dreams and my playground," which he has so far imagined to have "belonged to my grandfather ever since God's creation," turn out to have belonged once to Masood, the grandfather's helpless opponent in a ruthless game of power and ownership ("HD" 1969b, 25). As if this revelation were not shocking enough, the child discovers that the rules of that game contradict everything he has been learning in the Qur'anic school. The boy loves the mosque, where he is a favorite pupil: "the Sheikh always asked me to stand up and recite the Chapter of the Merciful whenever we had visitors, who would pat me on the head and cheek" (23). The boy would also recite the Qur'an to his grandfather, who was always "moved" (24). Surat al-Rahman (the Merciful) addresses both mankind and the *jinn*—the part of creation subject to judgment—reminding them of Allah's bountiful mercy; and after a brief warning to the unrepentant, the *sura* ends with a lavish description of the joys of Heaven. All of this centers on "mercy" as one of the most frequently evoked attributes of God in Islam. Yet to the boy's shock, mercy is what seems to be missing in the world of the same adults who encourage him to learn the Qur'an. This discrepancy is the first crack in the boy's image of a perfect world.

It is a fall from childhood innocence that comes about with knowledge—specifically, with the grandfather's articulation of his social philosophy for the first time. His is a self-righteous patriarchal discourse with a bourgeois ethic of "respectability" and accumulation, from which perspective his neighbor Masood is "an indolent man" ("HD" 1969b, 24). Masood, Hajj Ahmad explains to his grandchild, has wasted his inheritance on " 'women,' and from the way my grandfather pronounced the word I felt that 'women' was something terrible" (25). The boy contrasts that description with his own impressions of Masood: "I remembered Masood's singing, his beautiful voice and powerful laugh that resembled the gurgling of water. My grandfather never used to laugh" (25). The imposing stature and demeanor of the grandfather, which the boy dreams of acquiring in the future (24), now take on a different, unsavory dimension: the old man is stern and contemptuous; he despises men less powerful than himself, he despises women, and he despises the humor and beauty of life. He never laughs and has no compassion.[5] As a result, the boy feels "pity" for Masood and "fear" of the grandfather, who intends to buy up the rest of Masood's land (25).

By dramatizing the contradiction between the two modes of life, the story sets in motion the process of the young boy's ethical development. In Bakhtin's terms, the grandfather's way functions as *"authoritative discourse,"* whereas Masood's represents an *"internally persuasive discourse"* (1981, 342). These two distinct categories of discourse often conflict with each other. The grandfather's "authoritative discourse" is "religious, political, moral; the word of the father [or the Law of the Father], of adults and of teachers," the language of authority that projects a hierarchy of values and offers or withholds legitimation. Masood's "internally persuasive discourse" is "denied all privilege, backed up by no authority at all, and is frequently not even acknowledged in society (not by public opinion, nor by scholarly norms, nor by criticism), not even in the legal code. The struggle and dialogic interrelationship of these two categories of ideological discourse are what usually determine the history of an individual ideological consciousness" (342). For the boy, Masood's nonarticulated and delegitimized discourse has a pathos and a humanity that he can place within the Qur'anic discourse of "mercy." What this paradox reveals, then, is a split within authoritative discourse itself between the moral standard set by the law and the practices of its representative, the grandfather. This contradiction defines the problem of moral, social, and political authority throughout the Cycle. From this point on, the discourse of the Qur'an will play a central role in the ideological fabric of Salih's narratives as a standard that is always evoked but, with few exceptions, almost invariably ignored (as by the grandfather in this instance), distorted, misquoted (as by Wad Rayyes in *Season* [*SMN* 1969c, 78] and by Hamad Wad Halima in *Dau al-Beit* [*B* 1996, 22]), or exploited for personal gain (as by Ash 'l-Baytat in *Dau al-Beit* [*B*

---

5. This is a much sterner Hajj Ahmad than the one a nostalgic, newly returned Meheimeed describes at the beginning of *Season,* where the grandfather (now twenty years older then he is in the short story) is depicted as an ascetic, God-fearing man who spends much of his time on the prayer rug and often laughs with his friends. However, Hajj Ahmad's opinion that "women are the sisters of the Devil" (*SMN* 1969c, 123) is evident here.

1996, 40–43]). Thus it is not only the clash of two worldviews that disrupts young Meheimeed's "ideological assimilation" to his grandfather's worldview, but also the latter's own inner contradictions.

Nevertheless, Masood remains in large measure responsible for his own situation, and the grandfather is to some extent justified in denouncing Masood's polygamy—although apparently for the wrong reasons. In *Season,* the monogamy of Meheimeed, Hajj Ahmad, and their whole family makes them the butt of Wad Rayyes's sexist jokes. To Wad Rayyes, Meheimeed's uncle Abdul Karim is the only "real man" in that tribe because "he was much divorced and much married—and an adulterer to boot" (*SMN* 1969c, 80). For that, he is all but disowned by the family, and Meheimeed humiliates him in Hajj Ahmad's presence and with his tacit approval (*B* 1996, 85). Meheimeed's is a world with highly ambiguous moral and ethical standards, and he grows into an impotent observer of events, never an active participant.

Meheimeed's passivity sometimes gives way to complacency—for example, when he fails to rescue Hosna Bint Mahmoud from a forced marriage in *Season.* More often, however, he is riddled with doubts about the roles he chooses to play or not to play. In the scene where the grandfather and the others divide up Masood's harvest of dates among themselves, Meheimeed hears Masood making the rasping noise of a slaughtered animal and feels "a sharp sensation of pain in my chest" ("HD" 1969b, 28). This pain points to his sense of guilt: his grandfather has given him a handful of Masood's dates to eat, thus making the boy an accomplice in the "slaughtering" of Masood. In reaction, Meheimeed rebels against Hajj Ahmad for the first time: "I ran off into the distance. Hearing my grandfather call after me, I hesitated a little, then continued on my way. I felt at that moment that I hated him. . . . I reached the river bank near the bend it made behind the wood of acacia trees. Then, without knowing why, I put my finger into my throat and spewed up the dates I'd eaten" (28). Note that at moments of profound anxiety, such as in the final scene of *Season,* he always goes to the same symbolically laden place at "the bend of the Nile," where the treacherous cross-currents of the life-giving river become deadly. The dates he had innocently accepted have become emblematic of a complicity he is forced to acknowledge. But can he undo it by the symbolic rebellion, or would he rather forget and repress the painful episode, taking refuge in memories of a paradise lost? This is Meheimeed's dilemma in *Season.*

The psychological rupture in "A Handful of Dates" becomes a cultural and historical dislocation in "The Doum Tree of Wad Hamid." An entire generation lives to see its world fall apart under the pressures of modernity and outside influences. The story depicts the worldview of a generation of villagers who have survived the colonial era. They have resisted attempts by the British to "civilize"

them and by successive postcolonial governments to bring them Progress and Modernity. From the perspective of the old narrator, there is no difference between colonial and postcolonial governments; all display a colonial attitude in their various attempts to sever the villagers' spiritual moorings and to disrupt their way of life. The story is a powerful indictment of the postcolonial government's attempt to impose the project of the *Nahda* from the top down, with neither the creative vision to achieve modernization in adaptive and productive ways, nor the willingness to engage the citizens in democratic dialogue on how best to steer the course of change.

The most complex of Salih's short stories, "The Doum Tree" is, in the author's words, "one of the pillars of my work, such as it is. It was the first story to meet with success and to make me feel that I could become a writer" (IM 1976b, 122). Chronologically, the story in "The Doum Tree" is contemporaneous with the last years in the plot of *Season*—that is, with events preceding and following Sudanese independence in 1956. In technique, the story resembles the novel in that each contains two main narrators—Meheimeed and Mustafa Sa'eed in *Season,* the old villager and the young urban guest in "The Doum Tree." Yet the world of the short story gives the impression of greater historical remoteness than that of the novel because the main narrative voice, which goes unchallenged until the last page of the text, projects a worldview that belongs to the past. It is the voice of a tired old man rather than the youthful and optimistic Meheimeed. Thus, the story is unique among Salih's works in that he tells it from the perspective of an older generation that hands over the affairs of the village to young men in their thirties and forties (identified in "The Wedding of Zein" as "Mahjoub's gang"). That older generation then passes into oblivion, along with its distinct mode of perception. The old man and his peers have successfully resisted the relentless intrusion of modernity into their world; now they see it captivate the imagination of their offspring. In the rest of the Wad Hamid Cycle, the voices of the young will take charge of narration, and Meheimeed, the most anxious and divided among the younger characters, will record the tribulations of this cultural dislocation.

There are two distinct modes of narration in "The Doum Tree," oral and literary, and two competing ideologies, the old man's and the young urban guest's. The old man's narrative bears many of the characteristics of orality. First, of course, there is the form of address, "my son," which he uses almost on every page. Second, there is his attentiveness to his audience during the act of storytelling; consider his frequent observations on the state and the reactions of his companion, for example, his comments on the youth's face, which is swollen from sandfly bites ("DTWH" 1969a, 1, 2, 3, 6, 15). Third, there is the old man's gentle mockery of the urban guest, which serves to emphasize his theme of the relative physical strength of the villagers and the weakness of city dwellers; he laughs at what he sees as their proneness to bruises on the backside as a result of riding donkeys (2) and their rush to hospitals for any trivial injury (11). Fourth, and more importantly, the old man structures his narrative, composed of a dozen mini-narratives, around the young man's inquiries. These mini-narratives are shot through with the old man's ideological intentions: they illustrate the old man's thesis that the villagers are content with their lives, that they do not need change, that in fact they are so different from people in other areas that they have absolutely no use for modernization, and ultimately that they should be left alone. For example, the story of the old man bitten by a snake, which he then crushes in his hand (11), and that of the third dream narrative of a woman with fever, who is cured under the doum tree (11–13), both illustrate the idea that the villagers have no need for hospitals. This is voiced in response to the guest's inquiry about what the villagers do when they are ill.

The second narrator is a stranger to the village—perhaps a government official, a journalist, a historian, or simply a passer-by, but in any case someone capable of writing down the village stories, which as the old man is well aware may soon be forgotten and lost forever. The visitor does not speak in the story until the last page; he even refrains from reporting his own observations and impressions, or the questions he asks old man during the tour. Apparently the guest prefers to record only the old man's voice—a sign that the guest sympathizes with his host and wishes to allow the old man to describe his worldview freely. Nevertheless, the guest's exchange with the old man at the end of the story reveals that he holds the opposite ideological position to that of the old man, namely, that modernization is both salutary and inevitable. For his part, the old man understands the significant role played by the guest. For all the villagers' indifference to the world beyond their village, the old man is obviously concerned that the visitor "think well of [them] and judge [them] not too harshly" ("DTWH" 1969a, 20), even though the villagers never before cared what the officials and other strangers to the village thought of them. This change in attitude seems to result from the old man's understanding of the importance of writing in the preservation and representation of a fast-disappearing oral culture.

Such is the purpose of the old man's guided tour of the village and the stories he tells the young urban visitor. As Chinua Achebe's *Things Fall Apart* does, the old man's stories paint a colorful portrait of a self-contained society undergoing radical transformation as a result of both outside pressure and its own children's rebellion against traditional values. Nwoye, Okonkwo's son in Achebe's novel, escapes from his father's household to join the missionaries, who eventually bring about the destruction of his native culture; in much the same way, the old man's son in "The Doum Tree" runs away to the city, where he attends a modern school without his father's approval. (Note that Mustafa Sa'eed's first independent decision was to enroll in the colonial school, and only afterward did he tell his mother about it [*SMN* 1969c, 21]). The old man knows that modern, Western education will turn his son into a more powerful agent of change than the total strangers whom the villagers have resisted successfully until now: "it is my hope that he [the son] will stay where he is and not return. When my son's son passes out of school and the number of young men with souls foreign to our own increases, then perhaps the water-pump will be set up and the agricultural scheme put into being—maybe then the steamer will stop at our village—under the doum tree of Wad Hamid" ("DTWH" 1969a, 19).

The profound sense of inevitability in the old man's words lends urgency to his narration, which may be the last act of resistance available to him. The tree is a living presence for the villagers; yet the old man is aware that soon it will be a relic of the past, an object as remote from everyday life as a museum exhibit: "In the towns you have museums, places in which the local history and the great deeds of the past are preserved. This thing that I want to show you can be said to be a museum. It is the one thing we insist our visitors should see" ("DTWH" 1969a, 2). Indeed, in the end the tree becomes a fenced-off monument identified with a plaque. Modernization has succeeded in breaking the continuity between a museumized past and an alienated present in the village.

The old man's oral narrative consists of the following twelve mini-narratives, in the order of narration:

1. Fellow student of old man's son visits Wad Hamid (1)
2. Preacher's story (2–3)
3. Envoy of colonial government (4)
4. Dream #1 (6–7)
5. Dream #2 (7–8)
6. Envoy of first postcolonial government (8–10)
7. Old man in his youth: "the crocodile" (10)
8. Old man in his youth: snake bite (11)
9. Dream #3 (11–13)
10. Story of Wad Hamid (13–14)
11. Envoy of second postcolonial government (15–17)
12. Toppling of second by first postcolonial government ("DTWH" 1969a, 17–18)

These mini-narratives can be divided into two groups: six map the imaginary, psychic, and spiritual world of the village and its worldview (4, 5, 7, 8, 9, 10), and six depict historical, social, and political processes that threaten in the name of Progress to destroy that worldview (1, 2, 3, 6, 11, 12). The first group portrays the doum tree as the embodiment of the living, oral *memory* of the village; the second represents the forces of cultural *amnesia*. The clash between the forces of memory and amnesia (which later on, in *Bandarshah,*, becomes a pivotal concern), reveals the contradictions of the *Nahda* project of modernization, which from the old man's perspective is a colonial legacy. The two rubrics of "memory" and "amnesia" shall, therefore, guide my discussion of the mini-narratives.

Memory is the villagers' repository of cultural worldview and identity; both revolve around the doum tree. In the old man's discourse, the doum tree's divine origin defies natural law, human knowledge, and secular history: "No one planted it, my son. Is the ground in which it grows arable land? Do you not see that it is stony and appreciably higher than the river bank. . . ?" ("DTWH" 1969a, 6). According to the old man, the tree cannot simply be spoken of—it must also be seen, for its form makes a distinct impression on those who behold it. But ultimately, human perception and language cannot grasp it fully, since the tree stands on the border between that which can be known and that which cannot: "In the afternoon, when the sun is low, the doum tree casts its shadow from this high mound right across the river so that someone sitting on the far bank can rest in its shade. At dawn, when the sun rises, the shadow of the tree stretches across the cultivated land and houses right up to the cemetery. Don't you think it is like some mythical eagle spreading its wings over the village and everyone in it?" (3–4). Much like the date palm in Hajj Ahmad's courtyard (*SMN* 1969c, 2), the doum tree is an image of strength, pride, and rootedness. Yet unlike the crop-yielding date palms, the doum tree has no economic value. Its shape is asymmetrical, wild, with something of a supernatural or mythical eerieness about it. Its presence is linked to the sun, which in ancient times was worshipped by the Egyptians as the principal god Ra, and to the river, which "twists and turns below it like a sacred snake, one of the ancient gods of the Egyptians" ("DTWH" 1969a, 6). As such, the tree stands "as though it were some ancient idol" (4), both protecting and presiding over the village; the tree's dominion extends from the other bank of the river (the source of life), to the living spaces of the village, and to the resting place of the dead. The tree is the center of the villagers' existence in this world and the next, and it shapes their sense of themselves as individuals and as a community.

The tree also defines the villagers' knowledge of the world: it marks the beginning of consciousness for them, and it figures prominently in their earliest memories and in their developing awareness and understanding of the small world it commands, which is the only one they know:

> [N]o one remembers having known it other than as you now find it. Our sons opened their eyes to find it commanding the village. And we, when we take ourselves back to childhood memories, to that dividing line beyond which you remember nothing, see in our minds a giant doum tree standing on a river bank; everything beyond it is as cryptic as talismans, like the boundary between day and night, like that fading light which is not the dawn but the light directly preceding the break of day. My son, do you find that you can follow what I say? Are you aware of this feeling I have within me but which I am powerless to express? Every new generation finds the doum tree as though it had been born at the time of their birth and would grow up with them. ("DTWH" 1969a, 6)

In the villagers' own regional blend of Sufi and animist creeds, the doum tree makes intelligible and livable an otherwise "cryptic" world by drawing the line between order and chaos, light and darkness, Good and Evil. The tree is the living, tangible incarnation of the divine criterion that determines the proper conduct of life. And like any mystical Way, that criterion is not a universally applicable (orthodox) rule, but a highly personal one, fitted to each individual's particular needs and capabilities and growing in proportion to his or her spiritual development. Such a mystical bond, which seems to be the ultimate significance of the doum tree to each one of the villagers, cannot be logically or rationally explained; the old man is "powerless to express" it because it falls beyond the scope of language.

However, that bond expresses itself in the villagers' dreams, where it embodies their fears and hopes for salvation. The old man narrates three such dreams together with their interpretations. For the villagers, the meaning of the dreams is almost self-evident, for their elements, symbols, and signification are fairly well known in the Arab-Islamic tradition of dream interpretation.[6] The old man recounts the dreams in order to demonstrate the doum tree's immense significance for the psychic, emotional, and spiritual well-being of the villagers. The dreams demonstrate the power of the tree and its holy man over the villagers' imagination and psyche. This power, which orthodox Islam would deem to be a function of idolatry, nevertheless allies itself with traditional sources, such as those concerned with dreams and their interpretation. Yet whatever the mix of pagan animism, mysticism, and orthodox Islam that constitutes the villagers' worldview, the tree stands for organic continuity with the past, which modernity ruptures.

Fedwa Malti-Douglas cites the traditional distinction between the two types of "prophetic" dreams: there are dreams that are coded and that require interpretation, and then there are dreams that literally come true—that the dreamer lives out in real life—and hence require no analysis (1982, 22). The first two of the old man's dream narratives belong to the first type, the third belongs to the second type. In the first dream, a man is lost in vast, endless desert until he spots an oasis of doum trees; one of these trees towers over the rest. He hurries to reach that tree and finds underneath it a bowl of fresh milk; he drinks his fill yet the bowl remains full.[7] A friend to whom the dream is recounted says, " 'Rejoice

---

6. In her important study, "Al-'anasir al-turathiyya fi al-adab al-'arabi al-hadith," Fedwa Malti-Douglas points out that the three dreams and their interpretations as reported by the old man follow the same patterns of imagery and symbolism found in such classics of Arab-Islamic dream interpretation as al-Nabulsi's *Ta'tir al-anam fi ta'bir al-manam* and Ibn Sirin's *Muntakhab al-kalam fi tafsir al-ahlam* (Malti-Douglas 1982, 28).

7. This marvel is reminiscent of one of the Prophet's miracles, in which he is reported to have blessed a small quantity of food, whereby it seemed not to decrease as a large group of people ate from it. See Ibn Kathyr's *Al-bidaya wa al-nihaya* vol.4, 98–99.

at release from your troubles' " ("DTWH" 1969a, 7).[8] In the second dream a woman finds herself in a boat tossed by towering waves through a channel in the sea, on the shores of which dark, leafless trees bearing thorns like hawk's heads seem to be moving toward her. Terrified, she calls on Wad Hamid for help, whereupon a dignified-looking man with a long white beard, a radiant face, and spotless white clothes reassures her and leads the boat to a beautiful shore lined with fields of ripe wheat, water wheels, and grazing cattle. He docks the boat under a doum tree and places a doum in her hand, after gently striking her on the shoulder with his rosary, which is made of amber beads.[9] " 'That was Wad Hamid,' her friend says to her. 'You will have an illness that will bring you to the brink of death, but you will recover. You must make an offering to Wad Hamid under the doum tree' " (8).[10] The third dream reported by the old man requires no decoding, for its content becomes a reality. A woman suffering from severe fever takes refuge under the doum tree and invokes the holy man: " 'O Wad Hamid, I have come to you to seek refuge and protection—I shall sleep here at your tomb and under your doum tree. Either you let me die or you restore me to life; I shall not leave here until one of these two things happen' " (11). Then she falls asleep, and dreams of voices reciting the Qur'an, and sees a bright light and the tree prostrating itself. Then Wad Hamid appears exactly as he does in the second dream, strikes her with his rosary, and commands her to stand up. At that she wakes up cured, and she has never been ill since then. These and similar dreams follow the pattern of *"al-faraj ba'd al-shidda,"* or "relief after distress" (Malti-Douglas 1082, 23); they indicate that the tree and its holy man represent, for the Wad Hamidians, not only relief from poverty, sickness, and other calamities, but also psychic and spiritual well-being.

The story of Wad Hamid himself follows the same pattern. It resembles medieval European hagiographies as well as the stories of some early Muslims and companions of the Prophet, especially his black muezzin Bilal.[11] The story,

---

8. Malti-Douglas observes that this interpretation is almost identical to the one given to a similar dream reported by al-Nabulsi, where "walking on sand" signifies sadness, distress, quarrel, or complaint (Malti-Douglas 1982, 23).

9. This gesture is repeated in the third dream, as well as later on in *Season,* where Hajj Ahmad similarly strikes a disobedient child with his sandalwood prayer beads in order to "chase away the devil that had got into him" (*SMN* 1969c, 72).

10. Citing al-Nabulsi, Malti-Douglas explains that "entering the water" in dreams signifies serious illness (Malti-Douglas, 1982 23). In Salih's fiction generally, those who swim effortlessly are spiritually pure (e.g., Rabab in "A Blessed Day"), whereas those who struggle against drowning are in spiritual peril (e.g., Meheimeed in *Season* and *Meryoud*). Strangers to Wad Hamid are either thrown in the water (e.g., the government envoys in "The Doum Tree") or they drown during the flooding of the Nile (e.g., Dau al-Beit and possibly Mustafa Sa'eed).

11. Bilal was a converted Abyssinian slave of one of the Prophet's ferocious enemies who tortured their servants and other poor Muslims in an attempt to destroy the new religion. His owner used to place a huge rock on Bilal's chest to force him to renounce Islam, but to no avail. A wealthy

passed down from father to son to grandson ("DTWH" 1969a, 13), is of a pious slave whose owner was a sinner. Wad Hamid calls on God for deliverance. A voice answers, telling him to spread his prayer rug on the water and let it transport him. (Note the motif of the "magical rug" from *The Thousand and One Nights*; there is also an allusion to the Qur'anic story of baby Moses floating on the river in a wicker basket.) The rug stops at the rock on which the doum tree is to grow afterwards, and which is surrounded by a wasteland that later on, through Wad Hamid's *baraka* (blessing endowed with mystical power), will become the fertile fields cultivated by the villagers. Wad Hamid spends his days and nights in prayer and worship, and the village springs up nearby.

The old man is careful to place special emphasis on Wad Hamid's *baraka* as the creative force that begets the village and its fertile fields. That creative force is mystical—one may say mythical or magical in the sense that its work is accomplished instantly by divine intervention in the natural course of things—that is, by interrupting secular history:

> It is as though this village, with its inhabitants, its water-wheels and buildings, had come split off from the earth. Anyone who tells you he knows the history of its origin is a liar. Other places begin by being small and then grow larger, but this village of ours came into being at one bound. Its population neither increases nor decreases, while its appearance remains unchanged. And ever since our village existed, so has the doum tree of Wad Hamid; and just as no one remembers how it originated and grew, so no one remembers how the doum tree came to grow in a patch of rocky ground by the river, standing above it like a sentinel. ("DTWH" 1969a, 14)

The categorical denial of history in favor of a creation myth clearly smacks of a theological conception of genesis rather than sociological or economic notions of growth and evolution. Any such narrative of change or process is considered a lie, a falsification of eternal, metaphysical truth. This jealous guarding of the sacred origin of the village is a form of resistance to the official and totalizing narrative of the nation—not an effective resistance, certainly, but in any case one that arises from the villagers' worldview, for what is at stake is not only representation and its social and political implications, but also the villagers' very sense of who they are in a fast-changing world, and their worldview itself. They find their lives meaningful in a world that is governed by fixed, eternal, and metaphysical

---

Muslim eventually purchased Bilal's freedom. Later on the Prophet appointed Bilal as Islam's first muezzin, a great honor and a strong token of Islam's repudiation of racial and caste prejudice. As the Prophet's muezzin and a prominent black Muslim who often led the prayers in the Prophet's absence, Bilal has special significance in Islamic history and for African Muslims. See Ibn al-Athyr's *Usd al-ghaba fi ma'rifat al-sahaba* vol. 1, 243–45. Allusions to Bilal recur in *Meryoud*.

laws, where only divine intervention brings about positive change. It is a mark of Meheimeed's ideological confusion that despite his colonial education and espousal of the *Nahda* belief in Progress, he feels that "life is good" when and if "the world [is] as unchanged as ever" (*SMN* 1969c, 2). This contradiction is central to his identity crisis in *Season*. For the rest of the untraveled villagers—especially elders like the narrator of "The Doum Tree"—change is a reality that bodes cultural amnesia.

Let us turn now to the rubric of amnesia, which both here and throughout the Cycle—especially in *Bandarshah*—is a metaphor for cultural dislocation. In "The Doum Tree" this dislocation results from the government's aggressive interference in the affairs of the village. The struggle between the villagers and the government raises the question of authority in postcolonial Arab states—a question that will surface again in "Wedding" and become central to *Bandarshah*. The government is often perceived as inefficient, corrupt, and made up of self-serving politicians, and the villagers regard it with contempt: like "a refractory donkey" (*WZOS* 1969e, 77), it is "a hopeless government" (*SMN* 1969c, 64). Their credo is that whatever the government does must be ill-conceived, misguided, or in some way threatening to their collective well-being.

This hostility toward the government extends to the inhabitants of the capital. It expresses a conflict of worldviews, politics, and economics, and reflects a disparity in living standards. Four of the mini-narratives (1, 2, 7, and 8), and many of the comments addressed to the young narrator, illustrate the old man's belief that villagers and city dwellers are quite literally different species of human beings. This radical othering of the city is a defense mechanism that masks the villagers' deep-seated anxiety vis-à-vis the central authority and the people who represent it or live in its vicinity. Thus the villagers find themselves physically strong and resilient, while urbanites are weak and vulnerable despite the comforts they enjoy. Village life is lethal to them not simply because it lacks hospitals, electricity, paved streets, and comfortable vehicles, but because nature itself chases them away with its troops of sand flies and horse flies, which "obstruct all paths to those who wish to enter our village" ("DTWH" 1969a, 1–2).

This discrepancy between the villagers' and the city dwellers' resilience provides the old man with a source of satirical humor at the expense of the guest. More importantly, it strengthens the villagers' belief that their lack of modern amenities is proof of their hardiness, that what the government sees as their backwardness only demonstrates their strength. The old man's two autobiographical mini-narratives illustrate this: he tells his guest about the prodigious amounts of food he used to consume in his youth; his enormous strength, which earned him the nickname "the crocodile" (we learn in *Bandarshah* that he is called "Hassan the Crocodile"); and his invulnerability to snake bites ("DTWH" 1969a, 10–11). All of this offers proof of the villagers' superior physical health, which leaves them in no need of hospitals or other modern comforts. In contrast, "townsfolk hurry to the hospital on the slightest pretext. If one of you hurts his finger you dash off to the doctor who puts a bandage on and you carry it in a sling for days; even then it doesn't get better" (11). In the villagers' world, urbanites simply do not belong: *Tomorrow you will depart from our village,* of this I am sure, and you will be right to do so. What have you to do with such hardship? We are thick-skinned people and in this we differ from others. We have become used to this hard life, in fact we like it, but we ask no one to subject himself to the difficulties of our life. *Tomorrow you will depart, my son— I know that*" (2; emphasis added). Beneath the show of humility and self-deprecation is a genuine desire that the guest—and any stranger to the village—"depart from our village." These words are repeated several times by the old man in the course of the story like an incantation (2, 6, 15, 20). Likewise, the rest of his statements in the passage can be understood in two ways: as expressions of (explicitly) a humble or (implicitly) a condescending and mocking attitude. This doubling of language can also be discerned in the old man's repeated references to the guest's swollen face and his agony; here, expressions of sympathy and pity mask the old man's mockery and derision (3, 6, 15). This yoking together of clashing intentions (or "double-voicedness," in Bakhtin's terms) is the old man's main rhetorical strategy.

Appropriately, then, the old man's narrative begins with a description of the fearful insects and their effect on nonvillagers, illustrated by the first and second of the old man's twelve mini—narratives. That beginning serves as a warning to strangers to stay away from the village. The first is about a fellow student of his son's who visited the village, "stayed one night with us and got up next day, feverish, with a running nose and swollen face; he swore he wouldn't spend another night with us" ("DTWH" 1969a, 1). The next mini-narrative illustrates the same point but adds two further dimensions: the superiority of the villagers' own religious blend of animism and mysticism to the orthodox Islam adopted by the state, and the central authority's failure to control the villagers' lives. A preacher sent by the government arrives, as his fate would have it, "at a time when the horse-flies had never been fatter" (2). For the old man, the timing of the preacher's arrival is no coincidence; later on, he makes a point of observing that the insects helped them get rid of the first government envoy (4) and the prime minister and his cabinet (17). The preacher represents central authority and orthodox (official) Islam, which is hostile to shrines, saints, and animism; he prefigures the unpopular imam in "Wedding." Dogmatic and inflexible in doctrinal matters (and government employees besides), these characters are less attractive to the villagers than ascetic Sufi sheikhs and holy men (such as Wad Hamid in this story, Haneen in "Wedding," and Nasrullah Wad Habib in *Bandarshah*), who are characteristically tolerant and unaffected. After speaking to the villagers, as the old man remarks sarcastically, of "the delights of the primitive life" (2), this imam barely survived for three days, at the end of which he

sent a desperate telegram to his superiors beseeching them to "come to my rescue, may God bless you—these are people who are in no need of me or of any
other preacher" (3).

The authorities attempt to cut down the doum tree, not to persecute the
villagers or to trample on their beliefs, but to modernize the village and to con-
nect it to the emergent network of economic relations. The problem, as Barbara
Peters points out, is that the successive governments do not, nor do they try to,
understand the particular way in which the villagers organize their existence
(1989, 17–18). For the various government officials who survey the village to
determine the appropriate location for a steamer stop or a power station, the
doum tree is simply part of the terrain and an obstacle to be removed, regardless
of its significance for the villagers. The old man illustrates this idea in mini-
narratives about government officials who visit the village. The first official represents the colonial administration, the others postindependence regimes. One
civil servant tells them that "the national government wished to help [them] and
to see [them] progress, and his face was radiant with enthusiasm as he talked"
("DTWH" 1969a, 8). However, when the official speaks of cutting the doum
tree the villagers attack him and throw him in the river (9–10, 16). Isolated in
their world, the villagers make no distinction between colonial and postcolonial
governments, so they do not care "what form the government had taken, black
or white" (15); all governments rule them from the capital, treat them with arrogance and condescension, and try to manipulate their lives. But in their zeal to
achieve the goals of the *Nahda* and build a modern nation on European models,
the postcolonial governments are more aggressive than the colonial administration, which gave up its designs for the village after one attempt.

Despite themselves, the villagers play an important role in national politics,
helping topple the government that has jailed their leaders. It is a passive role
that demonstrates the extent of their unwilling entanglement in political battles
between parties that mean nothing to them. (In *Season*, Abdul Mannan ex-
claims, "All they're [the national government] good at is coming to us every
two or three years with their hordes of people, their lorries and their posters:
Long live so-and-so, down with so-and-so. We were spared all this hullabaloo in
the days of the English" [*SMN* 1969c, 64]). When the second postcolonial government, thinking itself stronger than the first ("DTWH" 1969a, 16), tries to
implement its program by force and jails the village leaders, the opposition seizes
the opportunity to rail against the prime minister, accusing him of tyranny and
impiety for desecrating the doum tree. The affair galvanizes public opinion because "in every village in this country there is some monument like the doum
tree of Wad Hamid which people see in their dreams. . . . And so the government fell . . . and the leading paper in the country wrote: 'The doum tree of
Wad Hamid has become the symbol of the nation's awakening' " (18).

Muhyiddin Subhi finds a strong satirical element in this episode: "How could the rejection of the power station and the agricultural project be considered a 'symbol of the nation's awakening?' Demagogy has no limit, and those hungry for power sacrifice the nation's best interests" (Subhi 1976, 20). For him, the crisis of the doum tree is a tragicomic situation: "both points of view are valid—the people are justified in defending their beliefs, and the government is justified in seeking development even if it means using force. How can this vicious circle, which benefits only opportunists, be broken?" (20–21). The answer to that question is embedded in the old man's words toward the end: "What all these people have overlooked is that there's plenty of room for all these things: the doum tree, the tomb, the water-pump, and the steamer's stopping place" ("DTWH" 1969a, 19). Contrary to Subhi's opinion regarding the use of force, a creative solution could be reached if the government were willing to engage in constructive dialogue with its rural citizens, provincial and uneducated though they may be, instead of attempting to impose on them something that insults their beliefs. As the old man indicates, the choice between "modernization" and "tradition" need not be compulsory; nor is this uninspired and sterile polarization. But this ideological bankruptcy goes unremarked, since the politicians take less interest in the villagers' spiritual or material well-being than in exploiting the crisis for their own ends. "Cleanly dressed . . . heavily scented and with gold watches gleaming on their wrists" ("DTWH" 1969a, 16), the new prime minister and cabinet members (like many "new rulers of Africa" [*SMN* 1969c, 118–20]) are no better than their predecessors.

In the end, according to the old man, the villagers' "life returned to what it had been: no water-pump, no agricultural scheme, no stopping-place for the steamer. But we kept our doum tree . . . and our village has acquired a marble monument, an iron railing, and a dome with gilded crescents," which the new government set up around the tree and the shrine of Wad Hamid ("DTWH" 1969a, 18). And once more the government officials are driven away by "the horse-flies which, that particular year, were as large and fat and buzzed and whirred as much as during the year the preacher came to us" (17). Yet it is far from certain that all of those battles seemingly won will result in the villagers' victory in the war against the forces of change, which threaten their beliefs and way of life. As Peters points out, "[t]he government, by memorializing the tree through a plaque and a railing, has symbolically closed off the villagers from their own historical legacy. . . . the plaque transforms the tree into a museum of heroic deed for the government" (1989, 25–26). As such, she concludes, "power is no longer found in cutting the tree; rather it is in being able to control how the tree is viewed" (36).

Moreover, change in "how the tree is viewed" will come about not only as a result of the "monumentalization" of the tree, but also from within the village itself as a result of a historical process which younger villagers eagerly embrace and to which the old man has resigned himself. When the urban visitor finally speaks, his question does not surprise the old man at all: " 'And *when*,' I asked, 'will they set up the water-pump, and put through the agricultural scheme and the stopping-place for the steamer?' He lowered his head and paused before answering me, 'When people go to sleep and don't see the doum tree in their dreams.' 'And *when* will that be?' " ("DTWH" 1969a, 19; emphasis added). It is only a matter of time, and the old man knows that. In fact, he underestimates the speed at which his world is changing. He believes that development will come about in the generation of his grandchildren (19), whereas those who now control the affairs of the village, Mahjoub and his "gang" (as they are called in "Wedding"), are already working to implement change. The docking place for the steamer and the agricultural project (which Mustafa Sa'eed helps Mahjoub's gang organize [*SMN* 1969c, 101–2]), with power generators and water pumps to replace water wheels, are set up only a few years later, in addition to modern schools and a hospital (*WZOS* 1969e, 77–78). Moreover, the government's new schemes, perceived by the old man and his generation as an attack on the spiritual values of the village, will be regarded by their children not only as beneficial, but also as miracles of the holy man Haneen. In the space of a few years before and after Sudanese independence, Wad Hamid not only witnesses a transfer of power from one generation to the next, but turns away from the traditional worldview of the elders and embraces the ideology of Progress. The new generation is less attached to a life centered around the doum tree and more desirous of economic development than their elders, who now represent the past. In *Season,* for example, Mahjoub considers Hajj Ahmad to be "an old windbag," while a nostalgic Mustafa Sa'eed regards him as "a part of history" (*SMN* 1969c, 102). For Meheimeed, his grandfather is "something immutable in a dynamic world" (48). In all cases, the old man is a relic from a bygone age. The attitude to the government has not changed ("a hopeless government" [*SMN* 1969c, 64], "a refractory donkey" [*WZOS* 1969e, 78]), but the attitude toward change has.

The introduction of water pumps, hospitals, electricity, and modern education announces not Progress as such, but the arrival of the tensions and conflicts of modernity, the dependency arising from unequal development, and the contradictions of the *Nahda.* The young Wad Hamidians believe in the need for development, but they are also under the impression that it can bring material progress while leaving old traditions and customs intact (*tawfiq,* in the discourse of the *Nahda*). They resist certain forms of change that affect their social structure, such as the patriarchal order. The steamer stop will crowd the doum tree in people's lives and in their imagination, but the result will not be a secular worldview: a new power station, a hospital, and a modern school will be perceived as miracles confirming the villagers' belief in the supernatural powers of the holy man Haneen. Thus popular Islam, as Ahmad Nasr argues, may mediate between "modernity and the strict adherence to tradition, between the village and the city" (Nasr 1980, 103), but it is a mediation that produces *talfiq* rather than *tawfiq*—a fabrication rather than a viable synthesis. The implications and repercussions prove to be well beyond the imagination not only of the old man and the elders who resist change, but also of the younger generation who embrace it.

"The Wedding of Zein"

Utopia and Narrative Procedures

SALIH'S THREE LONG NARRATIVES register the ideological shifts that occurred during the two decades from Sudanese independence in 1956 to 1976 (the year the last episodes of the Wad Hamid Cycle were published). The same period also witnessed the independence of most Arab and African countries. The novella "'Urs al-Zayn" (The wedding of Zein; 1962) expresses the boundless optimism generally characteristic of the early years of independence, and explores the conditions that could allow the *Nahda* project to succeed. Salih was writing as an immigrant, and his nostalgia (discussed in the previous chapter) infuses the entire narrative and sanitizes the fictional village of the very ills and conflicts he would depict so graphically in his later narratives. In sum, "Wedding" shows Salih at his most optimistic anywhere in the Cycle.

The novella was received warmly by Arab critics, partly because of its delightful depiction of the title character and the atmosphere of peace and harmony that his wedding represented. Typical of that critical acclaim is 'Ali al-Ra'i's unqualified praise of the novella as "a long ululation for life, a hymn of love" (al-Ra'i 1976, 117). "Wedding" was also so well received because of the great appeal of the *Nahda* vision of synthesis between Western science and Arab Islamic culture. The novella realizes that synthesis instead of advocating Westernization or rejecting Islam as an impediment to Progress, and it does so while celebrating the creative spiritual resources of the native culture. The argument that Arabs had to choose between the two, famously made by French Orientalist and racial theorist Ernest Renan, among others, and refuted first by the great *Nahda* religious reformer Jamal al-Din al-Afghani and by others after him, continues to haunt Arab cultural debate.[1] The novella was highly praised partly because it reassured its readers in the early 1960s that Westernization and the abandonment of Islam did not have to be the price of Progress.

---

1. See Jamal al-Din al-Afghani's "L'islamisme et la science," and *Al-rad 'ala al-dhahiriyyin*, in which he responds to Renan and other Orientalists. See also Qasim Amin's *Les Égyptiens: Réponse à M. le duc d'Harcourt*.

Salih's ideological project is valuable in combating cultural imperialism; however, it is also symptomatic of the inability of Arabic thought to move beyond colonial discourse. One result of this failure is that the West continues to dictate the terms by which the Arab world sees itself. The project of the novella is also problematic in its own right, in that it risks reinscribing what Abu Zayd calls the *Nahda*'s *"talfiq"* (fabrication) rather than *"tawfiq"* (synthesis). Thus the author's nostalgic idealization of traditional society, combined with the idealism of the *Nahda*, produces a utopia (etymologically, a "nonplace"), a fictional world idealized beyond the realm of possibility. Such utopianism has subversive potential, but it risks entrenching obsolete social practices.

In approaching the novella as a utopian text, I take my cue from two separate statements made by the author. In one interview, Salih said that "Wedding" "represents my hopes and dreams which I wish could be realized within human society . . . [when it] is calm and stable. . . . As for the disturbed, contradictory world as I sense it, it is the world of *Season*" (*TSS* 1982, 17–18). In another interview, Salih discussed his interest in English and Arab satirical writers, Jonathan Swift, al-Jahiz, and Ibrahim 'Abd al-Qadir al Mazini in particular. He spoke of satire in relation to the old man's mockery of city folk in "The Doum Tree," before proceeding to describe "Wedding" as "carnivalesque" (IM 1976b, 121–23). Utopianism, satire, and carnivalesque parody (if we recall Bakhtin's reading of the carnival as parodic reversal) are, of course, discursive modes denoting dissatisfaction with the status quo and highlighting the discrepancy between the way things are and the way they ought to be. This sort of literature is infused with the kind of optimistic rationalism that finds its clearest expression in the Enlightenment doctrine of Progress, a doctrine that lies at the heart of the *Nahda*, which was directly influenced by the Enlightenment. In that sense, "Wedding" ultimately affirms the project of the *Nahda* and embodies its hidden utopianism.

However, the novella departs from the project of the *Nahda*—and for that matter from much utopian literature since Plato's *Republic*—in that the state fails to be the agent of Progress. In "Wedding," and in line with the villagers' distrust of central authority seen in "The Doum Tree," the agents of Progress are pragmatic village leaders. If the synthesis of traditional culture and modern technology is nearly impossible for the old narrator in "The Doum Tree," it is not so for those of his son's generation, the generation of "Mahjoub's gang," who are eager for change and who assume power in the village in the early postcolonial era. However, their desire for modern things is coupled with their distrust of the government, which they see as corrupt, inept, condescending, and relatively indifferent to the people of the countryside. Thus "Wedding" is perhaps the most ideologically ambivalent episode of the Cycle with regard to the *Nahda*: on the one hand, the novella upholds the vision of adapting modernity to traditional culture; on the other hand, this is seen as impossible on the national level within the framework of the postcolonial state. This tension in the discourse of the novella is sublated, not resolved, through an ideological compromise that lies at the heart of the novella's utopianism: the village leaders carry out what the central government fails to achieve.

Salih skillfully enacts this utopianism through his approaches to narrative. Among these, perhaps the most salient are his subtle manipulation of narrative point of view and the interplay he establishes between narrative time and story time. Throughout the Wad Hamid Cycle, narrative point of view is intricately linked to discourse. Within each of the novels, the juxtaposition of narrative points of view proliferates narrative possibilities and pits several ideologies dialogically against one another. Most of Salih's novels and short stories employ a first-person narrator. *Season* has two first-person narrators (Meheimeed, the principal one, and Mustafa Sa'eed, whose narrative is embedded in Meheimeed's); *Bandarshah* features a third-person narrator as well as several first-person narrators whose narratives are embedded within Meheimeed's. Except in "A Blessed Day," Salih's first-person narrators have a tragic consciousness, an acute sense of loss marking their voices (e.g., the old man in "DTWH," Mustafa Sa'eed in *SMN,* and Meheimeed in "HD," *SMN, DB, M,* and "CM"). His third-person narrators, in contrast, tend to be detached observers; some of them are sympathetic and solemn (as in "DPS" and "BDCUB"), some scathingly satirical (as in "ISC"), others skeptical and moderately ironic (as in "WZ") and still others dispassionate chroniclers (as in *DB* and *M*). These third-person narrators are invariably outsiders who do not necessarily share the village worldview. I shall return to this point soon.

Like "A Date Palm" and "The Doum Tree," which focus on an older generation of villagers, "Wedding" is not narrated by Meheimeed, nor does he appear in it, even though his lifelong friends who make up "Mahjoub's gang" play a central role in the novella. In a sense, then, Meheimeed's total absence as narrator and participant in the events of the novella is quite conspicuous, since it is his life story from childhood to old age that constitutes the main narrative thread of the Cycle. But there is a reason for his absence: "A Date Palm" and "Wedding" present a vision of final reconciliation after an initial state of disequilibrium or crisis, whereas each of the other episodes in the Cycle depicts a falling apart or disintegration of the social and/or psychological order. Meheimeed's tragic consciousness qualifies him as narrator of the stories in which peace, tranquillity, and being at home in the world give way to alienation and psychic turmoil. As such, his life unfolds in a series of defeats and unresolved crises that sometimes signal the loss of childhood innocence ("A Handful of Dates"), the frustrations and bitterness of old age (*Bandarshah*), and sometimes coincide with and reflect larger historical forces beyond his control (*Season*). At still other times, his agony results from metaphysical speculations on the nature of good and evil ("The Cypriot Man"). Each of these narratives is in one sense a variation on the theme of human limitation and moral failure, and in another sense an exploration of the crisis of Arab modernity. In contrast, "A Date Palm" and "Wedding" contain a large measure of optimism, which Meheimeed is not well suited to communicate, ridden as he is with anxieties.

Hence the third-person narrator, whose role in "Wedding" must now be clarified. The novella opens with three short, consecutive scenes depicting the reactions of the villagers to the breaking news of Zein's engagement, in a manner that has been described as "using two familiar cinematic techniques: relating different events occurring simultaneously in different places, and successive flashbacks" (Subhi 1976, 31). The second technique, "narrative flashbacks," "suspends time and action" (Berkley 1979, 206). This suspension can be traced back to "A Date Palm" and "The Doum Tree," where story time is much longer than narrative time. Narrative time in "A Date Palm" lasts only for the few moments it takes Sheikh Mahjoub to reject the merchant's offer and to receive news from his son, whereas story time encompasses Sheikh Mahjoub's entire life, which is recalled in flashbacks. Likewise in "The Doum Tree," narrative time is the duration of the tour the old man gives to his urban guest; in the course of that tour the latter is treated to an overview of the village's history from its founding to the present, which comprises story time. Similarly, little happens in "Wedding" between the spreading of the news of Zein's engagement in the opening scene and his wedding two days later. The time in between is filled mostly with narrative flashbacks depicting Zein's life from birth to his wedding, as well as the stories of the imam of the mosque, the headmaster of the local school, Seif ad-Din, Ni'ma, and "Mahjoub's gang." Consequently, narrative time remains frozen in a seemingly eternal present, the moment of the "miraculous" event of the wedding. If the main narrative voice in "The Doum Tree" conveys a powerful sense of the past that accentuates the fast-disappearing world of the short story, the opposite takes place in "Wedding," where the present is privileged at the expense of both the past and the future. The emphasis on the present lies at the heart of the novella's utopianism, which suspends historical reality in order to dwell on the "miraculous" event of the wedding.

Coupled with this suspension, the quasi-anthropological gaze of the third-person narrator, who is clearly an outsider, functions to undercut the villagers' worldview. Witness, for example, how he distances himself from the villagers' beliefs in passages such as this one: "At first, *as is well known,* children meet life with screams. With Zein, however, it is recounted—*and the authorities for this are his mother and the women who attended his birth*—that no sooner did he come into this world than he burst out laughing" (*WZOS* 1969e, 33; emphasis added). The narrator reports the beliefs of the villagers, neither vouching for nor discrediting those beliefs, but insisting nevertheless on their peculiarity. At other times, the same effect is produced through the use of persistent, redundant phrases which follow on each other in quick succession. For instance, in the pas-

sage describing the villagers' opinion of the imam, phrases such as "in the opinion of the village," "they reckoned," and "in their minds" (used twice in less
than two lines [87]), relativize the description of the imam and suggest that the
narrator may doubt its validity; he poses as an outside observer who simply
records those phrases. Such distancing undermines the credibility of the villagers' beliefs and perceptions; it also allows for alternative interpretations of the
events, without validating any of the sometimes contending interpretations
given by characters. Consequently, the reader must also question the narrator's
own credibility when he offers his own version of events from time to time. For
instance, speaking of Zein's extraordinary marriage agreement, the narrator
says: "But how had the miracle happened? Accounts differed" (107); he then
goes on to report some of those accounts. Nevertheless, as if unable to resist the
temptation to evaluate those reports, in the manner of a historian evaluating
sources or an anthropologist interpreting primitive beliefs, he volunteers his
own rationalistic interpretation of what has been perceived by the characters as a
miracle: "It is, however, more likely that things happened otherwise" (108).

This distancing of narrative point of view is symptomatic of the tension—
never quite resolved in the *Nahda* discourse—between the two elements it seeks
to reconcile: scientific rationalism and the mythic-religious worldview. This tension is prefigured in the exchange between the urban guest and the old villager
in the final scene of "The Doum Tree," and earlier still in Yahya Haqqi's *Qindil
Umm Hashim* (1947), a classic depiction of the dilemma of the modern Arab intellectual, in which science and superstition are brought in direct confrontation
(to be discussed at some length in chapter 3). Salih's approach to this dilemma
in "Wedding" can be illustrated by his admission that he "accept[s] the world of
magic," and that in "Wedding" (but also in his other works), "the world is not
secular and things do not go according to scientific rules. . . . I do accept the beliefs of the people on condition that they must be transformed . . . into . . . a
new myth" (*TSS* 1982, 7). The nonsecular "world of magic" or miracles (which
later on would be described, in the context of Gabriel García Márquez's *Cien
años de soledad* [1969], as *lo real marveilloso,* or "the marvellous real," aka
"magical realism") derives from the popular beliefs of the villagers and their religious worldview. Miracles happen in Salih's fiction insofar as his characters believe in them and in the supernatural powers of saints. But unlike García
Márquez's superstitious narrator, who speaks of restless ghosts, levitating
priests, and flying carpets as commonplace events, Salih's rationalistic, educated,
third-person narrator distances himself from superstitious beliefs. He is interested in them as folkloric raw materials for inventing a "new myth," a satirical
utopia.

The juxtaposition of several unreliable versions of the same story that are
circulating within the village community has a different function in each novel.
In *Season,* Meheimeed's perception of Mustafa Sa'eed is effectively undermined

by Meheimeed's unreliability, by his anxieties, fears, and conflicting feelings toward Mustafa, by the villagers, and by his own identity. Mustafa's own account is no more reliable; nor are the many incompatible portraits of Mustafa painted by other characters (the Mamur, Mrs. Robinson, Richard, the minister of education, Arthur Higgins, Maxwell Foster-Keen, Mahjoub, Hosna Bint Mahmoud). Salih also presents multiple versions of events in the two parts of *Bandarshah*. In *Dau al-Beit,* the dream vision of Bandarshah's castle and the memorable dawn prayer in the mosque are narrated with some variation by several characters. In both cases, each version carries the personal stamp of its teller. In *Meryoud,* the third-person narrator resorts to a more subtle way of stating his preference for one version than the third-person narrator of "Wedding"—namely, by ascribing his opinions to Ibrahim Wad Taha, "a reliable chronicler of Wad Hamid's history" (*B* 1996, 107), who himself plays no role in the action—much like Cide Hamete Benengeli, the fictional "real author" of Cervantes's *Don Quixote.*

In Salih's longer narratives, such proliferation of irreconcilable versions of the same story rules out any certainty about "what really happened," thus complicating any possible resolution to the conflicts of the plot and delaying the progression of the narrative itself. In "Wedding," where very little actually happens in the time of narration, the effect is to postpone the final scene, announced in the opening lines. In *Season,* Mustafa becomes such an enigma as a result of the many irreconcilable reports given about him by other characters that the delayed revelation of his private papers at the end of the novel contributes to the mystery instead of solving it. In the third novel, the legend of Bandarshah and Meryoud pervades the characters' conscious and unconscious thoughts to such an extent that they all, in a sense, become Meryoud and Bandarshah, and the catalogue of folkloric, archaeological, and historical reconstructions of the legend toward the end of the novel has the effect of a puzzle. In each novel, this narrative strategy performs thematic and ideological functions (which will be analyzed in the appropriate places below). In "Wedding," the postponement of the title event and the divergence of the characters' and narrator's points of view prolong and deepen the meditation on the state of harmony created at the expense of sociohistorical reality. For the atmosphere of peace and love symbolized by the wedding celebration to be so pervasive, what Salih loosely calls the "secular" world, with its unequal power relations, injustices, and conflicts, must be suspended. Moments of revolutionary potential such as Hosna's killing of Wad Rayyes in *Season* and the bloody slave rebellion in *Bandarshah* are effectively precluded in the novella's utopian discourse.

This is not to suggest that the novella represents the fantasy of a nostalgic immigrant writer. On the contrary, there is a lot of truth in 'Osman Hassan Ahmed's argument that the novella "calls for love, tolerance, and sympathy between those who are in disagreement with one another, who live in the same village but are divided by different living conditions, temperaments, interests, and so on. It is also a call for tolerating different ideas, beliefs, and lifestyles without hateful bigotry." The political implications of this aspect of the novella are underscored by Ahmed's reading of it as an allegory in which the village of Wad Hamid stands for "Sudan with its conflicting tribes . . . classes, and warring cultures" (1976, 187). In a country torn by civil war along ethnic and religious lines since independence, such a message has a clear urgency; yet at the same time, the novella satirizes the failure of successive postcolonial Sudanese regimes to resolve this conflict.

It is perhaps for that reason that many critics focused their attention on this message of tolerance and peace rather than on the novella's ideological compromise. For those critics, social harmony is the essence of popular Islam. Berkley, for instance, holds that the religious world of Wad Hamid, centering on Haneen (the spiritual heir of the village's legendary founder, Wad Hamid), demonstrates "the syncretic merger of Islam with traditional African cosmologies, where there was always a holy man who had the power to intervene between ordinary man and nature. Through this special power the holy man could right the social malfunctioning in the community" (1979, 229). Citing A. Spenser Trimingham, Ahmad A. Nasr contends that "[p]opular Islam combines two extremes, namely the indigenous pagan religion as well as orthodox Islam. In it Islamic beliefs and animistic beliefs coexist" (1980, 91). Nasr further argues that "modernization can be achieved under the auspices of popular Islam" (90). Thanks to Haneen's miracles, Nasr argues, a school, a hospital, an army camp, and an agricultural project bring prosperity and modernization to Wad Hamid (103). This, Nasr contends, seconds the opinion of the old man in "The Doum Tree," who says there is enough space in the villagers' life for the doum tree, the tomb of Wad Hamid, the water pump, and the steamer's stopping place all at once. This argument reiterates the villagers' own perception of miracles, which fits within their worldview (subtly undercut by the urban guest's questions), but which does not explain how—short of producing dozens or even hundreds of holy men with supernatural powers—a society can achieve "modernization"! The serious implication of the argument is that such modernization—understood merely as the introduction of modern technology and institutions—can be made palatable to the uncouth masses if it is sugarcoated with religious superstition. This rules out democratic practice, which would engages those masses as citizens with the ability and power to decide for themselves on the course and pace of viable change.

Ahmad Shams al-Din al-Haggagi would perhaps disagree with Berkley and Nasr, arguing that it is Sufism and not ancient pagan religion that informs the villagers' unorthodox belief in the *wali* (the Sufi ascetic regarded as a holy man or saint): "The character of Zein is drawn as an enraptured dervish with all the familiar characteristics of a *wali* . . . as known in Arab villages" (1994, 100). Such characters are Sufis "who constitute an independent world, and they have a great influence upon the social life in the city, the countryside, and in oases" (99). Al-Haggagi goes on to interpret the novella in the light of Sufi cosmology, arguing that Zein assumes the role of the *qutb,* or the Pole (the highest spiritual guide in a Sufi order), which Haneen occupied until his death. This, for al-Haggagi, is reinforced in the novella's final images of Zein during his wedding celebrations:

> The clothes that the villagers give him—a white caftan and green sash—demonstrate their awareness of the entire situation. He stands amidst them, with a long crocodile-leather whip in his hands. . . . The crocodile is a symbol of fertility among the people of the Nile valley, as well as a source of bounty and a good omen. . . . It is also one of the ancient Egyptian deities representing the Nile. Thus, the figure of the crocodile had attacked Seif ad-Din, the evil-doer, to show him the punishment he would get if he persisted in his evil. Its skin in the hand of Zein is a whip that Zein can wield as he wishes.
>
> These images are enhanced further by the ring on Zein's finger which he wears that night. The ring has a ruby stone in the form of a snake head. The snake, which is not poisonous, represents to the masses the protecting Saint, and to some it is the Spiritual Pole. Zein has now fully introduced himself to his society. . . . Tonight, he is in control of their spiritual world. (al-Haggagi 1994, 129)

To that gloss, while developing a psychoanalytic reading of Zein's "individuation" from a Jungian perspective, Ahmad Harb adds:

> The psychological wholeness is doubly emphasized . . . by the image of the dancing circle itself, and the image of Zein, like a peacock, standing in the center. The circle is an ancient symbol of wholeness. Zein, now having completed his individuation, is the center of that wholeness. He becomes a new person. His comparison to the peacock signifies his rebirth, for the peacock is an emblem of transformation. The peacock also in Islamic iconography symbolizes the cosmos, viewed as a wheel that turns upon itself, taking on the contour of a mandala, another symbol of wholeness. Thus in the end we have two circles in total correspondence with each other; the microcosmic circle of Zein suggesting his personal wholeness against the macrocosmic circle of the dancers, the collective wholeness. (1986, 90–91)

Those two readings usefully foreground the iconography and structure of mystical thought, which is a fundamental source of inspiration for Salih not only in "Wedding" but also in "The Doum Tree," *Season, Bandarshah,* and "A Blessed Day."

Yet two fundamental aspects of the novella have generally been overlooked. The first is the narrowly circumscribed and conventional nature of its central event. The wedding of Zein, like any wedding or funeral, is an occasion for the coming together of heterogeneous and even conflicting groups at a gathering where conflicts and schisms are temporarily suspended. The novella ends at the climax of the celebrations; this signals the high point of unification, but also the beginning of its dissolution—something that takes place beyond the scope of the narrative. In this way, attention is called to the narrative's limits. As Peters observes, "the village is not devoid . . . of struggle, strife, conflict, all those layers of life that somehow manage to reach a temporary resolution and create at least a temporary catharsis" (1989, 234). This is indicated on the first page of the text, when news of the wedding offers some people the opportunity to exploit others. Amna's shock gives Halima the opportunity to give her a short measure of milk, and Shaykh Ali is able once again to avoid repaying his debt to Abdul Samad. These and other forms of exploitation are unlikely to disappear after Zein's wedding.

Second, for Zein's rehabilitation or individuation to occur, he must be transformed from village idiot into a fully socialized adult. This occurs under the auspices of two distinct though interrelated patriarchal orders, one spiritual and one secular. These two orders are never mutually exclusive in traditional societies, nor do they constitute separate, independent spheres, as modern Western social science construes them; rather, they interpenetrate each other, even though for analytical purposes it is useful to distinguish them from each other. The first is represented by Haneen, Zein's spiritual guide, the second by Mahjoub and his "gang," the village leaders who control the affairs of the village and befriend Zein. Critics have invariably privileged the spiritual. Within the narrative itself, however, the secular order, with its regulatory and pragmatic focus, is as central as the spiritual to Zein's life (and to the lives of the other villagers as well). The wedding itself is organized by Mahjoub's gang, whose members give Zein the clothes and emblems he dons in the final scene. In the novella, the (temporary) triumph of love over hate, of unity over divisiveness, is also a matter of efficient management of local worldly affairs.

In that sense, Zein is less a saint or a Sufi Pole than the personification of a social space traversed by the multiple, contradictory forces that make up the ensemble of a culture tethered equally to a complex material reality and to sometimes conflicting perceptions of the metaphysical world. Zein's contradictory images as buffoon and saint, therefore, make him, as a literary creation, similar to Mustafa Sa'eed and Bandarshah, who are also extraordinary and contradictory characters who embody the values, aspirations, and failings of a cultural worldview at a particular historical juncture. Zein's conflicting yet intertwined dimensions place him in the unique position of an outsider within, similar to Mustafa Sa'eed and Bandarshah. Indeed, just like Zein, Mustafa Sa'eed is likened to the prophet al-Khidr (*SMN* 1969c, 107), while at times Mustafa is a diabolic figure; likewise, the question of whether Dau al-Beit, the father of Bandarshah, is a devil or an angel in human form is never quite resolved (*B* 1996, 60–80); consequently, his son becomes part human and part myth. Such characters often expose the fissures in the community's social fabric, as Mustafa Sa'eed and Bandarshah do; alternatively (and rarely), they can strengthen the ties that pull it together. This is Zein's role.

Holy Fools and Social Space

"The Wedding of Zein" is about the incredible marriage of the village idiot to the most beautiful and desirable girl in Wad Hamid. Zein is a variation on the familiar literary character of the dervish, saintly idiot, or village buffoon. All of these are outsiders within. Two striking examples of this literary type in the works of other writers are worth noting here in order to situate Zein within that literary context. One is regarded as a holy man, the other as a semihuman monster. Those characters represent the two dimensions that converge somewhat paradoxically in Zein.

The first is Shaykh Darwish (literally, "dervish") in Naguib Mahfouz's *Zuqaq al-midaq* (1947, *Midaq Alley*). Shaykh Darwish is not certified by al-Azhar, Cairo's religious university; however, he is given the title of "Shaykh" by the residents of the alley, who regard him as a holy man. This fascinating character seems to be living in a world all his own, unconcerned by the goings-on of ordinary people. He emerges from a trance every now and then to utter cryptic or humorous statements which are not always clear but which occasionally turn out to have been visionary. For example, he predicts Abbas's tragic fate to his face, but the young man fails to comprehend Shaykh Darwish's meaning (Mahfouz 1947, 44). Earlier in his life, in the course of departmental restructuring, Darwish is demoted from his position as an English teacher to the less prestigious post of a clerk in the Ministry of Religious Endowments. There, he becomes bitter, rebellious, and increasingly negligent until one day he decides to write all official correspondence in English, to the bewilderment and exasperation of his superiors. One day, he enters the deputy minister's office to announce that "I am a messenger to you from God and I bring you a new [cadre]." Fired, he deserts his family and wanders off

> into a state of peace, contentment, and beatitude such as he had never known before. Even though he had lost his house, the whole world had become his home. Even though he had lost his salary, gone, too, was his dependence on money. Though he had lost his own family and friends, everyone he met became his family. If his gown wore out, someone would bring him a new one; if his tie became ragged, someone brought him a new one of those too. Everywhere he went people made him welcome. . . . He could not, despite what simple folk said, perform miracles nor predict the future. He was either distracted

and silent or extremely talkative without ever knowing particularly what [peo-
ple thought of what] he was saying.

Loved and honored, everyone always welcomed his presence amongst
them as a good sign and said that he was a fine and holy man of God, to whom
revelation came in two languages, Arabic and English. (Mahfouz 1947, 14)

Mahfouz does not hesitate to call those who believe in miracles "simple folk."
Shaykh Darwish and Zein share certain basic traits: both are half-witted individuals considered holy, and both are loved and cared for by their respective
communities.

The second character is Shaykh Shaykha (Shaykha is feminine for Shaykh),
the central character of a short story bearing his name by Yusuf Idris, the pre-
miere Egyptian writer of short stories.[2] The collection containing "Shaykh
Shaykha" was published in 1961, one year before the publication of "Wedding."
This time, the eccentric character

> could not be classed as human, nor yet as animal. . . . A curious creature with
> no name. Sometimes people called him Sheikh Mohamed, sometimes Sheikha
> Fatma . . . He was endowed with human features, nevertheless. Two eyes, two
> ears, a nose, and he walked on two feet, but he still wasn't anywhere near a
> human being. . . . Short, thick and woolly, his hair was neither that of a man
> nor of a woman, and his massive build reminded one of a sturdy wall. There was
> no trace of a beard on his face. His voice might have determined his sex except
> that he never spoke. He never moved either, unless he was hurt or in pain, in
> which case he would emit a low whine which was hard to attribute to anything
> sapient. (Idris 1961, 188–89)

This extraordinary character has much in common with Zein: both are androg-
ynous, both are described in animal imagery, and neither occupies a particular
place within society. Like Shaykh Darwish, however, both are accepted and accommodated within the community; moreover, they enjoy the freedom to cross
boundaries forbidden to normal adults. Thus Shaykh Shaykha stands wherever
he chooses, be it on the street or inside homes, and witnesses things done pri-
vately: "Women undressed before him and so did the men. Private affairs were
discussed in his presence, and men made love to their wives or other people's
under his eyes. Conspiracies were planned and false accusations plotted while he

---

2. The translator chose to render the title, "Shaykh Shaykha," as "The Freak," and throughout
the text the character's name is rendered in the same fashion, whereas it should perhaps have been
left untranslated. "The Freak" obscures the character's gender indeterminacy, which underlines not
only "his" (the masculine third-person pronoun is used out of linguistic necessity in the Arabic text)
eccentricity, but also his ability to move across gender (among other) barriers, which is an important
theme in the story.

looked on" (Idris 1961, 190). He is believed to be deaf, dumb, and all but blind. Though not invisible, his presence is as unthreatening as his absence. Though not saintly, he is significant within the religious worldview of the villagers:

> [N]obody looked upon him as someone abnormal, only different. And since he was living peacefully in our midst, doing no harm, no one had a right to mock or molest him. His deformity was a manifestation of God's will which none had a right to contest. His was a vast universe where all had a right to live, the maimed and the crippled and the wise and the insane. All moving in the same slow, fearful procession leading to their end and to infinity. It was simply that the people regarded [Shaykh Shaykha] with a special awe . . . inspired by those extraordinary phenomena that reveal the tremendous order of the universe. (189)

Chaos looms over the village, however, when rumors spread that Shaykh Shaykha not only hears and understands what goes on around him, but also talks. Everyone in the village has at some point over the years exposed a secret to him, and now they all fear scandal. If Zein is a catalyst that unites the community, Shaykh Shaykha's presence threatens to tear it apart. Thus one morning he is found murdered, no doubt by someone who fears the disclosure of some secret that Shaykh Shaykha may have known.

In contrast to Mahfouz's novel and Idris's short story, Salih's novella traces Zein's normalization and his successful socialization. Although the story describes how Zein unifies the village, the dynamics of the narrative suggest that Zein is ultimately co-opted and made to fit within the power structure of the village. His wedding symbolically unifies the village; it also serves as Zein's rite of passage into full membership in the community. This entitles him to privileges but also imposes on him the obligations and restrictions faced by "normal" adult males. Henceforth, he will no longer be an outsider within; on the contrary, by the time *Bandarshah* begins, he has become one of the village notables.

To understand this transformation, we must consider Zein in relation to the social space of the village and its power structure. Sociopolitical power circulates through two interrelated structures of patriarchal authority: religious and secular. These authorities are challenged by forms of resistance that threaten the established order. The novella's utopianism consists of maintaining a seemingly benign balance of power among the various authorities and the forces challenging them, and turning a potential agent of disruption (Zein as an outsider within) into a catalyst for social harmony. In this section of the chapter I will focus on Zein's location in the social space of the village; in the next, on the power structure of the village; in the final section, on how the discourse of the novella neutralizes other forces of disruption.

Initially, Zein has no particular location in the village's social landscape. His childishness, idiocy, or saintliness gives him free access to male and female spaces within the villagers' homes, as well as to the quarters inhabited by the various tribes and ethnic groups in and around the village. The opening sequence depicting the impact of the news of his engagement on its recipients indicates the degree to which he is believed to be socially dysfunctional. Ordinarily, Zein's marriage to his cousin Ni'ma would have been nothing unusual, for "the fact that a girl was reserved for marriage to her cousin was an irrefutable argument according to the conventions of village folk; it was an ancient tradition with them" (*WZOS* 1969e, 82). However, Zein's buffoonery and grotesque appearance disqualify him. Zein, whose name literally means "beautiful," is anything but good-looking. His features are disproportionate and exaggerated; they also contain a number of contradictions: prominent bones and sunken eyes, a childish (or feminine) hairless face despite his age and sex, powerful arms and shoulders and spindly legs, a concave chest and a hunched back. The rest of his features are at once human and animalistic: a neck like a giraffe's, arms like a monkey's, feet like a camel's (33–34). Later on his eyes are likened to those of a mouse, his laugh to the braying of a donkey, and his roaming the streets to the "running hither and thither [of] a bitch that has lost her puppies" (42–43). Furthermore, the seemingly "emaciated body concealed an extraordinary, superhuman strength" (61–62). These descriptions are punctuated by repeated mentions of the name Zein—"beautiful"—effectively making the man a walking paradox. His behavior matches his appearance. In the company of the village leaders he proclaims himself "the manliest chap in this place" (102), yet only moments later he "let[s] out a great burst of joyful ululation, like the women do at weddings" (104). His childish tomfoolery entertains the villagers but scandalizes the imam and the pious, who believe the villagers have spoiled him.

All of this is counterbalanced by the perception that he is a *darwish* (dervish), one of those entranced, roaming mystics whose devotion to God is believed to elevate them to a state of divine madness.[3] "[T]his belief was strengthened by Zein's friendship with Haneen" (*WZOS* 1969e, 44), the mys-

---

3. Trimingham describes different kinds of *darawish* (pl. of *darwish*): "a minority who are supposed to be wholly devoted to the religious life and to be following the 'Path' under the supervision of shaikh," and others who "own no allegiance to a particular order or a living shaikh; their shaikh is a dead saint who revealed himself to them in a vision and whose shrine they frequent . . . they carry around sand from his grave to drop into the hand of the faithful, who are then expected to reward them. *Darwish* is also applied in a general way to any half-witted or simple-minded person. Once when I spoke to a mentally-deficient child his mother explained him by saying, 'he's become a *darwish*' (*iddarwash*). None of these self-constituted dervishes know anything of Sufism and they are usually half-witted. They are beyond any recognized standard and their disregard of the laws of conventional Muslim morality and mental deficiency is ascribed to their being so absorbed in God that their bodies cannot be held responsible for their actions" (1965, 204).

terious ascetic who spends six months in the village praying, fasting, and talking
to no one except Zein, whom he calls "the blessed one of God." Haneen then
leaves the village for six months, carrying only his prayer rug and ablution
pitcher. Besides Haneen, "Zein had numerous friendships . . . with persons
whom the villagers regarded as abnormal, such as Deaf Ashmana, Mousa the
Lame, and Bekheit who was born deformed with no upper lip and a paralyzed
left side. Zein was fond of such people" (44). He is the only one of whom Ashmana is not terrified, and the only one to care for Mousa, the elderly ex-slave.
These characters are, like Zein, described in terms of animal imagery: Ashmana
clucked like a hen (45), and Mousa "lived on the fringe of life . . . like the old
stray dogs that howled in the waste plots of land at night, harassed by boys"
(46). Zein's affectionate care for them reinforces the image of a saint who acts as
an agent of God's grace: "The people of the village, seeing these acts of Zein's,
would be even more amazed; perhaps he was [God's prophet al-Khidr],[4] perhaps an angel sent down by God in lowly human form in order to remind His
worshippers that a great heart may yet beat even in one of concave breast and
ridiculous manner such as Zein. Some would say: 'He places His strength in the
weakest of His creatures' " (46). The proverb signifies that God's wisdom
sometimes finds the most unlikely agent to accomplish its plan. Thus Zein himself becomes to the villagers one of the mysteries of God's creation, like Shaykh
Darwish and Shaykh Shaykha.

Social identity in the village is determined by ethnic divisions as well as differences in the lifestyles and modes of production of settled, peasant tribes and
nomadic, herding ones:

[T]he bedouin who lived along the Nile in the north of the Sudan . . . came
down from the lands of the Kababeesh and the Dar Hamar, and from the en-
campments of the Hawaweer and the Mereisab in Kordofan. At certain seasons
water became scarce in their lands and they would journey down the Nile with
their camels and sheep in search of watering for them. . . . Most of them remained only until things got better, when they would return whence they had
come, though some of them, taking a liking to the settled life in the Nile valley,
stayed on. The bedouin of Koz were one such group. They continued to pitch

---

4. The "Prophet al-Khidr" is rendered in the English translation as "the legendary Leader."
Identified in the Qur'an as "one of Our slaves, unto whom We had given mercy from Us, and had
taught him knowledge from Our presence" (18: 66), al-Khidr is an immortal man (the name means
"Verdant," signifying his perennial existence) who performs good deeds that on the surface of
things seem to be evil. He represents esoteric knowledge and is, therefore, an especially significant
figure in Sufism. In the Sura of al-Kahf (The cave), Moses, who represents exotericism, seeks out
al-Khidr to learn from him, but fails to comprehend the wisdom behind al-Khidr's apparently irrational or wicked deeds (18:61–83). See Ibn Kathyr's *Al-bidaya wa al-nihaya* vol. 1, 295–9 and
325–37.

their tents on the edge of the cultivated land, where they pastured their sheep and sold the milk, collected wood for fuel, and hired themselves out at low rates in the date-harvesting season. They did not intermarry with the local inhabitants, considering themselves to be pure Arabs. The village people, however, regarded them as uncouth bedouin. (*WZOS* 1969e, 41)

Ethnic prejudice on both sides keeps these peoples separated into distinct communities; neither group wishes to contaminate itself by intermarrying with the other, even though the two maintain economic relations. It is a peaceful coexistence, but one that discourages social integration. Zein's special status exempts him from observing these barriers: "Always on the move, spending all day long wandering through the area from end to end," he may be found in the center of the village or wandering "for no particular reason [among] the people of the Koz" (41).

Another social barrier is gender. Children are exempted from segregation by gender until they reach puberty. Examples of this can be found in Salih's fiction: Ni'ma ("WZ") Hosna (*SMN*), Fatima bint Jabr ad-Dar (*DB*), and Maryam (*M*) were all (except for Fatima) childhood playmates of Meheimeed and Mahjoub's gang, and two of the girls attended boys' schools until their parents deemed that they "became women." Old age, too, can qualify some women, such as Bint Majzoub in *Season*, to join the company of men, though not vice versa. Outside of those two groups, keeping company with members of the other sex who are not spouses or family members is often frowned upon and considered immoral.

Zein, however, poses no threat to the honor and reputation of women, since he is not perceived as a responsible adult male. Rather, he serves as a bridge between the male and female spaces. For example, he is allowed to carry the food trays back and forth between the women in the kitchen and the men's quarters—a duty usually assigned to children (*WZOS* 1969e, 35). His free way with women (32–33) and his public proclamations of love, which would have scandalized and angered a conservative community, arouse laughter. Far from damaging the reputations of girls he admires, Zein publicizes their graces by claiming they have "slain" him; those girls get married so quickly that the mothers of marriageable girls begin to court his favor, hoping he will bring notice to their daughters (39–40). Everyone acknowledges "his impeccable taste, for he fell in love with none but the most beautiful girls, the best mannered and most pleasant of speech" (39). In this way he becomes an unwitting marriage broker: "In a conservative society where girls are hidden away from young men, Zein became an emissary for love, transporting its sweet fragrance from place to place. Love, first of all, would strike at his heart, then would be quickly transferred to the heart of another" (42). Astonishingly, one such marriage is that of Haleema, an "uncouth" Koz bedouin, to the son of the Cadi (judge), one of the notables of Wad Hamid. Yet Zein himself is never regarded as eligible for marriage either by the villagers or by the bedouin. Haleema's mother calls him a "dervish" (42), and when the news of his engagement reaches the headmaster, he declares indignantly that "Zein's a dervish of a man who shouldn't be marrying at all" (81)—an opinion seconded by the imam (103).

Zein's transgressions of social boundaries are not always tolerated and are sometimes severely punished. In fact, the first words he speaks in the novella tell the story of a scar on his right foot, the mark of an old wound sustained when, at a wedding, he attacked the bride and bit her on the mouth, only for one of her relatives to stab him in the ankle with a knife (*WZOS* 1969e, 34–37). The scar on his foot is a symbolic reminder of the consequences of overstepping social boundaries. A similar transgression earns him an equally symbolic wound, this time a near-fatal ax blow on the head, and marks the beginning of his transformation into a responsible adult. The description of the injury and the scene of Zein's return from the hospital suggest rebirth: "When Zein returned from the hospital in Merowi after a stay of two weeks, his face was sparkling clean and his clothes a spotless white. When he laughed, people no longer saw those two yellow [teeth] in his mouth, but a row of gleaming white teeth in his upper jaw and another row of pearly [teeth] in his lower.[5] It was as though Zein had been transformed into another person—and it struck Ni'ma . . . that Zein was not devoid of a certain handsomeness" (58).

The "miraculous" recovery of a full set of teeth reinforces the idea that Zein has attained manhood, since teeth, according to Freud, are phallic substitutes.[6] The story behind the two yellow teeth (according to his mother, as the narrator reminds us) adds to Zein's saintly aura: "His mother . . . says that his mouth was filled with pearly white teeth, but that when he was six she took him one day to visit some relatives of hers; at sunset, passing by a deserted ruin rumored to be haunted, Zein suddenly became nailed to the ground and had begun shivering as with a fever. Then he let out a scream. After that he took to his bed for several days, and on recovering from his illness it was found that all his teeth had fallen out—except for one in his upper jaw and one in the lower" (33). The characters understand this incident in light of their belief in *jinn* (creatures of fire invisible to human beings), a belief validated by the Qur'an, which teaches that there are good and evil *jinn,* those who are faithful and those who are the troops of the

5. The English translation reads, "yellow fangs . . . white teeth . . . pearly dentures," while in the Arabic the word for "teeth" is employed three times (first in the dual form, then twice in the plural). The translator perhaps wished to avoid using the word "teeth" three times in the same sentence, hence the choice of "fangs" and "dentures." Those two words, however, carry associations not evoked in the original.

6. See, for example, Freud's discussion of the significance of the growth of teeth in infantile sexuality (7: 181–2) and of the loss of teeth in dreams as symbolic castration (5: 357, 385–92).

Devil. The latter are believed to inhabit deserted areas, and what happens to Zein near the ruined building is immediately recognized as the work, not of ghosts as the word "haunted" in the English translation suggests, but of the evil *jinn,* who are always trying to harm humans. Zein's affliction, therefore, is the result of his confrontation with evil *jinn,* which he is able to resist because, as Haneen vouches, he is a "Blessed One of God." Zein's loss of teeth is also in line with a pattern regularly encountered in a number of mythologies—symbolic loss compensated for by a special gift. For example, in Greek mythology the priest Tiresias lost his eyesight but at the same time acquired the gift of prophecy. This acquisition was also associated with his crossing of the biological boundary between male and female, which brought him knowledge unattainable to ordinary human beings. Similarly, Zein's loss of teeth can be seen as a condition for his special status; in turn, his recovery of teeth suggests his arrival at the threshold of a new stage of his life—one in which he reacquires normalcy. The two illnesses marking those events frame the period of his life during which he is considered a *darwish.*

Seif ad-Din, who strikes Zein on the head with an ax, is like the evil *jinn* in that he is associated with the Devil. When he returns to the village to claim his inheritance, he has the appearance of a devil: "He carried a thick stick of the sort used in the east of the Sudan and had no luggage whatsoever. His hair was ruffled as a *sayal* acacia tree, his beard thick and dirty, and his face that of a man who has come back from Hell-fire. He gave greeting to no one and all eyes avoided him" (*WZOS* 1969e, 71). All of the villagers are scandalized by his appearance and by his withholding of the Islamic greeting of "Peace, mercy, and blessings of Allah be upon you." Thus his attack on Zein reenacts the incident by the ruins and Zein's affliction. Within the mythical scheme of the novella, Zein's recovery the second time can be understood as a spiritual victory—one that is achieved through divine intervention and that restores to Zein what he has lost in the battle with the forces of darkness, symbolized by the pearly white teeth. The victory becomes complete with Zein's own retaliatory attack on Seif, which in turn brings about a symbolic death and spiritual rebirth for the heretofore Devil's advocate.

Seif is the spoiled son of a wealthy, pious man who tries everything possible to reform his "dissolute boy—as he expressed it" (*WZOS* 1969e, 70). Having failed, the father finally throws him out after a sound beating. Upon the father's death, Seif returns in the above described manner to claim his inheritance before the mourning period is over. This scandalizes his mother, sisters, and uncles. As feared, he wastes a large part of his father's wealth and befriends the vagabonds and prostitutes of the oasis. When he invites these people to his sister's wedding, the villagers (headed by Mahjoub's gang) ambush them and give them "a good beating . . . with the best hiding of all . . . to Seif ad-Din. Then they threw them out into the street" (73).

Zein's later retaliation against Seif has the effect of a baptism by fire. It brings to an end the latter's life of depravity. Seif is reborn a penitent, reformed individual. This transformation is believed by many—including Seif himself—to be caused by a miraculous death and rebirth. With his customary skepticism at such moments, the narrator reports the event:

> In fact some of them [the witnesses] insist that Seif ad-Din had actually died, had breathed his last, and had fallen to the ground a lifeless corpse. Seif ad-Din himself affirms this and says that he did actually die; he says that the moment Zein's grip tightened he completely departed this world. He saw a vast crocodile the size of a large ox with its mouth agape; the crocodile's jaws closed upon him, then came a wave so large it seemed like a mountain, which bore off the crocodile . . . into a vast bottomless pit. It was then, Seif ad-Din says, that he saw [death] face to face, and Abdul Hafeez, the person closest to Seif ad-Din when he recovered consciousness, is adamant that . . . the first thing he said on opening his eyes, was: "I bear witness that there is no god but God, and I bear witness that Muhammad is the messenger of God." At any event, there is no doubt that from that moment Seif ad-Din's life underwent a change undreamed of by anyone. (*WZOS* 1969e, 66–67)

Whatever "actually" happened, Seif finally comes to face the consequences of his evil deeds (the crocodile, according to al-Haggagi, being a mythological figure of retribution) and to realize that he still has the chance to atone for the past. The Proclamation of Faith he pronounces on regaining consciousness, of course, signifies the spiritual rebirth of the Muslim convert; these words absolve past sins committed before conversion and indicate that he or she who speaks them is a new person with a clean slate. Again, the narrator cautions us that it is Abdul Hafeez who reports having heard Seif pronounce the Proclamation. Abdul Hafeez is the only member of Mahjoub's gang who attends prayers in the mosque, "a fact he would attempt to hide from the others" (*WZOS* 1969e, 99). Unlike Mahjoub, Abdul Hafeez "believed most firmly in Haneen's miracles" (74). Later on, in *Dau al-Beit*, Abdul Hafeez becomes openly devout, and replaces the imam in leading the prayers during the latter's illness, which leads Mahjoub's group to joke that Abdul Hafeez should lead the Friday prayers as well. His report on what "really" happened is thus less than reliable, since he is more predisposed than the others to believe in miracles. Yet the many unexpected changes in Seif's behavior—from frequenting the mosque, becoming its muezzin, and going on pilgrimage, to making up with his family, taking his father's aging former slave Mousa into his care, getting married, and reviving his father's business—all serve to confirm the faithful in their belief that the transformation of Seif is "a miracle . . . without a shadow of doubt" (75).

The incident marks a new beginning for both Zein and Seif; it also has a profound impact on Mahjoub's gang, who witness it, and on the village as a whole.

Haneen appears "out of the blue at the moment, the very instant, when Zein's grip tightened on Seif ad-Din and he had all but throttled him" (*WZOS* 1969e, 66). It is Haneen's presence, as if by a miracle, that turns Zein's blind anger into a benevolent force; left to his own devices, he would have killed Seif with the "immensely terrifying strength" that all of Mahjoub's gang combined had been unable to control (61). Haneen, Zein's spiritual guide and father figure, prevents him from committing evil. That he obeys Haneen while consumed with anger, and that at his injunction he makes peace with Seif "without protest" (64), confirms Zein in his "blessedness." Moreover, obedience to Haneen prevents Zein from stepping outside worldly laws. His newly acquired restraint—a sign of his capacity to be socially rehabilitated—is rewarded with Haneen's prophecy of marriage to "the best girl in the village" (64).

Seif also returns to the fold, both spiritually and socially. However, he turns to the imam for guidance rather than to Haneen—a sign that Seif enters the mainstream of the community's spiritual order, the realm of religious and social dogma, convention, and orthodoxy. His reform is spiritual but also very much social, manifesting itself in the public sphere of communal prayers at the mosque, where he becomes the muezzin. He also mends his relations with family and community and gets married; later, in *Dau al-Beit,* he is even elected to Parliament. His transformation from follower and agent of the Devil to follower and advocate of religion goes hand in hand with the one he undergoes from social pariah to active participant in the mainstream of social life in its religious, personal, economic, and political dimensions.

Spiritual and Secular Authority

Zein's socialization is not complete until he, too, is fully reconciled to both aspects of religious authority—orthodoxy and mysticism—as well as to secular authority. In particular, the imam's opposition to Zein's marriage *almost* constitutes a religious prohibition, for the imam represents orthodox Islam as an institution, and his opinions in matters of marriage and divorce are an informed interpretation of *shari'a* law. Besides, he is by profession the one who contracts marriages in the village. Still, Zein "treated him with rudeness and if he met him approaching from afar he would leave the road clear for him. The imam was perhaps the only person Zein hated; his mere presence at a gathering was enough to spoil Zein's peace of mind and start him cursing and shouting. The imam would react to Zein's outbursts with dignity, sometimes saying that people had spoiled Zein by treating him as someone unusual and that to regard him as a holy person was a lot of rubbish" (*WZOS* 1969e, 93).

The imam's authority as the representative of institutional Islam is counterbalanced by that of Haneen, the representative of popular Islam, and also by that of Mahjoub's gang, the secular authority in the village who virtually control its day-to-day worldly affairs, including the maintenance of the mosque and the payment of the imam's salary (which puts him practically "at their mercy" [92]). Furthermore, the imam is tacitly resented by the villagers themselves, who are suspicious of the government and its envoys (including imams), as we have seen in "The Doum Tree." The imam goes unnamed in "Wedding" because the villagers consider him as an "institution" rather than an individual (*WZOS* 1969e, 90). He is—and note the narrator's distancing of the villagers' perception of him—"in the opinion of the village, an importunate man, a talker and a grumbler, and in their heart of hearts they used to despise him because they reckoned him to be the only one among them who had no definite work to do: no field to cultivate and no business to occupy him, but lived off teaching children for a set fee collected from every family—a fee grudgingly paid" (87). The villagers' religious sensibility is at odds with the orthodox aspects of religion such as ritual duties, as well as with doctrinal matters such as "Judgment Day and punishment, Heaven and Hell-fire, disobedience to God and turning to Him in repentance—words that passed down their throats like poison." The imam's temperament adds to the problem, for he is the kind of preacher who deals in fear: "He used to chastise them harshly in his sermons as though avenging himself" so that they left the mosque "boggle-eyed" and "experience[d] no feeling of joy" (89). Moreover, "an abyss had grown up between them" because he is contemptuous of their provincial concerns about agriculture and "the particulars of life"; he prefers instead to discuss international politics (88–89). He is, in short, like the urban imam in "The Doum Tree," who cannot stay for more than a week and is unable to relate to the villagers.

Yet in spite of themselves, the villagers admire his eloquence and the extensive learning he acquired at al-Azhar University. Even though he takes away their peace of mind, "most of them would go back to listen to him and each time they would experience the same mysterious conflict. They would go back to him because his voice was strong and clear when he preached, sweetly melodious when he recited the Koran, terrifyingly awesome when he said prayers over the dead, thoroughly knowledgeable of all aspects of life as he performed contracts of marriage" (*WZOS* 1969e, 89–90). The villagers perceive him as idle—a result of his lack of a manual occupation—yet they need him to teach their children and to conduct their religious affairs and to infuse in them a sense of religious community. His very presence among them upholds its formal aspects; in contrast, Haneen—as much by his mysterious absence as by his sporadic, sudden appearances—infuses in them a sense of awe at divine mysteries.

In this way the spiritual authority in the village is shared by Haneen and the imam. Haneen represents what different people would variously call mysticism, esotericism, popular Islam, or superstition. The imam, for his part, represents orthodoxy, exotericism, and the religious establishment with its dual emphasis on worldly and otherworldly affairs—on legislation, jurisprudence, and ritual on the one hand, and doctrinal matters of faith and Judgment on the other. Indeed, the credit for the miracles attributed to Haneen seems to be shared in some measure by the imam, who is reported to have recited "a particularly auspicious and blessed" verse from the Qur'an at the same time that Haneen blessed the village (*WZOS* 1969e, 76). In that sense, Haneen and the imam are not antagonists, the one nourishing the spiritual life of the villagers, the other impoverishing it, respectively, which is how the two religious figures have often been represented by commentators on the novella. Rather, the two address different aspects of life in an essentially religious community of simple and mostly uneducated farmers.

The two religious men do, of course, contest each other at times and are themselves contested by the nonreligious. Like the imam in "The Doum Tree," who shows contempt for the tree of the title and for popular Islam in general, this imam does not recognize "the mystical side of the spiritual world" represented by Haneen (*WZOS* 1969e, 94); the imam regards him as a "holy man" (94) but does not acknowledge his miracles. According to the imam, Seif ad-Din's transformation is an "example . . . of how Good was in the end victorious. The imam paid no heed to the fact that Haneen . . . was the direct cause of Seif ad-Din's repentance" (94). Later on, *contra* Haneen's prophecy, the imam tries to stop Zein's marriage on the grounds that a *darwish* is "not a man for matrimony" (103). The imam reverses his position under pressure from Mahjoub's gang, who also teach Zein lessons in conduct and responsibility that qualify him "for matrimony" (as shall be demonstrated momentarily). In the end, the imam warmly congratulates Zein after contracting his marriage "in a voice charged with emotion," and prays that the marriage will prove to be "a happy and blessed union" (110). Thus, Zein's successful socialization is crowned by marriage and reconciliation with the imam.

As for Haneen, he dies shortly after fulfilling his role in the novella, which is to bring about the rehabilitation of Seif and Zein. Zein does not replace Haneen in the role of the Pole, as al-Haggagi argues, nor does he develop into a full-fledged mystic exempted from social obligations. Instead, his marriage to "Ni'ma, daughter of Hajj Ibrahim," which is "synonymous with noble birth, virtue and social standing" (*WZOS* 1969e, 106–7), leads him eventually—as indicated at the beginning of *Dau al-Beit*—to become, like Seif, one of the notables of the village. Through their reconciliation to the spiritual realm in its orthodox and mystical orders both, Zein and Seif become fully rehabilitated into the secular realm.

Secular authority is a function of three distinct orders. First of all, there is the national government, which makes economic and strategic policy decisions that affect the villagers in ways they cannot always comprehend. It sends its envoys to them, as in "The Doum Tree," and the Wad Hamidians must negotiate with those envoys in order to preserve a measure of autonomy for the village

(*WZOS* 1969e, 40). The younger generation of villagers, headed by Mahjoub's gang, attempt to maximize their benefit from governmental development schemes while maintaining that autonomy. To them, the government remains—as it was for the generation of their parents—omnipotent and unpredictable, and their attitude toward it is a mixture of awe and contempt. It has a mind of its own, like a "refractory donkey," and it does things "for no apparent reason" (79). But once "the government has made up its mind to something, it has the power to carry it out" (78). The villagers do not understand the political and economic conditions underlying the "refractory donkey's" decision to allow them to cultivate cotton at a time when its prices rise, or why a hospital is about to be built in their village, or why the army of a newly independent country would set up new camps, one of which happens to be near their village. The government's failure to gain their confidence and respect because of its condescending and patronizing posture (seen in "The Doum Tree") ensures that the *Nahda*'s project of modernization is achieved only on a superficial level—one that paradoxically serves to confirm the villagers in their superstitious beliefs: since nothing of good can be attributed to the wisdom of the government, the villagers consider the building of a hospital, a power station, and a school as so many of Haneen's miracles (78).

Next in the chain of power is the Omda (mayor) of the village. Both here and in *Season,* he is represented as rapacious and exploitative, as levying heavy taxes and plotting with the merchants to keep the peasants ignorant of the best means of cutting their costs and increasing their profits (which is why he "absolutely loathed" Mustafa Sa'eed, who "opened the villagers' eyes" [*SMN* 1969c, 101]). He exploits Zein's love of his daughter by promising to wed her to him, and for a whole month gives him "any number of arduous tasks which would have defeated the jinn themselves" (*WZOS* 1969e, 40).

But the Omda's authority is curbed by those who "wielded real power in the village" (*WZOS* 1969e, 91), Mahjoub's gang: "[W]hen the Omda came to collect taxes, it was they who would stand up to him and say that such-and-such taxes were too much for so-and-so, that this amount was reasonable, that unreasonable" (92). Furthermore, they constitute the link between the village and the government: "If some government representative descended on the village . . . it was they who received him and put him up, killing a sheep or lamb for him, and argued matters out with him in the morning before he met any of the villagers. With schools being set up in the village, also a hospital and an agricultural project, it was they who were the contractors and the overseers; they also made up the [committee] responsible for everything . . . no task could be carried out successfully, no work accomplished, unless he came to an understanding with them" (92). Furthermore, their leader, Mahjoub, has secret methods that even his close associates and "gang" members—Abdul Hafeez, Taher Rawwasi (Meheimeed's closest friend), Hamad Wad Rayyes (not the same Wad

Rayyes of *Season,* but apparently his son), Ahmad Isma'il, and Sa'eed the shop-keeper—cannot fathom. When a new district commissioner—an official with considerable authority over a group of villages—begins to criticize the gang for controlling the affairs of Wad Hamid, prompting some of its members to consider resigning from various committees, Mahjoub orders them to " 'stay put' . . . and no more than a month went by before the Commissioner was transferred. . . . Mahjoub has special methods of his own in extreme situations." His "stolidness showed itself in times of real emergency, when he would take over the captaincy of the ship, he giving the orders and they carrying them out" (101)—a scenario repeated in *Season* on the night Hosna kills Wad Rayyes (*SMN* 1969c, 127–28).

It would be difficult to overstate the importance of Mahjoub's gang in "Wedding," although their role has gone almost unnoticed by critics, who privilege the spiritual authority. Scenes depicting the gang occupy more space than any others in the novella with the exception of those depicting Zein; together, they comprise a fascinating portrait of a half-dozen men who control most aspects of life in the village. They are not the village elders by the count of years, for they were "between thirty-five and forty-five, except for Ahmad Isma'il who, though in his twenties, was one of them by virtue of his sense of responsibility and way of thinking." They are an unusual group who have attained power through their own craftiness, initiative, and sense of responsibility:

> They were the men you came across in every matter of moment that arose in the village. Every wedding was seen to by them; every funeral was organized and got ready by them; between them they would wash the dead man and take turns when bearing him off to the cemetery. It was they who would dig the grave, bring along the water, lower the dead man into his tomb, and pile the earth on top of him, after which you would find them receiving in the dead person's house those who came to offer their condolences, passing round cups of un-sugared coffee. When the Nile was in spate or there was a torrential downpour, it was they who dug the channels, set up barricades, and patrolled the village by night carrying lanterns, finding out how people were faring and making estimates of the damage. If someone said a woman or girl had glanced provocatively at a man, it was they who would reprimand, and sometimes even strike, her—it didn't matter to them whose daughter she was. If they learned that there was some stranger hanging round the village at sundown, it was they who would send him packing (*WZOS* 1969e, 91–92).

Their sphere of influence is the nitty-gritty of everyday life in all its aspects, and they manage it with an efficiency that foils the ineptitude of the national government. The imam officiates over the ceremonial aspects of events marking the continuation and the end of life, conducting the marriage ceremonies and funerary prayers over the dead, but it is the secular authority in the village that attends to the practical side of those matters, regardless of whose wedding or funeral it may be. They act as guardians to the entire village, and they undertake to protect it from those natural and human calamities—floods, strangers, small acts considered immoral—that are normally the responsibility of the government, the police, or parents. Women may go to Abdul Hafeez to complain to him of their husbands; Hamad Wad Rayyes may be "deputed to deal with women's problems in the village" (99). They are the ministries of Interior, Public Works, Agriculture, and Foreign Affairs, as well as border guards, police, and vice squad—a miniature government on a village scale. "[W]ith genuine admiration," Meheimeed says to Mahjoub in *Season,* "it's you who've succeeded, not I . . . because you influence actual life in the country. Civil servants, though, are of no consequence. People like you are the legal heirs of authority; you are the sinews of life, you're the salt of the earth" (*SMN* 1969c, 99). A member of the intellectual elite and a government employee, Meheimeed here wistfully testifies to the failure of the *Nahda* as an *official* project, although he suggests that local secular leadership holds the key to the future.

The narrator in "Wedding" seems to share this opinion to a certain extent. He often depicts them gathered at night outside Sa'eed's shop, conversing in a cryptic, elliptical manner that outsiders cannot comprehend. As if trying to control the traffic between two worlds, they often sit in "their favorite spot where the light form the lamp touched them with the tip of its tongue . . . the light and shadow danced above their heads as though they were immersed in a sea in which they floated and dipped" (*WZOS* 1969e, 96), or "as though they are drowning in a sea" (98). In Salih's fiction (specifically in *SMN, M,* "CM," and "BDCUB"), imagery of light and darkness, of floating and dipping in water, and of drowning always suggests confusion, loss, struggle, or moral uncertainty. Here the images suggest that the gang's power in the village, like their political and social vision, has its limits, even though they seem—in the explicit discourse of the narrator—to be all-knowing and all-powerful, much to the benefit of the village. Sometimes control of a situation is wrenched from them, as when Haneen's successful intervention to stop Zein from killing Seif foils their failure to do the same (62).

Haneen is the only person whose power they cannot curb; it is of an order outside their rational, ordered world. His appearance, sudden and uncanny, places them in one of those characteristically Salihian moments—so abundant in *Season* and *Bandarshah*—in which, for the "twinkling of an eye," the characters feel themselves transported to a region "outside the boundaries of time and space," the boundaries of the secular world they understand. Although not particularly religious and almost never performing the prayers, Mahjoub has "an innate awe of religious people, especially ascetics like Haneen, and [h]e used to remove himself from their path and have nothing to do with them. Yet he took warning of their predictions, feeling, despite his lack of outward concern, that they had mysterious powers" (*WZOS* 1969e, 64). When the gang members kiss Haneen's hand and receive his blessing, they are acknowledging his power and authority as surpassing theirs. Haneen's departure from the scene, like his sudden appearance, leaves them with the eerie impression that one order of existence has given way to another: "For an instant a shaft of light from the lamp hanging in Sa'eed's shop flickered above their heads, then slipped off them as a white silk gown slips from a man's shoulder. Mahjoub looked at Abdul Hafeez, Sa'eed looked at Seif ad-Din, and they all exchanged looks and nodded their heads" (65).

In contrast, Mahjoub and his group are in control of the imam, who depends on the villagers for his livelihood. While Mahjoub's gang and the imam share the management of the worldly and religious affairs of the village respectively, they dislike each other, and they coexist peacefully only for practical reasons. He calls them "the sinful" (*WZOS* 1969e, 88) because they do not pray behind him in the mosque or attend his Friday sermons, but "he knew he was at their mercy" (92). For their part, "they harnessed their tongues as best they could to avoid criticizing him and would render him 'the requisite courtesies' . . . Though they did not pray, at least one of them would attend prayers once a month . . . to give him his monthly salary and examine the structure of the mosque to see if it was in need of repair" (92–93). It is not the spiritual or religious significance of the mosque that interests them, but its physical structure and, by extension, the structure of the society in which the building occupies a position of central importance. To their pragmatic and socially conservative minds, the mosque (built through their efforts [*B* 1996, 7]) is one of the responsibilities of governance in the village of which they have taken charge. As for the imam, he is "a necessary evil" (*WZOS* 1969e, 92), just as the prostitutes of the "oasis" are to them "an inevitable evil" (95).

Indeed, their daily ritual of dining together at the end of the day coincides with, and almost parodies, the prayer of the congregation behind the imam. It is a secular ritual that affords them the same inner peace that the faithful find in the mosque:

> When the call to prayers had come to an end and they heard the imam's voice calling out in the mosque courtyard "To prayers, to prayers," each one of them got up to go home and bring his dinner. Just as other people prayed as a group in the mosque, so the "gang" dined as a group . . . When their plates were returned empty, tea would be brought and they would fill up their glasses and each would light a cigarette, stretch out his legs and relax. By then the people would have finished the evening prayer. They would talk quietly and contentedly, enjoying that warm, tranquil feeling which is also experienced by the worshippers as they stand in a row behind the imam . . . This is the time when Wad

> Rayyis suddenly breaks out into a single phrase, like a stone falling into a pond: "God is living" . . . and Taher Rawwasi gives a sigh from deep within him and says: "Time comes and Time goes." (*WZOS* 1969e, 104–6)

The imam considers the gang to be "sinful," yet they are not necessarily irreverent, and the parody is almost unconscious. Just as the five daily prayers give tempo to the lives of the pious, the group of six have their own rhythm to follow. If the religiosity of the imam and his followers is orthodox and based on ritual, if Haneen's is mystical, if Zein's is instinctive and unconscious, then the gang's is generic. They hold that "God is living," that miracles occur at the hands of holy men, and that the whole of life conforms to the moral lesson implied in the edict, "Time comes and Time goes"—one that is stated in Surat al-Rahman ("The Merciful" 55: 26–27): "Everyone that is thereon [i.e., on earth] will pass away. There remaineth but the countenance of thy Lord of Might and Glory." The six men experience the same kind of inner peace felt by the worshippers in the mosque, and the eyes of both groups wander away in the distance contemplatively: the worshippers' following their prayers, the gangs' meditating on the elusive line between light and darkness (*WZOS* 1969e, 105). Seated in that liminal, uncertain area where "light ends and darkness begins," Mahjoub's group are situated between what Salih calls "the world of magic" and that of history and material reality; they try to make sense of both as they strive to preserve order and maintain social equilibrium. They succeed in doing so here, but fail in *Season* and lose their power altogether in *Bandarshah*.

It is they, in the end, who are in charge of the wedding festivities, not Zein, as al-Haggagi and Harb argue. Mahjoub's gang share with Haneen the credit for preparing Zein for full participation in social life by teaching him how to behave like an adult. In that regard the gang has played the role of surrogate father to an orphan: "They were careful to get him out of trouble, and if he did get himself into a fix it was they who would come to his rescue. . . . They knew more about him than his own mother did, and they kept a watchful eye on him from afar" (*WZOS* 1969e, 93). They make sure that neither the hostility of the imam nor the opposition of the headmaster stops the wedding; at the same time they teach Zein responsible conduct: " 'The wedding ceremony's next Thursday,' Mahjoub told him firmly. 'After that there'll be no more fooling about and dancing and talking nonsense" (103). On the wedding day, Mahjoub, assuming the role of a father for the occasion, acts on behalf of Zein in contracting the marriage. Later, when Zein starts looking round him "in simple-minded fashion," surprised that the imam greets him warmly after the ceremony, "Ahmad Isma'il gave him a severe look," giving him to understand that his behavior should rise to the occasion (110). Besides that, of course, the group of six organize the wedding and give Zein the symbolically laden clothes and accessories he wears, for just as they maintain the physical structure of the mosque, they up-hold the mystical belief system. Finally, when Zein abandons the wedding for Haneen's grave, they search for him (Mahjoub, as usual, taking charge of a potentially disastrous situation) and bring him back, gently teaching him that there is an appropriate action for every occasion: " 'He [Haneen] was a man blessed of God. But tonight is your wedding night and no man cries on his wedding night' " (119).

The wedding functions as a symbol of social integration, a celebration on a grand scale that includes almost every house, community, and stratum of the village and its vicinity. The magnitude of the wedding and the juxtaposition of the imam and the prostitutes, the reciters of the Qur'an and the dancers, the digni-fied pious and the reveling drinkers, with Zein at the center of it all, paints a pic-ture of a community able to manage its internal conflicts, maintain its equilibrium, and produce its own symbols of peace and harmony. It may achieve that in the name of religion, mysticism, or miracles, but it would not be possible without efficient and able management of worldly affairs.

In fact, the novella's satirical utopianism consists of the secular authority's ability, versus the national government's inability, to harness social energies and to contain if not resolve conflict and dissent. This may mean, in practical terms, consolidating the existing power relations and eliminating or minimizing resist-ance. This necessarily raises the question of social justice and whether it can ever be guaranteed within the established order. More concerned with expediency than with justice, more with efficient management than with progressive change, the secular authority, in the final analysis, acts according to a socially conservative politics. The novella's utopianism dictates the success of that poli-tics, but when revolutionary forces violently disrupt the status quo, the villagers feel that "the world has turned suddenly upside down" (*SMN* 1969c, 134), that "the harmony in the universe had been disrupted" (*B* 1996, 9).

Utopian Erasure

In *Season,* the disruption of established social order results from female resist-ance to an oppressive, misogynistic patriarchal order (murder of husbands); in *Bandarshah,* patriarchal authority is shaken through Oedipal and caste conflict (parricide and slave revolt). Such forms of conflict never disturb the serenity of the utopian world of "Wedding," but they exist as lacunae in the discourse of the novella. Other forms of dissent and rebellion also remain at bay. This utopian erasure must now be exposed for the novella's ideological project to be understood.

In opposition to the elders of Wad Hamid, the "sensible-minded grown-up men . . . [who] treated the imam with reserved affection" (*WZOS* 1969e, 90), and Mahjoub's gang, who treat the imam with grudging civility, there is the "camp" of "young men under twenty who were openly antagonistic to the imam." These young men seem to have only two things in common—youth and nonreligiosity. That aside, they are drawn from various groups. "Some of them were students, others had traveled abroad and returned." Those are "the educated who had read about or heard of dialectical materialism" (90), the Westernized youth who in the opinion of the old narrator in "The Doum Tree" have "foreign souls." Another group of young men, "feeling the flame of life scorching hot in their blood . . . drank wine in private and gathered secretly at 'the Oasis' on the edge of the desert" (90–91). There are also "the mutinous" (like Seif ad-Din before his transformation) and simply "the lazy who found it difficult to perform their ablutions at dawn in the depths of winter" (91). All of these groups are headed by "a man in his seventies, Ibrahim Wad Taha by name, who did not pray, fast, or give alms, and who did not acknowledge the imam's existence" (90). Ibrahim Wad Taha "was a poet" (91)—something that evokes such figures as Abu Nuwas and Omar Khayyam, poet-rebels who defied religious prohibitions and raised the cry of *carpe diem*, an ethic clearly at odds not only with the two branches of spiritual authority (orthodoxy and mysticism), but also with the conservative politics of the village's secular authority. Abu Nuwas's poetry plays an important role in framing *Bandarshah*; for his part, Ibrahim Wad Taha returns in that novel as the "reliable chronicler of Wad Hamid's history" who is cited at length by the narrator (*B* 1996, 107–9). In other words, these "rebels" are not simply "bad guys" in the Wad Hamid Cycle; they contribute to shaping its ideological critique of Arab modernity. However, in "Wedding," none of the groups headed by Ibrahim Wad Taha is treated with any depth; the novella is too concerned with envisioning a utopian society.

The confluence of patriarchy, religious conservatism, and slavery as systems and discourses of power finds its clearest expression in the representation of the "oasis." The prostitutes of the oasis are "slaves who had been given their freedom, some of them having migrated from the village and married far away from the locality of their bondage; others had married freed slaves from the village and led a respectable life, a continuing affection existing between them and their former masters. Some of them, however, not finding a settled life easy, had stayed on the perimeter of life in the village, a place for those bent on pleasure and sensual enjoyment"[7] (*WZOS* 1969e, 67–68). 'Osman Hassan Ahmed is sensitive to this social problem: "the story of Mousa the Lame points to our double standard toward 'slaves,' for in spite of the official ban on slavery, we still regard them as slaves. Either they intermarry among themselves or move to the oasis" (1976, 189).

In a society with powerful sexual mores and narrowly circumscribed relations between the sexes, the (ironically named) "oasis" serves as a more realistic

---

7. On slavery in Sudan, see Abbas Ibrahim Ali and Muhammad Ibrahim Naqd.

alternative to Zein's eccentric and unsustainable approach to bridging male and female spaces. It also marks the boundary of the community: geographically, the oasis is at the edge of the desert, and separates the fertile farmland of the Nile Valley from the deadly, uninhabitable waste beyond it; socially, the oasis lies beyond the pale of both secular and spiritual authority. The villagers, therefore, are not content to ostracize the former slaves of the oasis, but tirelessly chase them away and burn down their houses. For the imam, "[t]he 'Oasis' had always been his chief concern, regarding it as a symbol of evil and corruption, seldom delivering a sermon without mentioning it" (94). As for Mahjoub's gang, the destruction of the oasis is "a matter of expediency" (95). Yet such measures always fail, for they try to suppress the symptom without curing the social malaise that produced the oasis in the first place. Consequently, the prostitutes' shacks reappear, "like the alfa plant that will not die," or more suggestively, "like flies alighting upon a dead cow" (69).

Clearly, the problem of prostitution lies beyond Zein's sphere of influence as a catalyst for social harmony. By virtue of his high profile, he helps bring some marginalized individuals to the attention of the community. When he cares for the poor, the downtrodden, and the disabled, such as Ashmana, Mousa, and Bekheit, he provides them with a much needed sense of human community and reminds the village of its collective responsibility toward them. But the prostitutes are outside the enchanted circle surrounding Zein, and even though they come to his wedding—the symbol of social unity in the novella—their status remains unchanged. In fact, they are beyond the reach of even Haneen's mystical powers, which, in the discourse of the novella as well as in much critical commentary on it, constitute the benevolent force that makes that unity possible. Haneen is credited with reforming Seif and bringing wealth and prosperity to the village, but his miracles stop short of the oasis. In fact, they worsen its plight: a reformed Seif turns against "his old friends" at the oasis, "exploit[ing] his knowledge of their inner secrets and so [becoming] their most dangerous adversary" (*WZOS* 1969e, 94). The oasis is not affected by the villagers' good fortune; it is only blamed for their misfortune.

Ni'ma is the utopian answer to the girls of the oasis, who are her dialectical counterpart. The characterization of Ni'ma is the final gesture of sanitizing traditional gender relations through a patriarchal fantasy of female self-sacrifice and devotion. She defies patriarchal authority by refusing to submit to her father's will on the question of marriage—a defiance similar to Hosna's in *Season*. Yet whereas Hosna is forced to marry against her will, Ni'ma is allowed to have her way. When she refuses one eligible suitor after another, her "father spoke furiously to her and was about to slap her. Suddenly, though, he stopped; something in the girl's stubborn countenance killed the anger in his breast. Perhaps it was the expression of her eyes, perhaps the calm resolution on her face. It was as though the man sensed that this girl was neither disobedient nor refractory, but that she was propelled by an inner counsel to embark upon something from which no one could deflect her" (*WZOS* 1969e, 54). The same independence of mind that could not be tolerated in Hosna's case is indulged in Ni'ma's when it is perceived as divinely inspired, as something that could be accommodated within the villagers' religious worldview though it is not the privilege of the vast majority of other women.

The difference between Ni'ma and Hosna lies in the source of their defiance of their fathers, and also in its scope and implications. Hosna's marriage to a "stranger" (*SMN* 1969c, 129) changed her so much that, in Mahjoub's words, "It was as though she were another person. Even we who were her contemporaries and used to play with her in the village look at her today and see her as something new—like a city woman" (101). Her rebelliousness is a direct threat to patriarchal authority. In contrast, Ni'ma has not been exposed to foreign ideas; her education took place in the Qur'anic school "where she had been a lone girl among boys" (*WZOS* 1969e, 52), and she despises modern education: when her brother urges her to continue her education and become a doctor or a lawyer, she replies, "education at school is a whole lot of nonsense. It's quite enough to read and write and to know the Koran and the rituals of prayer" (53). Unlike Hosna's, Ni'ma's independence of mind is inspired by precocious religiosity; thus her "stubbornness" breaches only the outward aspect of tradition, but conforms to it in a fundamental, mystical way through "inner council" or divine calling.

Moreover, Ni'ma's choice of a husband is less unusual than may appear at first. Zein after all is her cousin, which would have ordinarily made him the most socially approved candidate for marriage. Since his ambiguous status as an idiot or a dervish disqualifies him, her choosing him is a powerful assertion of social convention to the point of self-sacrifice. She finds inspiration in the Qur'anic Suras that describe mercy and motherhood—qualities with which she identifies—and in the ordeals and sacrifices of prophets:

> When she reached the verse 'And we restored unto him [Job] his family, and as many more with them, through our mercy,' she would picture 'Mercy' to herself as a woman, a woman of rare beauty, dedicated to the service of her husband, and she wished that her parents had named her Rahma, that is 'Mercy.' She used to dream that one day she would make some great sacrifice, though she did not know what form it would take, and then she would experience the same strange sensation that came over her when reading the *Chapter of Mary*. (*WZOS* 1969e, 52)[8]

8. Sura 55, Al-Rahman (the Merciful), describes some manifestations of mercy as one of God's qualities, and promises Heaven to the faithful. Sura 19, Maryam (Mary), glorifies motherhood in the figure of Mary, the mother of Jesus, features an Honor's List of prophets, and foretells punishment in Hell for unbelievers. Sura 28, al-Qasas (Stories [of the Prophets]), tells the story of Moses

And while Hosna rejects the idea of marriage on principle, Ni'ma thinks of marriage as something "unexpected and unplanned, just as God's divine decree falls upon His servants . . . a destiny fore-ordained by God for her . . . She felt no joy, fear or distress when she thought of it, merely that a great responsibility would be placed on her shoulders" (*WZOS* 1969e, 54). Marriage for her has little to do with romance of love, and much to do with a romance of martyrdom. It does not exclude a polygamous union, or one that brings her poverty and diminished social status. That romance is focused on Zein, the top candidate for marriage by social convention, yet the least qualified by material standards; thus her choice reaffirms social convention over vanity, wealth, and status. Since it is difficult to conceive of him in romantic terms, "when Zein came to Ni'ma's mind, she experienced a sensation of warmth in her heart, of the kind a mother feels for her children. Intermingled with it was another feeling: of pity. She would see Zein as being an orphan in need of being cared for" (55).

Yet if the lack of parental coercion in the question of marriage differentiates "Wedding" from *Season,* men's attitudes toward women in the two works are identical, and male supremacy prevails. Ni'ma being the exception that proves the rule, fathers have unlimited power to dispense of their daughters in marriage, as evidenced by the Omda and Mahjoub, each of whom promises to give his daughter to Zein (*WZOS* 1969e, 37, 40), and by Mahmoud in *Season,* who promises to give his daughter Hosna to the aged Wad Rayyes against her will. As Shaykh Ali puts it, "a man's a man even though he's drooling, while a woman's a woman even if she's as beautiful as Shajarat ad-Dur" (85). The same idea is expressed by Mahjoub with reference to Hosna (*SMN* 1969c, 99). Ni'ma challenges some of those attitudes, but she hardly threatens male supremacy. In fact, the example she sets foils other forms of resistance and undermines them by projecting a nearly impossible ideal of womanhood. Mahjoub's reaction to her conduct is quite revealing. A firm defender of patriarchal values who would have liked to throw Hosna's body to the hawks after she killed her abusive husband "if it wasn't for the sake of decency" (*SMN* 1969c, 133), Mahjoub expresses his admiration of Ni'ma's acts "with boundless enthusiasm": " 'She's certainly a woman to fill the eye all right . . . I'll divorce if there's another girl like that' " (*WZOS* 1969e, 103). Ni'ma's independence of mind serves not to challenge patriarchal order, but on the contrary to uphold it, thus validating it beyond the wildest dreams of its staunchest representatives. While the characterization of Ni'ma demonstrates the potential for social harmony inherent in traditional society, it effectively does so at the expense of those women who are oppressed or marginalized by it—not just the prostitutes of the oasis, but also ordinary

---

from birth to the Exodus. The verse from Al-Anbiya' (Prophets 21:83) speaks of God's mercy toward Ayyub (Job) after his ordeal.

women whose freedoms are curbed by the patriarchal order, the cruelty and rigidity of which are sanitized in the novella. The characterization of Ni'ma is the capstone on a utopian construct that despite its satirical, carnivalesque intent, delegitimizes progressive change.

The erasure of traditional patriarchy's abuse of women is thus indispensable to a vision of the *Nahda* project adapted to the actual conditions of the postcolonial state. The state's failure to win the trust of the people leaves it incapable of carrying out comprehensive, progressive change. The people adapt themselves randomly to superficial change, which serves only to strengthen traditional, premodern structures by giving them the updated form that Sharabi calls "neopatriarchy." We shall see that Salih's subsequent works abandon this utopianism and launch a more nuanced critique that de-idealizes the village and its traditional and neotraditional power structures.

Season of Migration to the North

Discursive Strategies and Ideological Projects

SALIH'S BEST KNOWN WORK, *Mawsim al-hijra ila al-shamal* (Season of migration to the north; 1966), established his reputation both in the Arab world and abroad as a major novelist. A radical departure from the utopianism of "Wedding," *Season* dialogically pits against one another several contending discourses and ideologies—colonial (Orientalist and Africanist), Arab (traditionalist and secularist), patriarchal (Western and Arab) and reveals the limitations, convergences, inconsistencies, and potentials of their respective logics. The novel is also an ominous prognosis, on the eve of the terrible Setback of 1967, of Arab reality and consciousness, beset as it was then by colonial hangover, heady pan-Arabism, and fateful obliviousness to the potentially catastrophic rifts within Arab society. If "Wedding"'s utopianism repressed all of that, *Season* presents an uncompromising figuration of "the return of the repressed"—one in which the wishful dream of the *Nahda* gives way to the nightmare of history.

In another departure from his previous works, Salih in *Season* quite explicitly addresses those issues through a web of intertextual connections to previous Arabic and European texts. The understanding that literary texts create meaning in relation to other texts has informed many theories of influence and intertextuality. This is true of those theories concerned mainly with aesthetic questions, such as Harold Bloom's notion of "the anxiety of influence," and also of those with explicit cultural-historical concerns, such as African-American "Signifying" and postcolonial "writing back."[1] These theories are genealogically linked to Bakhtin's concept of "double-voicedness," a mode of dialogic discourse that he theorized in his 1929 study of Dostoevsky. Bakhtin draws several distinctions between different kinds of appropriation of one speech act into another; among these is the distinction—essential to characterizing the intertex-

---

1. See Harold Bloom's *The Anxiety of Influence*, Henry Louis Gates's *The Signifying Monkey: A Theory of African-American Literary Criticism*, and *The Empire Writes Back: Theory and Practice in Post-Colonial Literatures*, by Bill Ashcroft et. al.

tual links between *Season* and its literary precedents—between "stylization" and "parody." In stylization,

> the author's thought, once having penetrated someone else's discourse and made its home in it, does not collide with the other's thought, but rather follows after it in the same direction, merely making that direction conventional.
>
> The situation is different with parody. Here, as in stylization, the author again speaks in someone else's discourse, but in contrast to stylization parody introduces into that discourse a semantic intention that is directly opposed to the original one. The second voice, once having made its home in the other's discourse, clashes hostilely with its primordial host and forces him to serve directly opposing aims. Discourse becomes an arena of battle between two voices. (Bakhtin 1984, 193)

Thus, while stylization creates convention and bestows authority on the original speech act, text, or discourse, parody, in contrast, calls into question the authority of the original. Bakhtin points out that everyday speech abounds in embedded statements that ridicule, mock, or cast doubt on the parodied statement. According to Bakhtin, however, there is a more subtle kind of (literary) parody, one that he calls "hidden polemic," in which

> the author's discourse is directed toward its own referential object, as is any other discourse, but at the same time every statement about the object is constructed in such a way that, apart from its referential meaning, a polemical blow is struck at the other's discourse on the same theme, at the other's statement about the same object. A word, directed toward its referential object, clashes with another's word within the very object itself. The other's discourse is not itself reproduced, it is merely implied, but the entire structure of speech would be completely different if there were not this reaction to another person's implied words. (Bakhtin 1984, 195)

Parody, in that sense, is a rhetorical strategy that undermines the truth claims of the previous text, but does so without explicitly evoking and attacking it.

The distinction between stylization and parody is relevant to my reading of *Season* because it allows us to see what the novel accomplishes: it parodies, through double-voiced intertextuality, previous European and Arabic texts that thematize the cross-cultural encounter between Europe on the one hand and Africa and the Arab world on the other. *Season* evokes works like Shakespeare's *Othello,* Gérard de Nerval's *Voyage en Orient,* Joseph Conrad's *Heart of Darkness,* Tawfiq al-Hakim's *'Usfur min al-sharq* (A bird from the east), Yahya Haqqi's *Qindil Umm Hashim* (The lamp of Umm Hashim), and Suhayl Idris's *Al-hayy al-latini* (The Latin quarter). Yet rather than simply stylizing the discourses of any of those antecedent texts—the way, for example, V. S. Naipaul's

A Bend in the River stylizes the structure of *Heart of Darkness*[2]—Salih undermines the colonialist premises of the European texts and radically revises the *Nahda* assumptions at work in the Arabic novels.

Consider, first, Salih's hidden polemic against earlier Arab novelists. The theme of love between a student from the colonies and a European woman is a vast topic in Arabic and African fiction that cannot receive an adequate treatment here, but a brief discussion of three important Arabic novels published before *Season* will help situate it in that context.[3] The central figure in Tawfiq al-Hakim's *A Bird from the East* (1938) is Muhsin, an Egyptian student of literature at the Sorbonne in the 1920s or 1930s. In the opening scene he is drenched in the rain while contemplating the statue of the French Romantic poet Alfred de Musset. Al-Hakim draws Muhsin, without irony, as a stereotypically romantic and dreamy Oriental. He is infatuated with a Parisian belle whom he knows only by sight. After a series of engineered coincidences and comically sentimental overtures, he becomes her lover. Two weeks later, he is shocked when this stereotypically liberated and pragmatic *femme fatale* leaves him to return to her French lover, with whom she has had a brief falling-out. Convinced of the heartlessness of European women, Muhsin is at a loss in trying to reconcile the moral and spiritual beauty of European art, music, and literature with the coldness and materialism of Europeans. Toward the end of the novel, his dying Russian friend, a revolutionary self-exile with deeply romantic notions of the East, delivers an impassioned speech on the East's moral and spiritual superiority to Western materialism; he claims that the best in European culture is rooted in Asian civilization. Muhsin understands that Ivanovitch's idealized East is simply the fantasy of a spiritually starved European; even so, the novel tirelessly reinforces the same essentialist conceptions of East and West derived from Orientalism, albeit reversing the hierarchy of values: the East is richly spiritual, while Europe is materialistic and depraved. In that sense, the argument represents al-Hakim's Orientalist answer to Léopold Sédar Senghor's and Aimé Césaire's Africanist concept of *négritude,* in that both notions are premised on essentialist theories of race and culture derived from colonial discourse.

Yahya Haqqi's conception of East and West is more dynamic, arising from the discourse of the *Nahda*. In *The Lamp of Umm Hashim* (1944), Isma'il, the protagonist, grows up in Cairo in the vicinity of the shrine of Umm Hashim, the Prophet's granddaughter Zaynab who is revered as a saint. Dardiri, the keeper of the shrine, tells him about the miraculous healing powers of the saint and the curative value of the oil used to light the lamp in the shrine, which he sells to the afflicted. The oil is supposed to cure only the faithful. After much hesitation,

2. See Peter Nazareth on Naipaul's appropriation of Conrad's novella.
3. See other treatments of this topic by Frantz Fanon, George al-Tarabishi, Issa Boullata, and Abd al-Fattah 'Uthman.

Isma'il's father decides to send his son to England to study medicine, admonishing him while there to observe religious rituals and to beware of European women. After getting engaged to marry his cousin Fatima, Isma'il leaves. Under the influence of Mary, a fellow student who becomes his lover, he loses his religion and acquires faith in science and contempt for superstition. Mary is described as a positive influence, opening Isma'il's eyes to the beauty of nature and art and teaching him independence and confidence. The relationship ends without hurt feelings or bitterness. Having distinguished himself in ophthalmology, Isma'il looks forward to returning home and serving his country. So far, the story embodies the *Nahda*'s conception of the ideal relationship between east and west, north and south: Europe radiates Enlightenment to the intellectual elite from the colonies, who are eager to carry that light back to their native countries.

The difficulties begin when the native intellectual tries to implement the new "enlightened" principles in his country. Isma'il shocks and dismays his parents when he blasphemes Umm Hashim on seeing his mother pour the sacred oil in Fatima's trachomic eyes. Enraged at such superstition, he enters the shrine and smashes the lamp, only to be beaten within an inch of his life by the offended worshippers. Isma'il then takes on the treatment of Fatima's eyes, but they deteriorate more and more until she loses her eyesight. Alienated, guilty, and deeply disturbed, Isma'il moves out of his parents' apartment and plunges into a period of self-questioning. On the holy night of Qadr toward the end of Ramadan, Isma'il has an epiphany while wandering near the shrine of Umm Hashim. He goes to Dardiri seeking some of the lamp oil, returns home, and treats Fatima again, this time restoring her eyesight. He sets up a clinic to treat the poor for a small fee, marries Fatima, has many children, and grows fat and happy until he dies many years later, loved and long remembered by his patients and neighbors.

The novel does not describe exactly how he uses the oil in treating Fatima—whether he applies it to her eyes or uses it as a spiritual aid while applying scientific medical treatment. Pondering the important question of "the precise nature of the compromise Haqqi offers," M. M. Badawi suggests that "perhaps we are not meant to consider this matter so closely and we should be satisfied with the general idea that science needs the support of religion, even though the particular symbol used here is a rather unfortunate one, since it stands not so much for religion as for harmful superstition" (1970, 159). Yet Haqqi's solution remains overly wishful and impractical; for the reconciliation, in this particular case, of the contradictory values of science and superstition can hardly be achieved at the level of "general ideas." This leads Muhammad Siddiq to conclude that Haqqi makes an "irrevocable bow to superstition" (1986, 144). The only practical alternatives would be a conception of modernity whereby the educated elite patronizingly minister to the masses, either by paying lip service to superstition and allowing the ignorant masses to perceive the fruits of modernity as miracles, as in Salih's "Wedding," or by urging the state to impose modernization plans through force, as postcolonial governments attempt to do in "The Doum Tree." In either case, the synthesis advocated by the *Nahda* lacks both a practical vision and a viable strategy for confronting the pressing problems of ignorance and the need for social change through education, participatory democracy, and creative syncretism.

Haqqi does not see any need to change social attitudes, and he allows Isma'il to concoct an absurd solution. For his part, Suhayl Idris locates part of the problem in outmoded social customs. Idris's message, in fact, is rather straightforward on that account. His protagonist is a Lebanese student living, together with other Arab students, in the Latin Quarter of Paris. Most of those students are preoccupied with sexual adventures. The segregation of the sexes in the Arab world and the resulting emotional and sexual frustrations are topics openly discussed by the characters. The protagonist meets Janine and they fall in love. When he returns home for the summer, his mother is dismayed at his affair and pressures him to write a letter to Janine disclaiming her, even though Janine is pregnant. Janine falls ill as a result but refuses to marry the protagonist when, back in Paris with a heavy conscience, he proposes to her. He returns home after graduation and braces himself for momentous struggles. As Issa Boullata observes, those struggles are not only political—even though independence and Arab nationalism are important concerns for the Arab students in Paris (the novel was published in 1954)—but also "socio-psychological," since "the hero . . . discovers his needs for individual freedom from the traditional conventions of Arab society in order to build up his personality and his nation on foundations of free will and not on coercion of any sort; this includes a liberalization of relations between the sexes as well as relations between parents and children" (1980, 59).

In several ways, Salih treats these issues differently. Both Mustafa Sa'eed and Meheimeed, like the protagonists of the other novels, return to Sudan and attempt to help their people, only to realize that no simple synthesis of Western knowledge and local customs is possible. Mustafa's education benefits the village in agriculture and trade, but at the same time he shakes its patriarchal authority through his influence on Hosna. And though Meheimeed makes a deliberate effort to erase from his mind the seven years he spent in England, he comes to discover that he no longer shares the values or worldview of the villagers. As we have seen, the old narrator in "The Doum Tree" anticipated this "soul change" in the young, educated villagers. In other words, in Salih we encounter a world that despite its relative marginality, insularity, and resistance to change, is nevertheless caught in a dynamic and unstoppable transformation.

Yet this transformation in no way resembles the idealism of the *Nahda* as enacted in Haqqi's novel and in Salih's own "Wedding." In *Season,* radical social change involves necessary but difficult negotiation and holds the potential for disastrous consequences, as Hosna Bint Mahmoud's tragedy demonstrates. *The Latin Quarter* stops short of such an assertion: the novel ends with the protagonist looking forward to participating in reforms, but the struggle itself does not begin in the novel. For Idris's protagonist, it is unthinkable to oppose his mother's will. In contrast, Hosna dares the unthinkable—and, for the villagers, the unspeakable. Her retaliation against the abuses of patriarchy—her castration and killing of Wad Rayyes, who represents the worst aspects of traditional culture—is payback in kind for her own genital mutilation, which until then had been the subject of casual remarks and jokes for the village patriarchs, though a taboo subject in Arabic literature and in public discourse generally. (It was not until the 1970s that Nawal al-Saadawi began to challenge that taboo publicly.) The significance of Hosna's vengeful assertion of her human dignity amounts to social revolution.

In brief, Salih's polemical revision of earlier Arabic novels is a two-pronged enterprise, similar to that of the great pioneer of African fiction, Nigerian Chinua Achebe. In *Things Fall Apart,* Achebe's main objective is to counter the racist and derogatory representations of Africa by writers like Joseph Conrad and Joyce Cary with an image of a highly developed society destroyed by colonialism. Yet at the same time that he rehabilitates the image of Africa, he does not idealize it; rather, he shows how certain social ills weaken a culture's resistance to foreign intrusion. Salih's project in *Season* parallels Achebe's. On the one hand, he shows how "things fall apart" in Wad Hamid as a result not only of colonialism but also of native patriarchy. On the other hand, he attacks colonial discourse and its representations of Africans and Arabs. In this he goes much farther afield than past Arab writers. He says, "I have redefined the so-called East/West relationship as essentially one of conflict, while it had previously been treated in romantic terms" (LAUB 1980a, 16). In other words, a correct assessment of the predicament of Arab culture from the nineteenth century until the 1960s must begin by recognizing what, according to Abu-Zayd, the *Nahda* failed to take into account: the imperialist face of Europe.

Yet by the same token, traditionalist discourse does not appreciate Europe's cultural contributions, and thus it too fails to offer a dynamic, dialogic conception of identity. In this connection, Saree Makdisi argues that the novel "points away from the traditionalism of the Arab past—as well as from the future that imperial Europe, through the ideology of modernity, once held out to its victims—and in an entirely new direction, finally escaping the narrow and tightly defined orbit of the debates surrounding the *Nahda*. Through this double negation, it offers tremendous liberating potential, allowing entirely new conceptualizations of social realities, and drawing an entirely new map of the present" (1992, 817). This reading is on target insofar as it describes the novel's intervention in the debates over traditionalism and modernity; however, Makdisi stops short of identifying those "entirely new conceptualizations" presented by the novel, or explaining what this "entirely new map of the present" looks like. By resituating the novel in its specific historical context, we could better understand the vision it presents.

Begun in 1962 and completed in 1966, the novel belongs to a period during which Arab nationalism—especially Nasserism—reached its heyday, before the devastating Setback of 1967. The novel can thus be seen as predictive of the final demise of the project of Arab unity (already looming on the horizon since the dissolution of the short-lived United Arab Republic, which by 1961 comprised Egypt and Syria and which was gradually to incorporate the rest of the Arab countries). The novel points to the conditions, present from the beginning of the movement, that would culminate in a major crisis of confidence analogous—but on the scale of the whole Arab world—to the one Meheimeed undergoes when he feels that "the world has turned suddenly upside down" (*SMN* 1969c, 134). In this sense, the novel does not point in a new direction—since Arabs believed they *were* heading in a new direction—so much as it anticipates the failure of that vision. Rather than "reinventing the present," as Makdisi argues, the novel reveals the bankruptcy of the present and suggests that a correct conceptualization of it lies not in the claims of Western modernity and its Arab champions, nor in those of the traditionalists, but in an often painful and difficult negotiation between old and new, north and south, that erases the discursive boundaries within which each has been construed as a timeless essence. As the novel's title suggests, a constant, relentless migration that erodes the monolithic conceptions of identity and that asserts the dynamic primacy of history is the answer to the challenge of modernity.

Salih says that while planning and writing the novel,

> I was pondering . . . [the] illusory relationship between our Arab Islamic world and Western European civilization specifically. This relationship seems to me, from my readings and studies, to be based on illusions [*awham*] on our side and on theirs. Illusion relates to our conception of ourselves first of all, then to what we think of our relationship to them, and then to their outlook on us as well. Western Europe imposed itself and its civilization on us . . . for a long time and became part of our cultural and psychological makeup whether we like it or not. (IM 1976b, 125)

In that sense, "tradition" and "modernity" are not alternative paths or free choices, but artificial constructs. The illusion lies in thinking about Arab modernity in terms of discreet dualities that depend on monolithic conceptions of Arab-Islamic and Western identities. Salih's significant contribution to the debate rests on his keen perception that any fruitful appreciation of that reality must begin by dispelling the illusions (*awham*) that cloud individuals' and societies' perceptions of themselves, of others, and of their inevitable relations to one another. The novel dramatizes the devastating consequences of those illusions.

Race and Gender in Colonial Discourse

The novel's dual critique of the discourses of colonialism and the *Nahda* can be discerned in the two interlocking narratives of Mustafa Sa'eed and Meheimeed, respectively. I shall focus on the former in this section and on the latter in the next one. Several critics have noted the structural parallels between Conrad's *Heart of Darkness* and *Season,* especially regarding the characterizations of Kurtz and Mustafa Sa'eed. There are two notable and diametrically opposite readings of Salih's treatment of Conrad: that of Mohammad Shaheen, on the one hand, and those of Edward Said and R. S. Krishnan on the other. Shaheen lists a number of structural and thematic parallels and contrasts between the two narratives. First is the identification between Kurtz and Mustafa Sa'eed, whose itinerary from south to north

> echoes Kurtz's journey, but in reverse. . . . Kurtz in the Congo is a colonizer and invader. MS announces himself in England as conqueror and invader. Both MS and Kurtz practice violence in the land they invade. . . . Each invader enjoys sexual orgies in the foreign land he invaded. Kurtz was partly educated in England; so was MS. The special intelligence with which each character is endowed receives particular emphasis in the narrative, and MS is, like Kurtz, a universal genius. The fathers of both are dead, and their mothers die while they are abroad. Both journeys begin out of poverty, which the protagonists leave behind. . . . The journey itself is pursued with dark yearning for the remote. (Shaheen 1985, 156–57)

Shaheen points out other correspondences between the two narratives: the narrators of both stories, Marlow and Meheimeed, are fascinated by the art of storytelling, besides being exceptionally gifted storytellers themselves. They are also captivated by their "secret sharers," with whom they partially identify while partially repudiating. Marlow is entrusted with carrying out Kurtz's deathbed wish; Meheimeed is entrusted with executing Mustafa's will. In this way, both narrators are made complicit with their sharers. Other parallels between the two narratives include recurrent images of darkness, both literal and metaphoric; the structural and thematic significance of a certain "lie;" and the preoccupation with the "popular theme of the colonial system" (160).

Shaheen contends that Salih's novel is an "unsuccessful attempt to integrate . . . Conradian elements into his fiction" (1985, 168). What underlies this judgment is the assumption that Salih's use of Conrad is merely imitative, meant simply to strengthen Salih's narrative so as to "produce a similar profound effect"

(160) to that achieved in *Heart of Darkness*. If, according to Shaheen's logic, Salih sought authentication for his art through mimicking Conrad's, then *Season* is a flawed imitation doomed to failure from the start. To use Bakhtin's terms, in Shaheen's reading there is no question of parody, only stylization. This reading denies any polemical intention on Salih's part, and even the very possibility of a literature that undermines colonial discourse or "writes back" to the imperial center. In contrast, Edward Said reads *Season* and Aimé Césaire's *Une Tempête* as deliberate postcolonial reversals of Conrad's *Heart of Darkness* and Shakespeare's *The Tempest,* respectively. Said defines such reversals as acts of literary "resistance" that participate in "the charting of cultural territory" and herald the "recovery of geographical territory" (1993, 209). Likewise, R. S. Krishnan writes that "Salih's work reclaims for itself both the fictive territory and the imagined topos of Conrad's Africa, and substitutes a postcolonial retelling, a new mythos for Africa, for a colonizing tale" (1996, 7). While analyzing Salih's hidden polemic against several European writers, I will demonstrate that *Season* does much more than reverse the structure, topography, and motifs of *Heart of Darkness* so as to paint an alternative image of Africa or the "Orient"; Salih's text in effect deconstructs colonial discourse itself.

Mustafa Sa'eed is many contradictory things at once: an intellectual prodigy and a villain; a selfish and diabolic Don Juan (in England); an enlightened and a selflessly patriotic reformer (in Wad Hamid); a wife killer (of Jean Morris); and an ideal husband (to Hosna Bint Mahmoud).[4] So much so that almost every character who meets Mustafa in the novel has a different impression of him, and their accounts are often contradictory. His former student, who becomes minister of education, sees him as "one of the greatest Africans I've known" (*SMN* 1969c, 120), yet Richard regards Mustafa as a "buffoon" (59). The retired Mamur remembers him as "isolated and arrogant" (52), yet for Mrs. Robinson he was a "tortured child" (147). Mansour believes that Mustafa was a spy for the British (56), while Hajj Ahmad finds him peaceful, pious, and "always ready to give of his labor and his means in glad times and sad" (7). Not only that, but Mahjoub (after a few drinks) goes so far as to declare that "Mustafa Sa'eed is in fact the Prophet [al-Khidr], suddenly making his appearance and suddenly vanishing" (107).

These conflicting reports render one another unreliable, but at least one thing is clear: everything about Mustafa's life in England has its referent in colonial history and discourse, and hinges on the notion of *wahm* or illusion, which

4. In Arabic "Mustafa" means "chosen" and is one of the epithets of Prophet Muhammad, denoting "the one chosen by God for prophecy;" "Sa'eed" means "happy" or "felicitous"—the irony of the name recalls that of Kurtz's: "Kurtz—Kurtz—that means 'short' in German, don't it? Well, the name was as true as everything else in his life—and death. He looked at least seven feet long" (Conrad 1988, 59).

for Salih mediates the relationship between Europe and its Arab and African colonies. In creating Mustafa, Salih explains that he

> knew that chances are the English reader of the novel will say, "This man from the Sudan, an Arab and a Muslim, says that we oppressed and misjudged them." No, I didn't want to do that. I accepted all of the misconceptions of Europeans. For example, when you read the books of European travelers to Africa in the nineteenth century, you find that they describe the African as lazy, a liar, a child who behaves like a child, an ingrate, and that all he cares about is sex. I imposed all those propositions on the main character, but in the hope that at some point the European reader will reconsider those accusations, and that the Arab reader, too, will not give in to the illusion [*wahm*] that things are clear-cut; things are ambiguous. (IM 1976b, 135)

In this sense, Mustafa is a composite of interconnected parodies of European stereotypes of Africa and the Orient, as well as a discursive destabilizer of Arab notions of identity.

Colonial discourse has internal contradictions. It casts Europe in a masculine role of dominating a feminized Orient (Said 1978), yet it represents African males as hyper-masculine (Fanon 1967). The convergence of colonial and racial stereotypes thus produces a troubled gender configuration in which an African male occupies at once masculine and feminine subject positions, and in which, conversely, a European female occupies the equally uncertain positions of masculinity and femininity. In other words, the category of race often destabilizes gendered colonial identities. *Season* depicts those ambivalent spaces where colonial power is dispersed and where a critique of patriarchy becomes indispensable to the critique of colonial discourse. If colonial discourse is necessarily masculinist, the novel clears a space for a radical rethinking of postcoloniality along nonhegemonic lines and beyond dualistic conceptions of self/other, north/south, masculine/feminine. Many forms of anticolonial and antiracist struggle have reinscribed patriarchy; Salih's novel demonstrates the futility of resisting one form of hegemony by consolidating another.

Mustafa's life coincides with the era of British colonization of Sudan: he is born on August 16, 1898, a date historically framed by the battles of Atbara and Omdurman (June and September of that year, respectively), in which Kitchener's army crushed the Mahdi's forces and completed the conquest of Sudan. His mother was a slave from southern Sudan, and his father belonged to a tribe that collaborated with Kitchener—a mixed Arab-African lineage marked both by social stigma and by treason (*SMN* 1969c, 54). He is born in Khartoum, "a city that was taken from Gordon and recaptured by Kitchener, i.e., a city whose history seems to be held suspended between the military might of two British generals" ('Abdalla 1999, 51). In 1916, while he was studying in England,

Britain and France signed the Sykes-Picot Agreement, which divided the Arab world into spheres of British and French influence; this, despite Britain's promise to Arab nationalist leaders of independence if they revolted against the Ottoman Empire (a promise that led to the Arab Revolt of 1917, orchestrated by Lawrence of Arabia). As a further betrayal, Britain issued the Balfour Declaration in 1917, which promised the establishment of a Jewish state on Arab land; and in 1922 the League of Nations formally recognized the British and French mandates to rule the area. In the same year, Mustafa is appointed lecturer at London University and begins a sexual crusade against Britain. Back in Sudan, Mustafa disappears from Wad Hamid in 1953, just before the end of the colonial period, the year of the formulation of a parliamentary system that would proclaim the country's independence in 1956. Major events of Mustafa's life coincide with milestones in the history of European imperialism in the Arab world; thus, he is metaphorically and psychologically a product of empire.

His public and professional life in England is defined in relation to colonialism. "In 1928 he was president of the Society for the Struggle for African Freedom" (*SMN* 1969c, 120). He couples this political activism with his research as an economist and with his authorship of books such as *The Economics of Colonialism, Colonialism and Monopoly, The Cross and the Gunpowder,* and *The Rape of Africa* (137). The convergence of revolutionary politics and masculine violence is clearly echoed in the title of the last book, which deploys the familiar trope of colonization as an exercise in masculine violence against women. As Edward Said points out, the sexual possession of the female is among the paradigms used to describe the colonial relationship (1978, 186–90). The convergence of colonial and masculine violence echoed in the title of Mustafa's last book prompts him to carry out a grim revenge on colonialism marked by sexism and misogyny "in the manner of Eldridge Cleaver's theory of the political uses of rape" (Accad 1985, 59; Cleaver 1968, 17–29). Mustafa vows jokingly to "liberate Africa with [his] penis" (*SMN* 1969c, 120), and he couches his sexual exploits in the rhetoric of battle, images of Arab desert warfare, and repeated references to the Arab conquest of Spain. For him, seducing women is a reclamation of masculinity, a metonymic equivalent of conquering territory, and a symbolic revenge on Europe for the crime that inspires the title of his book: feminizing and raping Africa. Symptomatic of the distorting effects of colonial discourse, this collapse of (colonial) metaphor into (sexual) metonymy is a function of "[o]bsessional neuroses, but also and differently psychoses, [which] have the distinctive feature of 'reifying' signs—of slipping from the domain of 'speaking' to the domain of 'doing' " (Kristeva 1991, 186). As an embodiment of the kind of psychological damage caused by phallocentric colonialism, Mustafa fails to grasp the metaphoricity of "the rape" of Africa, or the difference (otherwise obvious) between the discursive trope (the "speaking") and the reality it expresses (the "doing").

Thus colonial discourse distorts Mustafa's notions of gender and sexuality. The figure of the English woman evokes hostile anxiety for him because, notwithstanding the misogyny of colonial discourse, the British Empire expanded under the rule of a mighty woman, Queen Victoria, the eponym of the Age of Empire whose name denotes "victory" over those she subdues. Thus, "wherever Mustafa turns, he finds himself surrounded by Victorian images. Victoria Station, where his feet took him when he journeyed from South to North, is the same station from which armed troops had journeyed in the opposite direction, from North to South" (Ni'ma 1986, 234). There is also another Victoria in the south—Lake Victoria. For thousands of years the source of the Nile remained a mystery that ancient Egyptians attributed to the gods. "But the newcomers, with their weapons, modern equipment, and advanced technology, were able to bend the divine will . . . and divulge the secret. The womb-mother turned out to be a lake, and the lake turned out to be a woman. But she was not African or Sudanese; she was British, and her name was Victoria" (237). Thus, in a sense, "the rape of Africa" and the penetration of its secrets was committed by, or in the name of, a British woman, who thus takes on the phallic attributes of colonial violence. Colonialism made Victoria an omnipresent, omnipotent, and violent goddess, and thus for Mustafa every British woman becomes her proxy or substitute.

Woman also stands for the city. Colonial discourse appropriates the masculinist identification of the metropolitan site of power and law with the feminine. That identification is, of course, an ancient trope—one that goes back at least to the signifying cluster of the Trojan War, where the city is both the geographical and the metaphoric site of the feminine. Helen's body is a palimpsest inscribed with narratives of ethnic, cultural, and civilizational sovereignty, of honor, of masculine pride of ownership. It stands in metonymic relationship to Troy, the city to be defended or destroyed by men, while the contest itself assumes the archetypal form of organized masculine violence. More explicitly, the identification of city with woman is found in the New Testament book of Revelation, wherein Babylon is personified as the whore (17:1 ff.) and Jerusalem as the heavenly bride (21:2). Thus for Gérard de Nerval in the nineteenth century, when the old trope of the city/woman was appropriated to modern Orientalist discourse, Cairo is indistinguishable from its women. Indeed, in his *Voyage en Orient,* knowledge of Cairo is knowledge of its veiled women, who embody the mystery and contradictions of the "Orient." Significantly, therefore, the entire section devoted to his voyage to Egypt is entitled "Cairo's Women" and opens with the following passage:

> Cairo is the Levantine city where women remain the most jealously veiled. . . . Solemn and pious, Egypt is still the land of mystery and enigma, where beauty is wrapped, as of old, in veils and bandages. . . . Let us halt and try to lift a cor-

ner of the austere veil of the goddess of Sais. Besides, is it not encouraging to see that in countries where women are believed to be prisoners, they can be seen by the thousands on the streets, in markets and gardens, walking aimlessly by themselves, in pairs, or accompanied by a child? Truly, European women do not enjoy as much freedom. (Nerval 1980, 1:149–50)

This passage contains many of the tropes that Mustafa Sa'eed appropriates to his own masculinist anticolonial discourse. For Gérard (Nerval's semiautobiographical narrator), Cairo is "enigmatic" and "mysterious" (and therefore seductive: "Cherchez la femme!") because its women are veiled. The gallant and resolute European, however, will attempt to lift the veil and unravel the mystery of the city/goddess. The veil itself, for him, is a deceptive barrier, for while it forestalls the masculine gaze, both "Oriental" and European, it also gives "Cairo's women" a freedom of movement unattainable to European women in either Europe or the "Orient." For Gérard, this freedom constitutes a beckoning to adventure. The adventure, however, turns into a mockery several pages later when Gérard follows two such enigmatic Cairene women into their house, thinking to himself, "Here I am in the middle of *The Thousand and One Nights*" (1980, 1:176). They turn out to be French women in "Oriental" disguise, availing themselves of the "freedom" of movement enjoyed by "Oriental" women! This ironic twist does not deter the European adventurer, whose pursuit of the Other constantly leads him to confront the significatory lack which, for Lacan, is constitutive of desire. The performative Orientalness of the French women indicates that the mystery of "Oriental" women is a colonial construct. However, like the mirage always shimmering before Mustafa Sa'eed's eyes, that mystery continues to tantalize Gérard, who pursues it throughout the rest of the narrative—at a marriage broker's, in the slave market, and beyond Egypt in the Druz mountains of Syria.

In Mustafa's case, the identification of women and cities with colonial power begins very early in life. When he is greeted by Mr. and Mrs. Robinson on his arrival in Cairo, he suddenly finds himself

on the station platform amidst a welter of sounds and sensations, with the woman's arms round my neck, her mouth on my cheek, the smell of her body— a strange European smell—tickling my nose, her breast touching my chest, [and] I felt—a boy of twelve—a vague sexual yearning I had never previously experienced. I felt as though Cairo, that large mountain to which my camel had carried me, was a European woman just like Mrs. Robinson. . . . In my mind her eyes were the color of Cairo: gray-green, turning at night to a twinkling like that of a firefly. (*SMN* 1969c, 25)

The boy's discovery of sexual desire at the double encounter with Cairo and Mrs. Robinson is intertwined with his sense of being invaded by the intrusive intimacy of a European woman. From that point on, sexuality becomes for him, on a deep psychic level, associated with aggression, which later on he will redirect against the all-powerful woman/city/empire, the "large mountain" to be conquered.[5]

It is significant that Salih allows this crucial event in Mustafa's life to take place in Cairo rather than London. The ambivalent position of Cairo is noteworthy: an Arab city that was the cradle of the *Nahda* and a center for Arab intelligentsia, revolutionaries, and nationalists who helped the Mahdists in Sudan and other anticolonial movements throughout the Arab world, but at the same time Britain's "ally" in the conquest of Sudan.[6] This larger historical context may be beyond young Mustafa's ken as he is enveloped by Mrs. Robinson's embrace; even so, he is fascinated by Cairo before his arrival there. He explains that "the headmaster—who was English—said to me, 'This country hasn't got the scope for that brain of yours, so take yourself off. Go to Egypt or Lebanon or England. We have nothing further to give you.' I immediately said to him: 'I want to go to Cairo' " (*SMN* 1969c, 22–23). The headmaster equates England, the colonizer, with the northern Arab countries of Egypt and Lebanon, intimating to the boy that all three are superior to Sudan. At work here is the colonial strategy of instilling self-depreciation and self-hatred within the colonized; also at work is the divide-and-rule policy by which the British always strengthened their hold on the colonies. Thus when he arrives in Cairo, the young Mustafa identifies the Egyptian capital with the body of an English woman, not an Arab or an African one. This confusion in the play of identifications compounds Mustafa's pathologically colonial conception of gender and sexuality.

In London, Mustafa perceives European women in much the same way Gérard perceives Oriental women. In the objectifying gaze of the foreign male, women are deprived of individuality, branded with the mark of the plural, and identified with the city. Mustafa says of Isabella Seymour: "We walked along together; she beside me, a glittering figure of bronze under the July sun, a city of secrets and rapture. I was pleased she laughed freely. Such a woman—there are

---

5. Muhammad Siddiq argues that Mustafa's relationship with his peculiarly unemotional mother, who is clearly Mrs. Robinson's opposite, allows the latter to play the role of "mother surrogate" (1978, 74). Furthermore, Mustafa Sa'eed's "sexual promiscuity and his inability to invest any feelings in his relationships with women or to enjoy life in general" are all aspects of "[w]hat Jung calls Don Juanism [which] is the result of the mother complex" (78).

6. Ironically, Egypt was itself a British colony during the conquest of Sudan. The so-called Anglo-Egyptian Condominium government of Sudan meant that Britain governed the country while Egypt paid the expenses, including the salaries of British officials.

many of her type in Europe—knows no fear; they accept life with gaiety and curiosity" (*SMN* 1969c, 37). If Cairo's Oriental women, to Gérard, are stereotypically undifferentiated figures, as silent and mysterious as ancient mummies ("wrapped, as of old, in veils and bandages"), European women to Mustafa are equally homogenized creatures resembling the statues of European art—note the swift passage from Isabella as *a* woman to Isabella the figure in bronze who exemplifies a *type* of woman—and whose free attitude to life is the polar opposite to that of veiled and voiceless Oriental women.

Yet the fundamental difference between Gérard and Mustafa is clearly their disparate positions of power. Gérard is a European male in the Orient, while Mustafa is an African in Europe who audaciously declares himself an invader: " 'Yes, my dear sirs, I came as an invader into your very homes: a drop of the poison which you have injected in the veins of history' " (*SMN* 1969c, 95). For Gérard, the city/woman is the object of a knowledge to be attained from the position of the colonizer; even though he is a Frenchman in a British colony, he still enjoys the privilege of a European. In contrast, for Mustafa the city/woman *embodies* a power he lacks, and to claim that power he must gain control over its site, woman's body. He does so, however, by posturing as the embodiment of European fantasies about Africa and the Orient. He becomes a favorite in conservative, liberal, and Bohemian circles alike by spinning fantastic tales about the Nile crocodiles and streets teeming with elephants and lions. At one point he delivers a lecture on Abu Nuwas at no less than Oxford University:

> I read them some of his poetry about wine in a comic oratorical style which I claimed was how Arabic poetry used to be recited in the Abbasid era . . . all arrant nonsense with no basis of truth. However, I was inspired that evening and found the lies tripping off my tongue like sublime truths. Feeling that my elation was communicating itself to my audience, I lied more and more extravagantly. After the lecture, they all crowded round me: retired civil servants who had worked in the East, old women whose husbands had died in Egypt, Iraq and the Sudan, men who had fought with Kitchener and Allenby, orientalists, and officials in the Colonial Office and the Middle East section of the Foreign Office. (143)

The disgraceful irony is that even those who should have first-hand knowledge of Arab culture, from either lived experience or scholarship, are duped by Mustafa's deliberate lies simply because they reinforce cherished Oriental stereotypes. His London apartment evokes those same stereotypes:

> my house, the den of lethal lies that I had deliberately built up, lie upon lie: the sandalwood and incense; the ostrich feathers and ivory and ebony figurines; the paintings and drawings of forests of palm trees along the shores of the Nile,

boats with sails like doves' wings, suns setting over the mountains of the Red Sea, camel caravans wending their way along sand dunes on the borders of the Yemen, boabab trees in Kordofan, naked girls from the tribes of the Zandi, the Nuer and the Shuluk, fields of banana and coffee on the equator, old temples in the district of Nubia; Arabic books with decorated covers written in ornate Kufic script; Persian carpets, pink curtains, large mirrors on the walls, and colored lights in the corners. (146)

These articles belong to very different cultural, historical, and geographical contexts—from ancient Egypt to tropical Africa, medieval Arabia, Persia, and contemporary Sudan, not to mention the bordelloesque bedroom. What they have in common is their fetishism in sexualized Western fantasies about Africa and the Orient. Mustafa's bizarrely decorated apartment deliberately stages these fantasies.

This sort of masquerade involves the performance of two specific forms of masculinity associated in Western imaginary with non-Western males: the despotic, misogynist Oriental and the uncontrollably jealous and violent African, represented respectively by Shahrayar, the Persian king of *The Thousand and One Nights,* and Othello. These characters possess an exotic appeal that Mustafa exploits. For example, his apartment and the Arabic wine poetry he recites evoke, for Europeans, the atmosphere of *The Thousand and One Nights* and set the stage for the masquerade of master and slave girl that Mustafa and Ann Hammond perform (*SMN* 1969c, 143–46). On other occasions, he explicitly compares himself to Othello: " 'What race are you? . . . Are you African or Asian?' 'I'm like Othello—Arab-African,' I said to her. 'Yes,' she said, looking into my face. 'Your nose is like the noses of Arabs in pictures, but your hair isn't soft and jet black like that of Arabs.' 'Yes, that's me. My face is Arab like the desert of the Empty Quarter, while my head is African and teems with a mischievous childishness' " (38). Mustafa's reply to Isabella Seymour indicates the extent of his complicity with colonial discourse, in that it appeals to ethnic and racial stereotypes, and evokes the landscape images of postcards and picture books, as well as the racist designation of Africans as "children in need of discipline and guidance" (Krishnan 1996, 11). Moreover, he seduces Isabella in much the same way that Othello gains Desdemona's love; note the almost identical strategies of self-exoticization:

> *Othello.* . . . I spoke of most disastrous chances:
> Of moving accidents by flood and field,
> Of hair-breadth scapes i' th' imminent deadly breach,
> Of being taken by the insolent foe
> And sold to slavery, of my redemption thence

> And portance in my [travel's] history;
> Wherein of antres vast and deserts idle,
> . . . And of cannibals that each others eat,
> The Anthropophagi, and men whose heads
> [Do grow] beneath their shoulders. . . .
> My story being done,
> She gave me for my pains a world of [sighs];
> She swore, in faith 'twas strange; 'twas passing strange
> 'Twas pitiful, 'twas wondrous pitiful. . . .
> She lov'd me for the dangers I had pass'd,
> and I lov'd her that she did pity them. (*Othello* I.iii.134–68)

I related to her fabricated stories about deserts of golden sands and jungles where non-existent animals called out to one another. I told her that the streets of my country teemed with elephants and lions and that during siesta time crocodiles crawled through it. Half-credulous, half-disbelieving, she listened to me, laughing and closing her eyes . . . Sometimes she would hear me out in silence, a Christian sympathy in her eyes. There came a moment when I felt that I had been transformed in her eyes into a naked primitive creature, a spear in one hand and arrows in the other, hunting elephants and lions in the jungle. This was fine. Curiosity had changed to gaiety, and gaiety to sympathy, and when I stir the still pool in its depths the sympathy will be transformed into a desire upon whose taut strings I shall play as I wish. (*SMN* 1969c, 38)

The close structural parallel between these two passages, the lies about fantastic creatures and monsters described in Mandeville's *Travels,* and the sympathy elicited only to be transformed into passion for the exotic, reveal Mustafa's calculated performance of the kind of exotic masculinity that plays itself out at the edge of civilization and even humanity, feeding European fascination with barbarism and monstrosity, and confirming Europe's sense of civilizational superiority. In this manner, Mustafa parodies Othello, one of Europe's most notable literary depictions of the Other since Homer's Cyclops.[7]

Mustafa's elaborate masquerade succeeds in seducing women from all three classes of English society: Ann Hammond, a young aristocratic student of Ara-

---

7. In this connection, Barbara Harlow quotes Sir John Davies's 1603 *Microcosmos,* in which "Southward men" are described as "cruel, moody, mad,/ Hot, black, lean lepers, used to vaunt,/ Yet wise in action, sober, fearful, sad./ If good, most good, if bad, exceeding bad" (Harlow 1979, 164), and Richard Burton's "Terminal Essay" to his translation of *The Thousand and One Nights,* in which he writes that the tales show "the Arab at his best and his worst. In glancing over the myriad pictures of this panorama, those who can discern the soul of goodness in things evil will note the true nobility of the Moslem's mind in the moyen Age, and the cleanliness of his life from cradle to grave . . . nor is the shady side of the picture less notable. Our Arab at his worst is a mere barbarian who has not forgotten the savage" (Harlow 1979, 166; Burton 1934, 3653–55).

bic; Isabella Seymour, a forty-year-old wife of a middle-class professional and mother of three; and Sheila Greenwood, a waitress from a working-class family. All three are drawn to him under the spell of the fabled black sexuality and the allure of the exotic "Orient." The problematic nature of black sexuality in colonial/racial discourse crystallizes in the British ban on miscegenation in the colonies; in the American South, the punishment meted out to blacks for miscegenation was often castration and lynching. But notwithstanding all the theories about the inequality of the races and the dangers to Aryans of miscegenation (Young 1995, 90–117), the fear of black sexuality arises from the perception that it "is a form of black power over which whites have no control. . . . In fact, the dominant sexual myths of black women and men portray whites as being 'out of control'—seduced, tempted, overcome, overpowered by black bodies. This form of black sexuality makes white passivity the norm—hardly an acceptable self-image for a white-run society" (West 1993, 87). These perceptions are at the heart of Mustafa's interactions with English women. Salih's foregrounding of the strong link between sexuality and racism draws attention to the corresponding silence we encounter in Conrad's *Heart of Darkness*. Conrad's novella "flirt[s] with a radical critique of certain Western values, but stops short" (Torgovnick 1990, 154), and evokes only to "obscure ugly facts . . . like the African woman's relation to Kurtz, facts like her death at the end, which goes unmentioned . . . in any commentary on the novella" (152). Kurtz's relationship with the African woman would have constituted a breach of the British ban on miscegenation and serves as a concrete example of his lack of "restraint." However, Marlow's refusal to speak of or even to learn about Kurtz's actions (" 'I don't want to hear any of the ceremonies used when approaching Mr. Kurtz,' I shouted" [Conrad 1988, 58]) obscures the function of black sexuality in the economy of colonial discourse. In his study of the rhetoric of colonial discourse, David Spurr explains the British colonial officers' designation of African mistresses as "sleeping dictionaries" thus:

> [T]he metaphor suggests an entire series of unstated connections between the sexual and the lexical. It suggests, for example, that the African woman is a text to be opened and closed at will, and whose contents allow entry into the mysteries of African language; that this language, and by extension African culture, is itself both contained within and revealed by the female body; that sexual knowledge of her body is knowledge of Africa itself. The body as text, however, is read only as a series of lexical fragments, without regard to history or narrative. In yet another sense, the "sleeping dictionary" evokes Africa as a dormant or sleeping text, which can only be awakened and brought into definition by the intervention of the European reader. And finally, the metaphor suggests that the colonizer's own language derives from his erotic relations with "her," the pronoun in this case designating both the African continent and the African woman. (Spurr 1993, 171)

Besides serving as a metaphor for conquest, as Said has pointed out, the sexual possession of the female here works as a form of textual, discursive, and specifically *masculine* knowledge.

Such objectification of the feminine is a function of the classical notion of the transcendental masculine subject, which is the foundation of both colonial and traditional patriarchal discourses. It is evident in the Arabic novels discussed earlier, where the masculinist discourse of the colonized feminizes the colonizer. However, this feminized West remains inaccessible to the kind of knowledge that is gained from the position of power. The bodies of Victoria's daughters, and the culture they represent metonymically, remain unknowable, mysterious, offering only a "mirage" (one of Mustafa's favorite images) of knowledge. Al-Hakim's and Idris's characters, for example, resign themselves to the fact that the Western female body unlocks no textual or discursive power of the kind Said and Spurr describe; as for Haqqi's protagonist, his new knowledge is imparted by Mary, who acts as his mentor and remains in control throughout their relationship. Incapable of understanding Susie, al-Hakim's protagonist falls back on Kipling's idea of quintessentially different East and West, the latter personified as a merciless, oversexed *femme fatale*. In Halim Barakat's ʿAwdat al-taʾir ila al-bahr (The return of the flying Dutchman to the sea; 1969, translated as *Days of Dust*), the Palestinian male protagonist feels that he is being raped by a married American tourist, for whom the journey to the war-torn Arab world in June 1967 becomes a sexual interlude. Here, the reversal of gender roles is complete. Arab males are epistemically castrated; at the same time, their Western mistresses are endowed with phallic colonial power. Contrary to Nerval's narrative, these novels depict situations in which colonial and gender hegemony do not coincide, and effective power is bestowed by colonial rather than gender relations.

In that sense, Mustafa's English mistresses "read" him as an African, Oriental "text," and they do so even in the very act of submitting to his perceived black sexual power. For Ann and Sheila, Mustafa's body metonymically encodes exotic landscapes like those depicted in Orientalist paintings, evokes mental associations with the primitive and the obscene, and represents transgressive desire that is directly related to the construction of black sexuality. Sheila says to him, "Your tongue's as crimson as a tropic sunset. . . . How marvelous your black color is! . . . the color of magic and mystery and obscenities" (*SMN* 1969c, 139). "[A]s though intoning rites in a temple," Ann says, " 'I love your sweat . . . I want to have the smell of you in full—the smell of rotting leaves in the jungles of Africa, the smell of the mango and the pawpaw and tropical spices, the smell of rains in the deserts of Arabia' " (142). To the church-going Isabella, he is a symbol of transgression so powerful that she renounces her religion for his sake: "The Christians say their God was crucified that he might bear the burden of their sins. He died, then, in vain, for what they call sin is nothing but the sigh of contentment in embracing you, O pagan god of mine. You are my god and there is no god but you" (108).

These extremes of passion lead all three women to suicide. Mustafa claims that these women "met him and discovered deep within [themselves] dark areas that had previously been closed" (*SMN* 1969c, 140); that "the infection had stricken these women a thousand years ago, but I had stirred up the latent depths of the disease until it had got out of control and had killed" (34); and at another point, that "there is a still pool in the depths of every woman that I knew how to stir" (31). "Dark areas" and "still pool" are familiar images of the unconscious, while "disease" is Mustafa's metaphor for the danger lurking in the "depths" of a collective identity constructed in opposition to exotic, primitive, oversexed, irrational, uncivilized, non-European Others. The "dark areas" are also inseparable from a mental image of Africa as the "heart" of psychological and moral darkness. Salih would seem to be echoing Fanon, who wrote that "in the remotest depth of the European unconscious an inordinately black hollow has been made in which the most immoral impulses, the most shameful desires lie dormant. And as every man climbs up toward whiteness and light, the European has tried to repudiate this uncivilized self, which has attempted to defend itself. When European civilization came into contact with the black world, with those savage peoples, everyone agreed: Those Negroes were the principle of evil" (Fanon 1967, 190).[8] Kristeva's "abjection" (Kristeva 1982, 1–11) and Conrad's "fascination of the abomination" (Conrad 1988, 10) arise from this aspect of the encounter with the Other; by enacting colonial stereotypes, Mustafa mobilizes psychic forces that undermine colonial Europe's sense of moral, cultural, and civilizational superiority.

That Mustafa's mistresses come from different social classes indicates that they share a cultural and racial, if not a class identity. As in Conrad, the fascination of the abomination puts that collective European identity to the test. However, Salih further shows that the complicated masquerade of forbidden desires shatters the colonial mask of cultural, moral, and civilizational superiority that lies at the heart of Conrad's "redeeming idea." Mustafa's mistresses realize that in worshipping him they have fallen from civilization into savagery. Savagery, of course, is the demonic face of the exotic; the allure of one inevitably leads to the "horror" of the other. In demonstrating such *inevitability*, Salih responds most forcefully to nineteenth-century male European travelers to the East, such as Flaubert and Nerval, for whom a feminine Orient offered the prospect of exotic and unrestrained sexuality, unavailable in Europe. Likewise, Salih redefines Conradian darkness: the "fascination of the abomination" emerges from the

---

8. Salih said in an interview that he had read Fanon after writing the novel, and had found himself in full agreement with him (IM 1976b, 130).

contradictions of colonial constructions of gender and race, not from some sort of ontological evil connected with a feminized Africa, metonymically represented by Kutrz's native mistress.

Mustafa Sa'eed himself is in turn destroyed by colonial discourse at the hands of Jean Morris. Unlike the other women, she resists his advances, humiliates him, and reinscribes him in the demonic representation of the Other. She does not allow him to play the exotic and desirable Shahrayar or Othello; instead she forces him to be the impulsive, uncontrollably and murderously jealous "Southward man," in John Davies's phrase. Whereas Isabella, Ann, and Sheila "read" Mustafa Sa'eed in terms of the exotic, Jean "rewrites" him, so to speak, in terms of negative stereotypes. She is motivated by the urge to contest and suppress Mustafa's sexual power over English women, which for her is an unacceptable form of black power over whites (West 1993). What draws Jean to Mustafa is the same thing that draws Mustafa to English women—namely, a struggle for imperial power and hegemony, one that unfolds in terms of a masculinist discourse on sexuality, working in alliance with colonial discourse.

Jean does not attempt to undermine socially constructed gender roles; she is not a feminist crusader against Mustafa's masculinism and misogyny. Such sexism and misogyny are deeply entrenched in the rhetoric of colonial discourse, which Jean appropriates wholesale. Just as Mustafa inscribes himself in the degrading terms of Africanist and Orientalist stereotypes, Jean conforms all the more closely to patriarchal gender roles and stereotypical representations of women in her effort to undermine Mustafa's claim to colonial power. If he plays Shahrayar, she plays Scheherazade; if he claims to be like Othello, she becomes Desdemona. Yet Jean revises those roles, differentiating herself from her female models by switching their moral function within the patriarchal value system that produced them, but without actually contesting that system. As literary characters, Scheherazade and Desdemona are idealized projections of male desire; Jean parodies them. Like Scheherazade, who succeeds in halting Shahrayar's daily execution of a new bride to avenge the infidelity of his queen, Jean ends Mustafa's psychological destruction of English women. Yet just like Scheherazade, Jean does so by conforming to patriarchal gender roles, even though the two women embody diametrically opposite stereotypes of women: Scheherazade is ever the obedient and dutiful wife, even in her craftiness, which aims at the moral, social, and spiritual reformation of her husband; the English Scheherazade is the *femme fatale* who destroys him.

In Mustafa's cryptic refrain, Victoria Station is always identified with "the world of Jean Morris" and not with any of the other women. This is because in her stubborn and humiliating resistance to his advances, she merges more fully than the other women with the city as a psychic function and a trope of empire.

Unlike Ann, Sheila, and Isabella, Jean seems to belong nowhere in particular in English society. Her family, class, and origin are uncertain: "She did no work and I don't know how she managed to live. Her family were from Leeds; I never met them, not even after I married her, and I know nothing about them except for the odd bits she used to tell me. Her father was a merchant, though I don't know of what. . . . She used to lie about the most ordinary things. . . . I wouldn't be surprised if she didn't have a family at all" (*SMN* 1969c, 155). Her mysteriousness epitomizes the allure of the metropolis. Victoria Station, London, and the empire are her "world" insofar as she is, like them, ungraspable, unattainable, a "mirage [that] shimmered before me in the wilderness of longing" (33). The other women are "an easy prey" (142); Jean, in contrast, is the only one who sees through his masquerades and fixes him with her "unreadable" gaze. Meheimeed reflects on her portrait in Mustafa's secret room: "Though he had kept photographs of all the other women, Jean Morris was there as he saw her, not as seen by the camera. . . . The expression on the face is difficult to put into words: a disturbing, puzzling expression. The thin lips were tightly closed as though she were grinding her teeth, while her jaw was thrust forward haughtily. Was the expression in the eyes anger or a smile? . . . Was this, then, the phoenix that had ravished the ghoul?" (154–55). The objectifying lens of Mustafa's camera is able to fix his "prey" in a way that bespeaks his possession of them—willing slaves, idolaters, or creatures money can buy—and feeds his fantasy of conquering the north. Painting in this context, however, involves the exploration of a mystery rather than an expression of mastery, and Jean's portrait reveals—if anything at all—his inability to "read" her. The willful inscrutability of the tightly closed lips and the defiance, arrogance, and mockery in the eyes are the lasting impression that Jean leaves on Mustafa, a reminder of his ultimate defeat and of the meaninglessness of his earlier "conquests."[9]

For Mustafa, Jean's actions are contradictory, intriguing, and confusing. She pursues him, teases him, rejects his advances, humiliates him, taunts him, marries him, refuses to sleep with him, and cheats on him. She destroys the emblems of his self-exoticizing, undermines the confidence with which he plays his various parts, and robs him of his sense of control. One night, after insulting Ann Hammond and kicking her out of Mustafa's apartment, Jean

9. Siddiq points out that Jean's inscrutability parallels that of Mustafa's mother, and that both withhold love from him (1978, 82–4). The obscurity of the two women's family backgrounds and the mysteriousness of their faces, argues Siddiq, are traits of the "negative anima" (82). Thus, "[o]n the one hand, as unattached women they are the typical universal female, the mother-prostitute who belongs to no man and to all men. On the other hand, detached as they are from a human setting, they may be seen as the embodiment of the female principle in the male personality; and as such they originate in and inhabit the unconscious" (83).

stripped off her clothes and stood naked before me. All the fires of hell blazed within my breast. . . . As I advanced towards her, my limbs trembling, she pointed to an expensive Wedgwood vase on the mantelpiece. "Give this to me and you can have me," she said. If she had asked at that moment for my life as a price I would have paid it. I nodded my head in agreement. Taking up the vase, she smashed it on the ground and began trampling on the pieces underfoot. She pointed to a rare Arabic manuscript on the table. "Give me this too," she said. My throat grew dry with a thirst that almost killed me. I must quench it with a drink of icy water. I nodded my head in agreement. Taking up the old, rare manuscript she tore it to bits, filling her mouth with pieces of paper which she chewed and spat out. It was as though she had chewed at my very liver. And yet I didn't care. She pointed to a silken Isphahan prayer-rug which I had been given by Mrs. Robinson when I left Cairo. It was the most valuable thing I owned, the thing I treasured most. "Give me this too and then you can have me," she said. Hesitating for a moment, I glanced at her as she stood before me, erect and lithe, her eyes agleam with a dangerous brightness, her lips like a forbidden fruit that must be eaten. I nodded my head in agreement. Taking up the prayer-rug, she threw it on to the fire and stood watching gloatingly as it was consumed, the flames reflected on her face. This woman is my quarry and I shall follow her to Hell. I walked up to her and, placing my arm around her waist, leaned over to kiss her. Suddenly I felt a violent jab from her knee between my thighs. When I regained consciousness I found she had disappeared. (*SMN* 1969c, 156–57)

The price she sets on her body is never stated up front; rather, it is collected in installments of increasing material, aesthetic, and spiritual value so that the more he pays, the greater the sacrifice, the less likely he is to walk away from the transaction. The objects represent layers of identity, which she strips from him. The fine English pottery signifies Mustafa's Anglicized identity; it is as though Jean is gloatingly telling him in a single gesture that the colonial promise of assimilation for the "civilized" native is a deception and a trap in which he has been caught. The next layer is Arab-Islamic, symbolized by the old and rare manuscript. In spite of his claim that he "didn't care," he finds that letting go of the manuscript is more traumatizing than giving up the vase: the manuscript is like a piece of his "liver." Jean's tearing and chewing of it is metaphorically cannibalistic. Obviously, such a way of describing the act assigns to Jean one of the most horrifying traits of barbarism that gave Europeans the moral justification for conquering Africa and America. The European's fear of being eaten by cannibals is experienced by Mustafa as a nightmare come true at the hands of this savage Victoria, who does not hesitate to destroy other cultures and civilizations in her lust for power. Mustafa's heightened sensibility with regard to Jean's destruction of the manuscript is the beginning of his awareness of his own degeneration—an awareness that is brought about in associations of violence and that will culminate later on in his attempt to exorcize colonialism's effects on him by murdering Jean. His denial that he cares, at this point, shows the degree of his complicity, and his realization as a reminiscing fifty-year-old that he was an accomplice in his own degradation.

The last thing she asks for—which he agrees to give her—heightens his anxiety because of its spiritual and emotional value. Having given up the prayer rug, Mustafa is now determined to "follow her to Hell." The rug has additional emotional significance for Mustafa: it is a token of the one genuine human relationship he has with an English person, Mrs. Robinson. Her importance in his life as surrogate mother is undeniable, despite his first reaction to her while still an adolescent. Her sincerity and maternal affection transcend the rigid bounds of colonial relationships. The nature of her gift to him is evidence of that. Mrs. Robinson is critical of colonialism (*SMN* 1969c, 148), and her husband is not a typical Orientalist, but one who admires the culture he studies. Not only that, he converts to Islam and is buried in a Muslim cemetery (111). Mrs. Robinson's gift to "Moozie" is a token of his cultural and spiritual roots. Jean's obvious satisfaction at burning the rug places the two women in opposite roles with regard to Mustafa: they represent the forces of light and darkness fighting for his soul. Of course, he is not a passive player at all, for he chooses his "quarry," and the result of that choice is a kick in the source of his hubris—a punishment that puts him in his place, so to speak, as an emasculated native vis-à-vis the phallic mother, Victoria.

Jean also rewrites Mustafa as "a slave Shahrayar." In the frame story of *The Thousand and One Nights,* the disproportionate jealousy of the Persian king incites him to kill his unfaithful wife, her maids, and their lovers, and to order the execution of each new bride he takes. Mustafa himself invites the comparison: his fantastically decorated home evokes the atmosphere of the *Nights* and sets the stage for Mustafa and Ann to play the roles of master and slave. Yet the images describing his failure to possess or control Jean ("grasping at clouds . . . bedding a shooting-star . . . mounting the back of a Prussian military march" [*SMN* 1969c, 34]) are in sharp contrast to those expressing his possession of other women: a king in his harem or a victorious Tariq Ibn Ziad subduing the armies of Iberia. This failure contrasts with Shahrayar's control over the life and death of the maidens in his capital city, a control that Mustafa exercised over Ann, Sheila, and Isabella. Moreover, Jean tells him incredible and fabricated stories about herself that mimic and parody both the Othellian lies with which Mustafa seduces other women (38–39) and the fanciful tales with which Sheherazade entertains and educates the king: she "was like some mendicant Scheherazade [who] used to lie about the most ordinary things and would return home with amazing and incredible stories about incidents that had happened to her and people she'd met" (155). These are not edifying tales that lead to his redemption; rather, they are deliberate and humiliating reversals that transform the self-proclaimed Shahrayar from master into "slave" and his great Sasanian capital (Mustafa's apartment being its analog) into "the rubble of a city destroyed by plague" (34).

Jean likewise effaces the exoticism of the Moor by creating humiliating situations in which he reacts in the irrational, violent manner stereotypical of jealous "Southward men" like Shahrayar and Othello: "She used to like flirting with every Tom, Dick, and Harry whenever we went out together. She would flirt with waiters in restaurants, bus conductors and passers-by. Some would take courage and respond while others would answer with obscene remarks, and so I'd get myself into fights with people, and exchange blows with her in the middle of the street" (*SMN* 1969c, 161). In fact, she turns Othello into a true cuckold by playing a role that blends Desdemona and Iago into an unfaithful, spiteful Desdemona:

> I knew she was being unfaithful to me; the whole house was impregnated with the smell of her infidelity. Once I found a man's handkerchief which wasn't mine. . . . On another occasion I found a cigarette case, then a pen. "You're being unfaithful to me," I said to her. "Suppose I'm being unfaithful to you," she said. "I swear I'll kill you," I shouted at her. "You only say that," she said with a jeering smile. "What's stopping you from killing me? What are you waiting for? Perhaps you're waiting till you find a man lying on top of me, and even then I don't think you'd do anything. You'd sit on the edge of the bed and cry." (*SMN* 1969c, 162)

Desdemona's handkerchief, which Iago steals and plants as evidence of her infidelity, becomes in Jean's case real evidence that she hardly denies. Moreover, she dares him to kill her and be a veritable Othello, a "real man" instead of a crying child. The racist provocation (Africans said to behave like children) demonstrates the extent of Jean's complicity with masculinist, even misogynistic, discourse in her attempt to destroy Mustafa's claim to colonial power. The provocation does indeed lead to the reenactment of Othello's murder of Desdemona: the above passage is followed immediately in the novel by the scene in which Mustafa kills Jean.

Jean's desire for death is evident in the imagery she uses to describe Mustafa's persistent courting: "You're a savage bull that does not weary of the chase. . . . I am tired of your pursuing me and of my running before you. Marry me" (*SMN* 1969c, 157). It is not surprising that she describes him as *thawr mutawahhish,* a wild bull (read: threatening, violent, enraged, oversexed). What is strange is that she would want to marry him once she inscribes herself within the same (incongruously mixed) image as a hunted prey that gives up on life out of sheer exhaustion. The irony, of course, is that she is more of a bullfighter than a maiden in distress. This contradiction is the product of her conflictually gendered status in colonial and racial discourses—like Mustafa, she is both masculinized and feminized, both "hunter" and "quarry" (159). She surrenders not so much to Mustafa, but to the discourse that has inscribed both of them in stereotypical images which both of them reproduce, project, and enact.

Thus the murder is the realization of both their roles, and hence the intense psychosexual fulfillment they experience at the consummation of their relationship: "She continued to look at the blade-edge with a mixture of astonishment, fear, and lust. Then she took hold of the dagger and kissed it fervently. . . . 'Darling,' she said painfully, 'I thought you would never do this. I almost gave up hope of you.' . . . I pressed down the dagger with my chest until it had all disappeared between her breasts. . . . she called out imploringly: 'Come with me. Come with me. Don't let me go alone' " (*SMN* 1969c, 164–65). The melodramatic language of "truth and tragedy" (162) is belied by the fact that both Jean and Mustafa are actors parodying literary embodiments of cultural stereotypes. The incongruity of this tragic farce is the reason why he does not kill himself— an act that would have completed the simulacrum of tragedy for which she yearns. Jean never steps outside her various roles; she remains incapable of passing a judgment on her life because she cannot see through the lies of stereotype. Mustafa, for his part, is able to see that Jean's rewriting him in terms of negative stereotypes brings self-exoticizing full circle. By killing her, he is trying to rid himself of stereotypes; by refraining from suicide, he is repudiating Othello.

With the murder, Mustafa's life reaches a turning point; after it, he begins an uncertain quest for redemption. Both the verdict of the English court and his own self-judgment bring into focus the themes of cultural illusions and colonial lies, and Salih's parodies of Shakespeare and Conrad. As he recounts his life story to Meheimeed many years later, Mustafa says that "everything which happened before my meeting her was a premonition; everything I did after I killed her was an apology, not for killing her, but for the lie [*ukdhuba*] that was my life" (*SMN* 1969c, 29). If "illusion" (*wahm*) has been, until this point in Salih's fiction, the prism through which identity and difference are constructed, "lying" as the deliberate creation and/or perpetuation of "illusion" adds an ethical dimension to the process that links Mustafa's "lies" to Othello's and Marlow's lies, and by extension the lie of "the civilizing mission."

In the courtroom, Mustafa feels an urge to scream, "This Mustafa Sa'eed does not exist. He's an illusion, a lie" (*SMN* 1969c, 32), and also "I am no Othello, Othello was a lie" (95). As a product of European imagination, Othello is a lie—an embodiment of a false representation of what Sir John Davies calls "Southward men" who are "[i]f good, most good, if bad, exceeding bad" (Harlow 1979, 164), and "a composite representation of an Arab-African mercenary

fabricated by an English playwright in 1604 and played almost exclusively by
white actors in and out of blackface for the first 340 years of his stage history"
(Cartelli 1999, 148). Othello is a lie in another sense: in lying about his adventures among medieval humanoids, he is falsely represents himself to the Venetians and to Desdemona.[10] Thus, as Barbara Harlow observes in elaborating on
Othello's final words ("Speak of me as I am"), Othello's identity was conferred
on him by the Venetians according to their needs and to their medieval notions
of the Other: "His parts, his title, perhaps even his 'perfect soul,' have been conferred on him, the stranger in their midst, by his hosts, his employers. When he
has killed their daughter, those parts and title are revoked. His perfect soul is sul-
lied" (1979, 163–64). Similarly, Mustafa's identity is conferred on him by the
British—that is, by overt racists who see him as a black savage, by infatuated
lovers for whom he is a "pagan god" (*SMN* 1969c, 108), and by "members of
the aristocracy who in the twenties and early thirties were affecting liberalism"
and for whom "he was a show-piece" (58).

Mustafa's professor at Oxford, Maxwell Foster-Keen, speaking with the
prestige of "one of the founders of the Moral Rearmament movement in Oxford, a Mason, and a member of the Supreme Committee for the Protestant
Missionary Societies in Africa," reinforces this when he says to him "with undis-
guised irritation, 'you, Mr. Sa'eed, are the best example of the fact that our civilizing mission in Africa is of no avail. After all the efforts we've made to educate
you, it's as if you'd come out of the jungle for the first time' " (*SMN* 1969c,
93–94). For Foster-Keen, what is wrong with the civilizing mission is not that it
has disrupted cultures and uprooted individuals, but that it is directed at savages
who cannot forget the jungle. The optimism inherent in the racist idea of the
civilizing mission thus gives way to the cynical disillusionment behind Kurtz's
final judgment on Africans, postscripted to his report to the International Society for the Suppression of Savage Customs: "Exterminate all the brutes" (Conrad 1988, 51). Yet Mustafa is not one of the faceless crowd; he is, like Kurtz, a

10. Salih's reading of *Othello* is worthy of note here: "I have always felt that the weakness in
[the characterization of] Othello is that whatever became of him, he couldn't have accepted his role
so easily that the conflict becomes centered around Desdemona alone—and I think some critics
point that out. It is perhaps presumptuous toward Shakespeare to say that Mustafa Sa'eed should be
the true Othello. You have noticed that the motives for Mustafa Sa'eed's murder of Jean Morris are
clearly explained in the novel: he didn't accept his role [in British society]; he was acting another role
and he linked himself to a huge illusion [wahm]. . . . He said, 'I am no Othello.' Othello was a lie,
and this is my point of view. Here there is a confrontation between characters from two different
ages. He [Mustafa] . . . was highly aware that the role played before him [by Othello] was a failure.
And I think that he went to the village [of Wad Hamid] not to act another role, but in all sincerity to
search for his roots. Sadly, however, having acted for too long he could not simply become authen-
tic and he had to create another theatrical role for himself in the village. . . . In fact, what happened
in London repeats itself in the village" (IM 1976b, 133).

"universal genius" (71)—brilliant scholar, capable painter, poet, and worldly all-round savant. Hence the acute sense of failure that laces Foster-Keen's remarks. It is that sense of failure, perhaps, which prompts the court to sentence Mustafa to only seven years' imprisonment instead of to the gallows, at a time when it was possible for "a man who stole four bananas [to be] sentenced to three years' penal servitude" (*SMN* 1969c, 150).[11]

It matters not that this is a deliberate failure on Mustafa's part, an abrogation of the civilizing mission as an imperialist project, one that Macaulay defined in his infamous 1835 "Minute" on Indian education and that reverberates in Foster-Keen's words: "We must at present do our best to form a class who may be interpreters between us and the millions whom we govern; a class of persons, Indian in blood and color, but English in taste, in opinions, in morals, and in intellect" (Macaulay 1952, 729). Yet Mustafa's rebellion against the colonial educational system remains futile, for in exploiting stereotypes he remains a mimic man in another sense. Macaulay's is essentially a "good" native; Mustafa chooses the role of the trouble-making native, yet he fails to question the discourse that constituted him as a "native" in the first place. Thus even while abrogating the kind of mimicry that Macaulay's program of education aims at producing, and even while deliberately becoming a living parody of it, Mustafa is so completely a product of colonialism himself that his revolt is confined within the bounds of colonial discourse on the Other. Thus when Foster-Keen, acting as his defense lawyer, tries to represent Mustafa to the trial jury as "a noble person whose mind was able to absorb Western civilization but it broke his heart" (*SMN* 1969c, 33), he is evoking Caliban, the monstrous semihuman hybrid who can learn the tool of civilization but cannot put it to good use: "You taught me language; and my profit on't/Is, I know how to curse" (*The Tempest* I.ii.363–64). Foster-Keen's contradictory attitudes toward Mustafa are consistent with the West's twin representations of the non-European: noble and exotic, as is found most notably in Montaigne, Shakespeare (Othello), and Rousseau; yet also base and diabolic, as in Mandeville, Shakespeare (Caliban), and Conrad. In other words, there is no identity for Mustafa outside of colonial discourse.

Mustafa's stubborn silence during the trial expresses a rebellion that cannot be articulated within the discursive registers of prosecution and defense: "Once it occurred to me in my stupor . . . that I should stand up and shout at the court: 'This Mustafa Sa'eed does not exist. He's an illusion, a lie. I ask of you to rule that the lie be killed' " (*SMN* 1969c, 32). He remains silent because to proclaim the murder and suicides as his personal responsibility would be to propagate the

11. The reports in the "only newspaper" found in Mustafa's library, *The Times* of Monday, 26 September 1927, are all actual news. The bits about the elephants, the cattle breeder gored to death, and the banana thief, who was a repeat offender, appear under "News in Brief" on page 9. Mustafa's trial takes place the following year.

"illusions" and "lies" into which he has been inscribed. Had he defended himself by marshaling Jean's infidelity as a motive for murder—something he seems not to have mentioned to Foster-Keen, who would have probably built his defense on it—he would have reinscribed himself in the stereotype of the noble but murderously jealous Othello. Therefore, "killing the lie" cannot simply mean sentencing Mustafa to death; it must also mean condemning the process by which imperialist Europe has defined itself in opposition to its Others. Mustafa's silence in the courtroom points to his awareness that such a judgment would never be passed by an English court.

Yet he yearns for the death sentence because it would at one stroke expiate his guilt for having been a lie and confirm his self-perception (itself another *wahm*) as the tragic hero in a grand historical drama—not Othello, but a liberator of Africa and colonizer of the north. However, the fact of the matter is that he has played the fool:

> When Mahmoud Wad Ahmed was brought in shackles to Kitchener after his defeat at the battle of Atbara, Kitchener said to him, "Why have you come to my country to lay waste and plunder?" It was the intruder who said this to the person whose land it was, and the owner of the land bowed his head and said nothing. So let it be with me. In the court I hear the rattle of [Roman] swords in Carthage and the clatter of the hooves of Allenby's horses desecrating the ground of Jerusalem. The ships at first sailed down the Nile carrying guns not bread, and the railways were originally set up to transport troops; the schools were started so as to teach us how to say "Yes" in their language. . . . Yes, my dear sirs, I came as an invader into your homes: a drop of the poison which you have injected into the veins of history. (*SMN* 1969c, 94–95)[12]

Wounded historical memory gives him the sense that everyone in the courtroom—including Ann's father and Isabella's husband—"conspired" to deny him the presumed victory of having taken charge of their fantasies about Africans and Orientals, and turned those stereotypes into weapons against empire. Mustafa's insoluble paradox is that he clings to an empty heroic stance while simultaneously knowing that he has been a "lie."

Nevertheless, after Mustafa is released from prison he tries to redeem himself from lies by not seeking a prominent government position in Sudan, as his old schoolmate, the retired Mamur, anticipated. Had he done so he would have been joining the corrupt, hypocritical class of Macaulian mimics, handpicked and groomed by the British (*SMN* 1969c, 53–54). Instead, he tries to live like a simple farmer in an obscure village, frequenting the mosque, getting married, and employing his knowledge in the service of the villagers (some of whose faces

---

12. See Thomas Cartelli's reading of the trial scene 151–55.

he draws "with a clarity of vision and sympathy approaching love" [151]). Mahjoub remembers him regretfully: "God rest his soul. . . . His death was an incomparable loss . . . he gave us invaluable help in organizing the [Agricultural] Project. He used to look after the accounts and his business experience was of great use to us. . . . I asked him more than once to take over the Chairmanship, but he always used to refuse, saying I was better suited. The Omda and the merchants absolutely loathed him because he opened the villagers' eyes and spoiled things for them" (101).

Yet Mustafa lives another lie by hiding his past from the villagers. This leads him to repress his Anglicization, symbolized by a library that contains "not a single Arabic book" (*SMN* 1969c, 137)—despite the considerable knowledge of Arabic he displays when he recites Abu Nuwas's poetry and when he composes a poem that follows the conventions of classical Arabic poetry. When he decides to tell the story of his life to Meheimeed, he begins to dismantle the edifice of lies surrounding him. His poem expresses a conflicted desire to escape from lies:

> The sighs of the unhappy in the breast do groan
> The vicissitudes of Time by silent tears are shown
> And love and buried hate the winds away have blown.
> Deep silence has embraced the vestiges of prayer,
> Of moans and supplications and cries of woeful care,
> And dust and smoke the traveler's path ensnare.
> Some, souls content, others in dismay.
> Brows submissive, others . . . (152–53)[13]

The poem resembles the devotional poetry of mystics except for the existential angst that reduces to "vestiges" the ritual repetition of prayer. Even though the

13. The translation succeeds in capturing the general sense of the poem while duplicating, as best as possible, the rhyme scheme of the original. Much is lost, needless to say, in any translation of poetry, and it would be useful here to point out, for the benefit of the Anglophone reader, some of the nuances of the Arabic original. The pathos of the original gives way to a certain monotony and flatness in the English which reinforces Meheimeed's judgment that this is "a very poor poem." The first line in the translation, for example, contains an unnecessary emphasis ("do groan") that serves only to complete the rhyme of the English verse, while the passive voice in the second line serves to establish the rhyme scheme at the expense of the energetic force of the Arabic. The word *'arbadat* (rendered as "groan") literally means "reveled" and denotes drunkenness, misbehavior, and sinfulness; the word choice, therefore, emphasizes the inner struggle of the would-be repentant who is torn between his inclination to pleasure and his spiritual aspiration. This contrast is reinforced by the arrangement of images in the two hemistiches of each verse, a division that characterizes classical and neoclassical Arabic poetry. Finally, the Qur'anic image of *jibahun saghiratun* (rendered as "bows submissive") evokes the suffering and humiliation of sinners in Hell, not the submissive stance of the faithful, as the translation suggests. Overall, there is in the original poem a heightened sense of tension and inner conflict that does not come across very well in the translation.

soul has been, in the mystical idiom, "emptied" of love and hate, which is a requirement for the ascetic on a spiritual "path," Mustafa's path is bedimmed with
"dust and smoke." He has finally exorcized the feelings that motivated his past
actions; what is left inside him, however, is not the serenity of enlightenment,
but darkness and despair. His state of mind is similar to that of Claudius in *Hamlet,* who tries to pray but cannot: "My words fly up, my thoughts remain
below:/Words without thoughts never to heaven go" (III.iv.97–98). Significantly, Mustafa is unable to finish the poem or to reach the serenity of faith and
vision.[14]

Mustafa's disappearance is not explained in the novel. The villagers, of
course, know nothing of Mustafa's life that would suggest that he may have
killed himself or fled to some unknown destination; they conclude that like Dau
al-Beit, he must have drowned in the Nile during "one of those floodings that
occur once every twenty or thirty years and become legendary," even though he
is known to be "an excellent swimmer" (*SMN* 1969c, 45), and even though his
body is never found. He may have drowned himself or taken advantage of the
flood to leave the village, knowing that he would be presumed dead. "The pangs
of wanderlust" he writes of in the letter he leaves behind for Meheimeed bespeak
his inability to repress the past any longer or to feel at home in Wad Hamid. He
wishes his sons to have a life unlike his own, to "grow up imbued with the air of
this village, its smells and colors and history, the faces of its inhabitants and the
memories of its floods and harvestings and sowings" (66). He wants them to
have "a normal upbringing and to take up worthwhile work" (65). As for himself, desertion of the village and his family is the logical consequence of his dias-
poric consciousness and his endeavor to correct "the lie that was [his] life," since
his life in Wad Hamid is based on yet another lie. Suicide would be an escape
from lies; departure into the unknown turns Mustafa into a symbol for the irre-
versible exile that is the legacy of colonialism. He writes in his letter to
Meheimeed: "I do not know which of the two courses would be the more selfish, to stay on or to depart. In any event I have no choice . . . It is futile to de-
ceive oneself. That distant call still rings in my ears. I thought that my life and
marriage here would silence it. . . . Rationally I know what is right: my attempt
at living in this village with these happy people. But mysterious things in my soul
and in my blood impel me towards faraway parts that loom up before me and
cannot be ignored" (66–67). The conflict here is no longer between essential-

---

14. Meheimeed's Romantic sensibility is behind his judgment that this is "a very poor poem
that relies on antithesis and comparisons; it has no true feeling, no genuine emotion" (*SMN* 1969c,
153). See Badawi's account of the attacks on neoclassical Arabic poetry by the Arab Romantics who,
in the 1920s to 1940s, attempted to revolutionize Arabic poetry (1993, 34–52). Meheimeed's
judgment is typical of their attitudes. Not surprisingly, his attempt to complete the poem reveals his
misunderstanding of it.

ized identities, but between what Mustafa knows "rationally" to be right and what he feels compelled to do. Wholly new is the very concern for right and wrong, for avoiding "the more selfish" choice, for being true to himself, and for the futility of self-deception. That is why he releases Meheimeed from the pledge of silence, and why he instructs Meheimeed to reveal to the two boys the truth about their father (66). All of Mustafa's life up to that point has been enveloped in *wahm*. In giving up his peaceful life in Wad Hamid, confessing the truth to Meheimeed, and permitting him to reveal it to the world, Mustafa finally repudiates illusions and lies.

Undoubtedly, Meheimeed misses the point and misjudges Mustafa, believing the latter to have "undertaken the most melodramatic act in the story of his life" (*SMN* 1969c, 67). This has to do with Meheimeed's own carefully guarded insecurity and self-deception—attributes that Salih makes plain in the subtle delineation of Meheimeed's story. But in concluding Mustafa's story in this manner, Salih is putting the last touches on his rewriting of Conrad: the latter's tale is sealed with Marlow's lie, another layer of darkness to envelop a tale of "horror." Salih lays bare what Conrad veils in his effort to uphold "the redeeming idea" of the civilizing mission. What Meheimeed cannot understand at this point is that Mustafa has taken charge of exposing his own lies. Mustafa was perhaps aware of the pitfalls of writing his own autobiography (150–51), and the temptation to construct himself in it, textually, as another illusion; therefore, he prefers to tell it incomplete to Meheimeed, whose curiosity will lead him to gather scraps of the narrative from other sources, such as the Mamur, Richard, Mrs. Robinson (who herself plans to write a book "about Rickie and Moozie" [148]), and the minister of education, each of whom has a different version. These irreconcilable versions of Mustafa's story make for an open-ended narrative and paint a more nuanced picture of Mustafa than he would have been capable of doing on his own. Kurtz's story is not so open; he seals it with two enigmatic words ("The horror, the horror"), having beseeched Marlow to protect his reputation. In compliance Marlow declares Kurtz's acts "unspeakable" and refuses to expose them to the Intended or to the crew aboard the *Nellie*; he discovers the infamous postscript to Kurtz's report on "savage customs," but chooses to tear it off, thus sealing Kurtz's lie with another of his own. In contrast, Mustafa opens up his own life to scrutiny and spells out his own "horror," thereby forcing Meheimeed to reassess his own migration to the north.

Postcolonial Culture

Mustafa's revenge intertwines structurally and thematically in the novel with another patriarchal drama that unfolds in Wad Hamid, significantly in 1956, the year of Sudanese independence, thus pointing to the consolidation of patriarchy in postcolonial culture. It involves the subjection of women to epistemic and physical violence. This oppression, which is sublimated in the utopian discourse of "Wedding," is here revealed as perpetrated by false appeals to religion that do not hesitate to distort the sources of Islamic *shari'a* itself, as Wad Rayyes does when he misquotes the Qur'an to justify his womanizing (*SMN* 1969c, 78).[15]

Cultural resistance to colonialism tends to reinforce that order. For example, clitoridectomy—a custom dating back to Pharaonic times—now becomes not only mistaken for an Islamic practice, but also a marker of a hierarchy of identity and difference; witness Bint Majzoub, a woman, teasing Meheimeed who has just returned from England: "We were afraid you'd bring back with you an uncircumcised [Christian] for a wife" (*SMN* 1969c, 4).[16] (Just as Jean Morris in England accepts phallocentrism wholesale, so does Bint Majzoub in Wad Hamid. Witness her, this time teasing Wad Rayyes: "What's come over you? For two years now you've contented yourself with a single wife. Has your prowess waned?" [77]). Rape can be the subject of boastful anecdotes (74–75). Fathers can barter their daughters away willy-nilly in marriage, and husbands can marry and divorce as often as they may change donkeys (100). And no sooner does a woman rebel against these norms than pronouncements such as the following uncover the basic tenets of a patriarchy that hijacks religion: "God curse all women! Women are the sisters of the Devil" (123).

In this context, Mustafa settles in Wad Hamid. Paradoxically, his Sudanese wife, Hosna Bint Mahmoud, finds in him an ideal husband, one who treats her with a respect unparalleled either by his treatment of British women or by the villagers' attitudes toward their wives and daughters. In England, Mustafa's misogyny fed on the epistemic violence of colonialism; in Sudan that misogyny apparently has given way to a liberationist impulse on behalf of Sudanese women. In fact, Mustafa seems to have transformed Hosna into what Mahjoub describes contemptuously as "a city woman" (*SMN* 1969c, 101) that is, a modernized woman who is not afraid to defy tradition. On Mustafa's presumed death, Hosna's father marries her off against her will to the aged womanizer Wad Rayyes, in a flagrant violation of her rights under Islamic law, which explicitly forbids forced marriage.[17] When she refuses to let Wad Rayyes touch her, he attempts to rape her. Herself badly injured in the ensuing struggle, Hosna stabs

15. In "The Two-Sided Image of Women in *Season of Migration to the North*," Sonia Ghattas-Soliman shows how the villagers' attitudes toward women predate Islam, and how that religion in fact restored to women many of the rights and privileges which, ironically, are still denied them in patriarchal societies by false appeals to religion. For an extended treatment of the subject, see Leila Ahmed's *Women and Gender in Islam*.

16. See note 3 to chapter 1.

17. Sonia Ghattas-Soleiman explains this point by quoting the Qur'an, which instructs male relatives that if widows "go out (of their own accord) there is no sin for you in that which they do of themselves within their rights" (2:240), and the Prophet, who rules that "[t]he widow shall not be

Wad Rayyes to death, castrates him, and takes her own life. Thus, just as the violence of phallocentric colonialism is literalized in the trail of suicides and murder Mustafa leaves behind in the north, so does the violence of traditional patriarchy assume a horrifically concrete form in the south. The mutilated bodies of Hosna and Wad Rayyes bear witness to a destructive form of patriarchy that normalizes the systematic violation of human rights. At the same time, those bodies dramatize the effects of the sudden disruption of social order under the auspices of imperialism.

The binary terms of the symbolic geography that frame the novel's trajectory from the opening lines to the closing scene collapse into a universal masculinist tyranny. From the perspective of gender, north and south are allies. Colonialism, anticolonial struggle, and traditional society have all been sustained by a foundational misogyny. Himself a scholar who has returned from England at the dawn of independence, Meheimeed is equally horrified by Mustafa's past (which signifies the colonial legacy Meheimeed would rather forget) and by the disastrous consequences of the abuses of traditional patriarchy (which he would all too readily delete from his idealized image of the village): "I imagined Hosna Bint Mahmoud . . . as being the same woman in both instances: two white, wide-open thighs in London, and a woman groaning before dawn in an obscure village on a bend of the Nile under the weight of the aged Wad Rayyes. If that other thing was evil, this too was evil" (*SMN* 1969c, 86–87). Located almost at the exact middle of the novel, this passage expresses most clearly Salih's dual critique of colonialism and patriarchy.

Despite this painful realization, Meheimeed is powerless to help Hosna or to oppose the villagers. His indecisiveness and failure to take action can be seen as Salih's indictment of the Arab intelligentsia's failure to struggle for the implementation of a vital part of the *Nahda*'s social reform project. Note here that although women were at the forefront of nationalist, anticolonial movements in countries like Egypt and Algeria, their demands for equality were ignored after independence. Hosna's story—especially as it relates to Meheimeed's failure to defend her rights—is linked in the novel to his problematic conception of history, identity, and agency, to which I shall devote the remainder of this chapter.

As British-educated Sudanese of two successive generations, Mustafa and Meheimeed exhibit strikingly different attitudes toward history. Mustafa articulates his identity in the context of the history of African and Arab contact with Europe, and his narrative establishes an unambiguously historical and political frame of reference. In contrast, Meheimeed's narrative contains not a single historical allusion, even though his life coincides with no less important events than

---

married until she is consulted, and the virgin shall not be married until her consent is obtained" (96–98).

those marking Mustafa's—the loss of Palestine in 1948, Sudanese independence in 1956, the Algerian War of Independence (1952–63), and the many other liberation struggles throughout the Arab world and Africa. If Mustafa turns colonial "history into a pimp" (*SMN* 1969c, 144), Meheimeed represses that history, for reasons that have to do with his characterization in the Cycle as a whole, and also for ideological reasons related to the *Nahda*'s failure to reconcile Enlightened with imperialist Europe—a failure that fostered a simplistic notion of synthesis between Arab culture and Western modernity.

The same pattern emerges in *Season* as in each of the other works narrated by Meheimeed: his world is always dominated by a powerful figure (the grandfather, Mustafa, the Cypriot Man, Bandarshah) who draws him into a violent confrontation with himself, so that the relative peace and harmony with the world that he feels at the beginning of each story is disrupted at the end through the clash of contradictory psychic forces and value systems. In "A Handful of Dates," he recounts an early incident that led him, while still a child, to rebel against his grandfather, whom he loves and still holds in great esteem in *Season*. In *Meryoud,* an adolescent Meheimeed has a greater conflict with Hajj Ahmad, who insists that his favorite grandson continue his education in England and become an "effendi," notwithstanding both the opposition of his father and the boy's own desire to stay in the village, become a farmer, and marry his childhood playmate, Maryam (*B* 1996, 90). Meheimeed's relationship with Hajj Ahmad borders most of the time on friendship and love, but occasionally also on "hatred" ("HD" 1969b, 28; *B* 1996, 85). In *Season* that ambivalence does not surface until the incident of Hosna Bint Mahmoud. Nostalgic and homesick, Meheimeed returns to Wad Hamid after seven years in the north. During that time Hajj Ahmad becomes for him a symbol of continuity, stability, spirituality, and tradition: "I go to my grandfather and he talks to me of life forty years ago, fifty years ago, even eighty, and my feeling of security is strengthened" (*SMN* 1969c, 5). In England, a nostalgic Meheimeed idealizes his grandfather in order to assuage an exile ironically decreed by Hajj Ahmad himself.

Many critics—most notably Ali Abbas, Siddiq, and Khairallah—have been sensitive to the multilayered relationship between Mustafa and Meheimeed. Raja' Ni'ma argues that the key to understanding Meheimeed lies in what she calls the "pendulum-like movement" of his narrative between the two opposite poles of Mustafa on the one hand and the grandfather on the other; or between night time (Mustafa's world and the realm of the unconscious, marked by negativity) and the dawn of day (the time of the grandfather's ablutions and prayer, which signify spiritual and moral purification and also the sphere of rational, ordered reality) (Ni'ma 1986, 77–114). Following Freud, Ni'ma goes on to argue that this vacillation speaks to a tension arising from Meheimeed's repressed libidinal drives: "Mustafa is no more than a substitute for restless needs lying in the innermost depths of the Narrator" (83). If Mustafa is a parody of Orientalist and Africanist stereotypes—a parody that provides an index to the alliance of imperial and patriarchal hegemonies—Meheimeed is a child of the *Nahda* who is forced to relinquish the illusion of monolithic cultural identities that are taken for granted in the novels of al-Hakim, Haqqi, and Suhayl Idris. Rather than the achievement of cultural identification ('Uthman), successful individuation (Siddiq), or visionary insight (Khairallah) for Meheimeed through his encounter with Mustafa, the novel depicts the disintegration of Meheimeed's conception of identity. He understands his migration not as a potentially dynamic mediation between south and north, but rather as a time lag, a passage between two static worlds. Not unlike Mustafa's fatalistic vision of eternal antagonism, Meheimeed believes in irreducible cultural relativism. And just as the novel dramatizes the failure of Mustafa's vision, so it does Meheimeed's.

The opening scene of the novel, in which Meheimeed describes his return, powerfully dramatizes his certitude about who he is and where he belongs. Yet Meheimeed also betrays his anxiety at having been dislocated from his culture, and the grand affirmation of identity succeeds only in calling attention to its artificiality. Underneath the serenity of the opening pages in *Season,* the psychic forces of exclusion and repression can be seen wrestling with undesirable memories that disrupt the construction of a unitary, monological identity. During his exile in the north, he takes refuge in a sanitized memory of Wad Hamid:

> It was, gentlemen, after a long absence—seven years to be exact, during which time I was studying in Europe—that I returned to my people. I learnt much and much passed me by—but that's another story. The important thing is that I returned with a great yearning for my people. . . . For seven years I had longed for them, had dreamed of them, and it was an extraordinary moment when I at last found myself standing amongst them . . . and it was not long before I felt as though a piece of ice were melting inside of me, as though I were [a man feverish and cold on whom] the sun had shone—that life-warmth of the tribe which I had lost for a time in a land "whose fishes die of the cold." . . . Because of having thought so much about them during my absence, something rather like fog rose up between them and me the first instant I saw them. But the fog cleared and I awoke, the second day of my arrival, in my familiar bed in the room whose walls had witnessed the trivial incidents of my life in childhood and the onset of adolescence. . . . I looked through the window at the palm tree standing in the courtyard of our house and I knew that all was still well with life. . . . I experienced a feeling of assurance. I felt not like a storm-swept feather but like that palm tree, a being with a background, with roots, with a purpose.
>
> My mother brought tea. My father, having finished his prayers and recitations from the Koran, came along. Then my sister and brothers came and we all sat down and drank tea and talked, as we have done ever since my eyes opened on life. Yes, life is good and the world as unchanged as ever. . . . Suddenly I recollected having seen a face I did not know. (*SMN* 1969c, 1–2)

As Amyuni points out, the first word in the Arabic text is the verb *'udtu* (I returned) (1985, 19), which foregrounds the end of migration as one of the novel's titular signifiers. I argue that the verb also points to the most crucial psychic operation to unfold within Meheimeed in this novel: the return of the repressed. The "return" of the "I" to "my people" and the place of origin is foregrounded to emphasize the conclusion of an undesirable "long absence," a lacuna during which his very life was suspended as though his heart had turned into "a piece of ice" and he became feverish and ill. His return to his people is a return to life, since the south is the place of health, sunshine, and the life warmth of the tribe. In contrast to this, Europe is cold and deadly both to human beings and to nature itself. This evenly balanced distribution of values between north and south denies Meheimeed both a productive interaction with the north and a clear assessment of his position in and toward the south. He makes no claim that racism experienced in Europe may have contributed to his withdrawal, but he still refuses to speak of his life there. What he learned and what passed him by is the subject of "another story"—one that he never really tells because he would like to forget it; he represses it, contending that it is less "important" than the fact of his return. (Note the contrast with the speaker in "A Letter to Eileen," who seems to have been a preliminary sketch of Meheimeed, and whose sense of alienation is expressed much more directly as a rejection of the south.) Not surprisingly, that repressed story immediately surfaces to "fog up" the clarity he so insistently seeks. The "fog" rising in front of his eyes is not a proverbial Arabic expression; rather, it is an image that specifically evokes London (nicknamed "the foggy city" in Arabic). This image suggests that the estrangement he feels is related to that "other story." His evocations of his "familiar bed," "room," "childhood and the onset of adolescence," function to negate the hybridized, split, and alienated self that he refuses to acknowledge; they are also affirmations of the self he desires (even though, as we learn from "A Handful of Dates" and *Bandarshah,* he really was not so much at home in the world back then as he now thinks). Similarly, the sight of the palm tree reassures him because it allows him to negate what he fears and to affirm what he desires: "I felt not like a storm-swept feather but like that palm tree, a being with a background, with roots, with a purpose." The assertion itself, of course, from a psychoanalytic perspective, betrays Meheimeed's anxiety at being precisely the opposite—rootless and without purpose. The domestic scene further allows him to dispel his fear and to articulate it: he fears change, and life is good so long as things remain familiar and static, as in a childhood idealized through the prism of nostalgia. Meheimeed's wish to return to childhood at the same time that he looks forward to the future indicates a dislocation from the present as well as a profoundly problematic sense of history.

Meheimeed reminisces to his audience of gentlemen that in the few days after his return, "I was happy . . . like a child that sees itself in the mirror for the first time" (*SMN* 1969c, 4). This comparison is highly significant from a psychoanalytic point of view, since it alludes directly to Jacques Lacan's concept of "the mirror stage." Lacan explains that the moment of self-recognition, when an infant recognizes itself in the mirror for the first time, marks the birth of identity; at that point the infant begins to develop a sense of distinct, autonomous being. It is also, ambivalently, the first moment of alienation for the infant, who recognizes its separation from the mother, its "otherness." Thus for the twenty-five-year-old who has just returned from what he perceives as an exile, the moment of return signals his irrevocable separation from the village—a separation acutely felt by the speaker in "A Letter to Eileen," who has no illusions about his own alienation. In that sense, Meheimeed's newfound sense of identity is something that paradoxically points to his alienation from the object of his identification. In Lacanian terms, that identity is a *Gestalt*, a form of fixed, symmetrical exteriority disguising the turbulent movement that both inspires Meheimeed's narrative and anticipates the destruction of his phantasmic world.[18]

The image of that destruction appears also in a mirror when he enters Mustafa's library and for a fearsome moment imagines seeing the latter's face instead of his own reflected back to him. Meheimeed's desire to burn the room betrays a self-destructive urge that he will satisfy in the novel's final scene. For Meheimeed, Mustafa is the projection of his own sense of alienation, to the same extent that the grandfather is a symbol of the stability and belonging that Meheimeed yearns for; Mustafa and Hajj Ahmad represent the psychic forces whose clash destroys Meheimeed's comfortable illusion (*wahm*) of identity and wholeness. This *wahm* is always disrupted by the sudden return of the repressed ("suddenly" is one of Meheimeed's most frequently used words in this novel): Mustafa appears suddenly like a phantom amidst the crowd of welcoming villagers, and is remembered just as suddenly at the climax of the opening scene, when the exile's dream of home reaches fulfillment in the family gathering around tea cups. The next time he remembers Mustafa, Meheimeed associates him with the legendary Bandarshah: "My grandfather was talking to me of a tyrant who had ruled over the district in the days of the Turks. I do not know what it was that brought Mustafa to mind but suddenly I remembered him." Mustafa at that moment becomes the absolute Other; he merges with a fearful

18. Lacan writes, "the total form of the body by which the subject anticipates in a mirage the maturation of his power is given to him only as *Gestalt*, that is to say, in an exteriority in which this form is certainly more constituent than constituted, but in which it appears to him above all in a contrasting size . . . that fixes it and in a symmetry that inverts it, in contrast with the turbulent movements that the subject feels are animating him. Thus, this *Gestalt* . . . by these two aspects of its appearance, symbolizes the mental permanence of the I, at the same time as it prefigures its alienating destination; it is still pregnant with the correspondences that unite the I with the statue in which man projects himself, with the phantoms that dominate him, or with the automaton in which, in an ambiguous relation, the world of his own making tends to find completion" (Lacan 1977, 2–3)

myth, while the grandfather—symbol of the *Heimliche,* the homely and the familiar, who is (appropriately) "very knowledgeable about the genealogy of everyone in the village and even of people scattered up and down the river"—significantly "knew nothing about [Mustafa]" (*SMN* 1969c, 6).

Mustafa's uncanniness is not simply a function of his hidden past; his very presence is disturbing. He seems to Meheimeed to have grafted himself successfully onto the community, whereas the newly returned wrestles with his repressed feelings of alienation from it. The stranger seems to have replaced him in the village; he plays the active role in its public life of which Meheimeed's exile deprived him; and he leads the simple life of a farmer which Meheimeed wanted for himself. It is no wonder that Meheimeed later falls in love with Mustafa's wife (*SMN* 1969c, 104). Moreover, Mustafa deflates Meheimeed's pride at his "achievement" when he mocks Meheimeed's study of poetry—"We have no need of poetry here. It would have been better if you'd studied agriculture, engineering or medicine." Admitting that "I had in those days . . . a rather high opinion of myself," Meheimeed is "furious . . . Look at the way he says 'we' and does not include me, though he knows that this is my village and that it is he—not I—who is the stranger" (9). Mustafa's provocative remarks do more than challenge Meheimeed's claim to his village; they highlight his alienation from it and question the value of any contribution he might make to its welfare. Meheimeed is no longer a simple villager, but a new member of the colonial bourgeoisie, whose questionable qualifications for power make them ineffective rulers if not outright exploiters of their own people. This is emphasized when Mahjoub complains about the dire lack of health and educational services in Wad Hamid and chides Meheimeed: "And you, what are you doing in Khartoum? What's the use in our having one of us in the government when you're not doing anything?" (118). Meheimeed has not joined the "pack of wolves" who are "the new rulers of Africa" (118), but he fears becoming, and being seen as, one of them.

Mustafa also uncovers in the familiar an excess that defamiliarizes it, and thereby forces Meheimeed to see what he knows with different eyes. The first such instance involves no less than the very symbol of the familiar, Hajj Ahmad himself: " 'Your grandfather knows the secret,' he said to me with that mocking phantom still more in evidence round his eyes . . . 'What secret does my grandfather know? My grandfather has no secrets' " (*SMN* 1969c, 11). Later on, Mustafa's drawings of the villagers demonstrate that he understands them better than Meheimeed: "Bakri, Mahjoub, my grandfather, Wad Rayyes, Hosna, my uncle Abdul Karim, and others: their faces looked at me [in Mustafa's drawings] with the penetrating expressions I had long been aware of but which I had been incapable of defining" (151). This "excess of signification," which is never quite articulated, remains as disturbing secrets and undefinable qualities, cryptic and uncanny, fissuring the *wahm* of a unitary identity.

In this way, Mustafa forces Meheimeed to face his crisis of identity, under-mines his illusory sense of security, and further destabilizes his grasp on reality. Meheimeed defines himself as everything that Mustafa is not, and his affirma-tion of identity is predicated on the negation of that which he fears—being up-rooted like Mustafa. The profoundly disturbing effect of Mustafa on Meheimeed arises from the fact that the former embodies—and is a constant re-minder of—everything that the latter seeks to repress within himself, but that keeps coming back "suddenly," in moments that seem "outside the boundaries of time and place." This is a recurring phrase that describes the experience of the uncanny, or the Other's sudden, disturbing appearance.[19] In fact, Mustafa seems to cast a spell not only over Meheimeed, but also over many of his generation, such as Mansour, the young Sudanese lecturer at the University of Khartoum whom Meheimeed knew in England, and who asks him an implausible question: whether he is Mustafa's son. At that moment, Meheimeed has the sense of be-longing to a community of British-educated Sudanese whose grasp on reality has been weakened by a peculiar bond to colonial history, embodied in Mustafa (*SMN* 1969c, 57).

Not surprisingly, Mustafa always seems to be the opposite of what Meheimeed thinks: a killer, and a man with an acute historical memory rather than an amnesiac.[20] Meheimeed asserts, "No, I am not a stone thrown into the water but seed sown in a field" (*SMN* 1969c, 5). In contrast, Mustafa cherished, as a child, "a warm feeling of being free, that there was not a human being, fa-ther or mother, to tie me down as to a tent peg at a particular spot"; rather, he "was like something rounded, made of rubber: you throw it in the water and it doesn't get wet, you throw it on the ground and it bounces back" (20). Meheimeed's exile to the north was no voluntary migration like Mustafa's, and in sharp contrast to him, Meheimeed's sexual behavior there is virginal (Wad Rayyes teases him about it [80]), but such reversals of expectations shake Meheimeed's self-assurance. His sense of identity is intuitive, filiative, based

19. Kristeva writes, "While it surely manifests the return of a familiar repressed, the *Unheim-liche* requires just the same the impetus of a new encounter with an unexpected outside element: arousing images of death, automatons, doubles, or the female sex . . . uncanniness occurs when the boundaries between imagination and reality are erased. This observation reinforces the concept—which arises out of Freud's text—of the *Unheimliche* as a crumbling of conscious defenses, resulting from the conflicts the self experiences with an other—the 'strange'—with whom it maintains a con-flictual bond, at the same time 'a need for identification and a fear of it' " (Kristeva 1991, 188). This sort of bond occurs twice in the novel: between Meheimeed and Mustafa as his Other, and between Mustafa and Jean as his Other. Jean also erases the boundaries between the real and the imaginary for Mustafa: "in an instant outside the bounds of time, I have bedded the Goddess of Death and gazed out upon Hell from the aperture of her eyes" (*SMN* 1969c, 153).

20. "I dismissed the idea that he was a killer—the use of violence leaves a mark on the face that the eye cannot miss" (*SMN* 1969c, 17). "As for having lost his memory, this was a possibility" (17).

merely on the geographical and biographical facts of birth, and rather determin-
istic and static: "I am from here—is this not reality enough? . . . I had lived with
them [the English] superficially, neither loving nor hating them. . . . I must be
one of those birds that exist only in one region of the world. . . . Over there is
like here, neither better nor worse. But I am from here, just as the date palm
standing in the courtyard of our house has grown in *our* house and not in any-
one else's" (49). As a result, Meheimeed leaves Mustafa's house after listening
to his story and begins seriously to doubt himself and his hitherto secure knowledge of the world: "Was it likely that what happened to Mustafa Sa'eed could
have happened to me? He said that he was a lie, so was I also a lie?" (49).

Meheimeed's denial of the effects of colonialism on himself is contradictory, for although his conscious identification with the villagers is total, he feels
superior to them. For example, it is not without some condescension toward the
villagers that he responds to their questions about England—questions that betray their ignorance of life beyond their village and reveal their prejudices, especially those related to their own moral taboos and social customs. Even though
he lived among the English "superficially," he now describes them to the villagers as "just like them" and seems amused by the villagers' lack of exposure to
foreigners (*SMN* 1969c, 3–4). His spoken and unspoken responses indicate an
affinity with "Negroes who return to their original environment convey[ing]
the impression that they have completed a cycle, that they have added to themselves something that was lacking" (Fanon 1967, 19). His life in Europe makes
him feel superior to the villagers. He seems to think that they may not understand even the most basic things about human life—that all people live, die,
dream, fear, love, hope, despair, and so on—as if such things required a special
intelligence that he has attained by virtue of studying in Europe (*SMN* 1969c,
3–4). By the same token, his attitude toward the English is contradictory: they
are "just like us," yet he describes the north as hostile to life itself, and his interaction with the people there seems to have been minimal. Paradoxically, equality is compatible with essentialism, common humanity with rigid cultural
boundaries.

This dubious logic leads Meheimeed to an impasse that lies at the heart of his
identity crisis. At the same time that he is aware of the change he has undergone
in England, he refuses to acknowledge that England has had any effect on him,
positive or negative: "The fact that [the British] came to our land, I know not
why, does that mean that we should poison our present and our future? Sooner
or later they will leave our country, just as many people throughout history left
many countries. The railways, ships, hospitals, factories and schools will be ours
and we'll speak their language without either a sense of guilt or a sense of grati-
tude. Once again we shall be as we were—ordinary people—and if we are lies we
shall be lies of our own making" (*SMN* 1969c, 49–50). The intent is existentially
courageous and liberatory, but the effect is mystifying. In contrast to Mustafa,

Meheimeed denies all effects—indeed, the very relevance—of colonial history. This ahistorical conception of cultural contact as various people taking turns at occupying and then leaving the lands of others, without that game of musical chairs ever affecting their "ordinariness," falls short of al-Tahtawi's conscious effort to examine critically Western civilization and its institutions in order to select those aspects of it which Arab society would find it beneficial to adopt. The *Nahda* project, whatever its shortcomings, envisioned a productive interaction between cultures; in contrast, Meheimeed betrays a thoroughly colonialist conception of East as East and West as West that shares Mustafa's fatalism but lacks his anticolonial fervor. The implausible claim that he, the recipient of a first-rate colonial education, does not know why the colonists came to his country hardly fits with his assertion that once they leave, an unproblematic transfer of ownership of the colonial tools will leave his people safe in their "ordinariness."

This denial of history constitutes, of course, a denial of historical agency. Nevertheless, he returns to Sudan at the dawn of independence, brimming with hope and optimism about his life and his country: "I want to take my rightful share of life by force, I want to give lavishly, I want love to flow from my heart, to ripen and bear fruit. There are many horizons that must be visited, fruit that must be plucked, books read, and white pages in the scrolls of life in which to inscribe vivid sentences in a bold hand" (*SMN* 1969c, 5); "This is the land of poetry and the possible—and my daughter is named Hope. We shall pull down and we shall build, and we shall humble the sun itself to our will; and somehow we shall defeat poverty" (112–13). Characteristic of the moment of independence (and this event takes place in 1956, the year Sudan gained independence), these grand hopes and noble sentiments are ill founded both in knowledge and in material reality. He does not know how to turn hope into action or how to "defeat poverty," but he is certain that a way will be found.

The immediate context of the euphoric moment in which he makes that proclamation is just after sunset during the desert journey back to Khartoum, after the passive role he has played in Hosna's marriage negotiations. A few hours earlier in the journey, he was "in a state close to fever" from the heat of the sun (*SMN* 1969c, 106). The sun was to him the embodiment of absurd cosmic cruelty that leaves humanity powerless: "an old blood feud existed between it [the sun] and the people of the earth" (105); the sun "melts" the brain and "paraly[zes]" thought (106) and leads Meheimeed to think that "this is the land of despair and poetry but there is nobody to sing" (110). The description serves to justify passivity vis-à-vis the inevitable, on the view that human choice and action mean nothing in the grand order of the universe: "The sun is the enemy. Now it is exactly in the liver of the sky, as the Arabs say. What a fiery liver! And thus it will remain for hours without moving—or so it will seem to living creatures when even the stones groan, the trees weep, and iron cries out for help. The weeping of a woman under a man at dawn and two wide-open white thighs.

They are now like the dry bones of camels scattered in the desert. No taste. No smell. Nothing of good. Nothing of evil" (111). In Meheimeed's reasoning, there is slippage between the moral indifference of nature on the one hand, and on the other, violence and rape in the human world (note, for instance, that nature is anthropomorphized through pathetic fallacy in images of weeping trees and groaning stones). Oppression becomes the law of the universe, absolving human beings of any guilt and responsibility. With the setting sun, however, "suddenly the war end[s] in victory" (a victory that has nothing to do with human effort to "humble the sun" and is thus no victory at all). The sky becomes "beautiful, compassionate" (112); then follows the boundless optimism, singing, poetry, the tearing down and building up, and the optimism expressed in naming his daughter Hope. The "festival to nothingness" may be a spontaneous affirmation of life in the face of a cruel environment, as Khiarallah argues convincingly, but the entire episode serves to portray the total dependence of Meheimeed's moods on his environment (natural in this scene, but also social and cultural elsewhere). His mood swings and even his worldview itself—his sense of identity, history, and agency—depend on the time of day, and vacillate between the extremes of total cynicism and boundless optimism.

Consequently, he fails to play an effective role either in the capital or in the village. "Civil servants like me can't change anything," he says defensively to Mahjoub. "If our masters say 'Do so-and-so,' we do it" (*SMN* 1969c, 121). Although he holds a doctorate in English literature, he is appointed to teach pre-Islamic poetry in secondary schools. He notes the corruption and hypocrisy of "the new rulers of Africa" (118), but he is powerless to do anything except participate in the system. Those frustrations produce the bitter and disillusioned early retiree who returns to Wad Hamid two decades later at the beginning of *Dau al-Beit*. In *Season*, he does realize, in a moment of truth, that he never made a single free choice (134).

Likewise, he feels the injustice inflicted on Hosna but withholds his support from her because of divided allegiances. He has idealized the village and its people; now, however, the evil of patriarchal hegemony not only clashes with his sense of justice but also erases the boundary between north and south: "I imagined Hosna Bint Mahmoud . . . as being the same woman in both instances: two white, wide-open thighs in London, and a woman groaning before dawn in an obscure village on the bend of the Nile under the weight of the aged Wad Rayyes. If that other thing was evil, this too was evil, and if this was like death and birth, the Nile flood and the wheat harvest, a part of the system of the universe, so too was that" (*SMN* 1969c, 87). Despite his anger, he chooses to do nothing and takes refuge in the complacent, pseudophilosophical view that both good and evil, justice and injustice, are "part of the system of the universe." Even when Mahjoub advises him on a course of action that would protect Hosna, he does nothing. She herself suggests a *pro forma* marriage with

Meheimeed "to save her from Wad Rayyes and the attention of suitors," so that she would be left alone (132). Yet instead of averting the tragedy through this kind of negotiation between oppressive custom and emancipatory impulse, he escapes to Khartoum by the short desert road ("this time I was, for no particular reason, in a hurry" [105]) and ignores the pleading voice ringing in his ears: " 'Why the hurry?' she had asked me. 'Why don't you stay another week?' she had said" (106). He refuses to take seriously Hosna's threat to kill Wad Rayyes and herself if she is forced to marry him. When he hears the ominous news that another woman killed her husband, he absurdly ends the conversation by suggesting that the man was not killed by his wife, but died from sunstroke (110). Only nature acts; humans cannot, as T. S. Eliot's Prufrock puts it, "disturb the universe." No wonder that when Hosna acts on her threat, he feels that "the world has turned suddenly upside down" (134).

In her analysis of the narrative mode of the novel, Ni'ma observes that Meheimeed avoids directly relating the incidents involving murder and sexuality. He leaves that function to the "narrative mediation" of other characters—Mustafa, Bint Majzoub, and Wad Rayyes—whose combined narration occupies almost half the novel by the count of lines. Ni'ma concludes that Meheimeed is unable to confront those issues directly (1986, 268–71). Instead, he displaces his sexual and murderous drives onto Mustafa and Hosna, both in fantasy and by the negative action of failing to rescue Hosna, thereby consigning her to act on her threat out of sheer desperation. In this way, Meheimeed indirectly participates in the murder, satisfying his desire for it through Hosna (272–75).

This unconscious "cunning" brings about a compromise between contradictory urges. First, it allows Meheimeed to express indirectly his outrage at the misogyny perpetrated in the name of Islam. Second, it permits him to participate in Hosna's revolutionary stance without antagonizing the village himself. Third, in symbolically killing his own "rival" and double—Mustafa—in the figure of Wad Rayyes, who is a crony of Meheimeed's grandfather, Meheimeed satisfies an Oedipal urge by eliminating the two father figures of Mustafa and Hajj Ahmad. Fourth, Meheimeed loves Hosna (or believes he does, for in *Bandarshah,* he remembers Maryam, not Hosna, as the only woman he ever loved), and feels contaminated by an emotion that links him to Mustafa and Wad Rayyes (*SMN* 1969c, 104). This time, it is the mirror of those two that reflects back to Meheimeed a disturbing *Gestalt,* one which he blames on a universal condition of evil that, like the burning sun (described in the scene immediately following) bears the burden of blame, absolving him of all guilt.

Yet when the unthinkable does occur and Hosna accomplishes what he never could or would contemplate, he blames Mahjoub. Furthermore, he flies into a violent rage for the first and only time in the Wad Hamid Cycle when Mahjoub demands, "Why didn't *you* do something? Why didn't you marry her? You're only any good when it comes to talking" (*SMN* 1969c, 131–32). Or he blames Mustafa, whose respect for his wife allowed her too much independence and dignity for her to accept being bartered away in a marriage transaction. Meheimeed's ethical judgment has collapsed, and he realizes that his "world has changed" (130), "turned suddenly upside down" (134). He reads on one of Mustafa's scraps of paper sentences that seem to allude to Hosna: "We teach people in order to open their minds and release their captive powers. But we cannot predict the result. Freedom—we free their minds from superstition. We give people the keys to the future to act therein as they wish" (151). This statement also reflects on Meheimeed insofar as he is a teacher by profession and a member of a class that sees itself as educating a new nation. If Mustafa did not claim membership in that class when he chose the life of a farmer, he at least put his precepts into practice. It remained for Meheimeed to fulfill his part.

Thus, even though he does not seem to jump in the river on leaving Mustafa's room with the conscious intention of ending his life, Meheimeed flirts with death in a symbolic reenactment of his migration to the north. The final scene of the novel sums up Meheimeed's predicament in terms of middle states and in-betweens. The river in Salih's fiction always seems to wash away the aliens from Wad Hamid: the villagers throw the government envoys in the river in "The Doum Tree," and Mustafa is believed by the villagers to have drowned in the river—a fate that decades earlier befell Dau al-Beit, another stranger to Wad Hamid.

To fully understand the significance of this scene, one must recall another scene that precedes it chronologically but is recounted in a flashback later on in the first chapter of *Meryoud* (*B* 1996, 88–89). As a boy of seven who has recently learned to swim, Meheimeed is told by his grandfather that the time has come for him to swim to the other (northern) bank across a dangerous whirlpool at the bend of the Nile. This near-fatal challenge is met successfully, to the wonder and admiration of the whole village and the immense pride of the grandfather. The boy, however, emerges from the trial with hatred in his heart for Hajj Ahmad. This time, Mustafa is the one who indirectly leads Meheimeed to the river, but this time, Meheimeed fails to save himself and desperately shouts for help. The river itself is in between states, "not in full spate as during the days of the flooding nor yet was it at its lowest level"—just like Meheimeed himself, who is no longer a villager, but not a stranger to the village, either. The river also gives indications of a hybridization that undermines Meheimeed's essentialist conceptions of Self and Other. The water is "cold," although in the opening scene of the novel he established the cold as a property of the north. The only sounds he hears are the "old familiar voice" of the river and the new, foreign "puttering of the water-pump." Objects on both the northern and the southern banks are "half visible, appearing and disappearing, veering between light and darkness" (*SMN* 1969c, 166). Soon, Meheimeed also "veered between seeing and blindness. I was conscious and not conscious. Was I asleep or awake? Was I

alive or dead?" Migration as a potential dialogic exchange and cultural mediation gives way to a fatal clash between the conscious and the unconscious, which
threatens to drown him. At that point he has a half-articulated vision: "Then it
was as if I were in a vast echoing hall. . . . The hall expanded and the answering
echoes quickened" (167). Nowhere in *Season* is there another mention of "the
hall," but it sets the stage for two crucial dream-visions experienced by
Meheimeed and Sa'eed Asha 'l-Baytat in *Dau al-Beit,* which will be discussed at
some length in the next chapter. Suffice it here to say that both scenes take place
in Bandarshah's mansion, where he offers the two visitors the choice between
redemption and damnation. Characteristically, Meheimeed does not understand the significance of what he sees, and concludes that he has been invited
simply to be an uncomprehending witness (*B* 1996, 32). Thus, the reference to
"the hall" at the end of *Season* indicates that Meheimeed's soul is at stake, not
just his life or cultural identity.

Here the choice is much more immediate and contingent—to die or to
live—and hence its urgency is signaled (not surprisingly for one who hesitates
before important decisions) on a biological level by "a violent desire for a ciga-
rette" that shakes him awake

> from the nightmare. The sky settled into place, as did the bank, and I heard the
> puttering of the pump and was aware of the coldness of the water on my body.
> Then my mind cleared and my relationship to the river was determined.
> Though floating on the water, I was not part of it. I thought that if I died at that
> moment, I would have died as I was born—without any volition of mine. All
> my life I had not chosen, had not decided. Now I am making a decision. I
> choose life. I shall live because there are a few people I want to stay with for the
> longest possible time and because I have duties to discharge. It is not my con-
> cern whether or not life has meaning. If I am unable to forgive, then I shall try
> to forget. . . . Like a comic actor shouting on a stage, I screamed with all my re-
> maining strength, "Help! Help!" (*SMN* 1969c, 168–69)

The passage deftly reverses Meheimeed's initial conceptions of identity without
suggesting that he reaches a better assessment of his predicament. As he regains
consciousness, the sound of water pumps (modernization) and the coldness of
the water (coldness of the north) assume their function as signs of hybridity. In
an image that recalls Mustafa's description of himself as a rubber ball floating on
the water without getting wet—which in his mind Meheimeed contrasts with
his own self-perception as seed sown in a field rather than a stone thrown in the
water—he now finds himself as precisely that which he negates—Mustafa's
image. But Mustafa made his first decision at the age of nine, while the twenty-
eight-year-old Meheimeed has yet to make a choice.

Yet it is doubtful that in asserting his choice he is being any less "melodramatic" than Mustafa. The cry for help is not so much a free choice as a desperate plea of one who, having unconsciously flirted with death, discovers that he cannot face it. Therefore, Meheimeed acknowledges that his decision does not resolve any of the questions that brought him to the bend in the Nile in the first place—questions about his problematic sense of history, identity, and agency—that his is not so much a heroic stance as a melodramatic performance by a screaming comic actor. He never quite recovers from that discovery: *Bandarshah* is an extended meditation on the past by a regretful and disillusioned old man. He will have discharged his duties, raised his children, and returned to spend his retirement among his friends, Mahjoub's gang, but that will not relieve his bitterness and sense of loss.

In the final analysis, the novel rejects the notions of cultural identity that informed both colonial and Arab discourses. Culture is not a discrete choice between the icy fields of the north and the burning desert of the equator, as "those who see with one eye, speak with one tongue, and see things as either black or white, either eastern or western" would understand it (*SMN* 1969c, 150–51). Through the metaphor of migration, the novel invites a reading of the postcolonial culture as a fluid, dialogic negotiation of historical legacies, social boundaries, and cultural encounters. No other perspective can liquidate both Western racism and the tired conceptions of identity that inform the spectrum of Arab ideology. At the bend of the Nile, water flowing from south to north turns sharply from west to east, and it is at the cross-currents of that symbolic geography, as the site of the potentially deadly negotiation between opposites, that Meheimeed's cry for help assumes its proper significance: not as a victory or an affirmation, but as the failure of Arab ideologies of modernity to reinvent the present.

Bandarshah

The Poetics of Amnesia

AFTER THE NOSTALGIC IDEALISM of "Wedding," *Season* announced the failure of the *Nahda* as an intellectual project. One can also make the case that the novel anticipated the demise of the official policies of those Arab regimes which adopted that project in the guise of socialism and nationalism. *Bandar Shah* (comprising *Dau al-Beit* [1971] and *Meryoud* [1976] and published in English as *Bandarshah* [1996]) is the most complex novelistic representation of the crisis of Arab ideology in the decade following the Six Day War of 1967, and one of the most ambitious experiments in Arabic literature since Mahfouz's Trilogy. During the 1970s, Salih anticipated that the novel might reach as many as five parts (*TSS* 1982, 48); however, no sequels have appeared since *Meryoud* was published, except for one short story, "Al-rajul al-qubrusi" ("The Cypriot Man" 1973, revised 1976), which seems to have been intended as an episode in a third part. Salih considers the novel to be his most important work (*RTS* 1997, 118) and still hopes to finish it (UIWH 2002). The novel's incompleteness could be seen as a literary testimony to a culture in turmoil during a critical decade in its recent history.

Bandarshah belongs to a body of Arabic texts that in the late 1960s and 1970s registered in myriad ways the crisis of consciousness that the Six Day War of 1967 caused in the entire Arab world. In the ideological vacuum that ensued, religious fundamentalism, which had been kept in check during the heyday of pan-Arabism with its secular, socialist orientation, began to gain ground and to acquire a popular, grassroots base as an "emotive ideology" (Sidahmed 1996, 120).[1] The fundamentalist argument was (and continues to be) that a "return" to Islam in the form of a theocratic state is the only way out of the crisis. This was by no means a new idea—the Muslim Brothers in both Egypt and Sudan had

---

1. In Sudan, Nimeiri's complete turnabout in the early 1980s from socialism to fundamentalism exemplifies this trend (Sidahmed 1996, 119–20). In Egypt, however, fundamentalism was a populist movement that, after the demise of Nasser's socialism, opposed Sadat's pro-Western orientation.

held that position since the 1930s; that said, the renewed appeal of this position was directly related to the failure of secularism. Around the same time, however, many intellectuals began searching for new paradigms for understanding the Arab predicament. The ongoing Arab-Israeli conflict, the Lebanese Civil War, the Sudanese Civil War, and other social and regional conflicts within the Arab world have all demonstrated beyond any possible doubt that Western modernity and its ideal of Progress can no longer be entertained with the optimism of Rifa'a al-Tahtawi and Taha Husayn.

A full discussion of the issues involved and of the radical ways in which Arab intellectuals have been reformulating them lies beyond the scope of this study. Suffice it here to cite the Lebanese novelist and critic Elias Khoury's succinct description of the intellectual climate of the 1970s. In *Al-dhakira al-mafquda* (Lost memory), he argues that "modernity as a political project was an attempt to . . . combine two pasts, Arab past and Western past." This notion of modernity developed "within the confines of the project of building the nation-state" (1982, 30). But the nation-state was a European model imposed on societies with different dynamics of interaction and distinctive networks of sectarian and tribal relations (as the Lebanese and Sudanese civil wars made abundantly clear); furthermore, the borders of the newly independent nations had been drawn by the colonial powers while they were dividing among themselves the Arab territories formerly occupied by the Ottomans after World War I. Thus while pan-Arabism was first and foremost an anti-imperialist project, it was also in part a colonial legacy in that it was predicated upon the project of building a nation-state after a model and an ideology that were never adequately adapted to local conditions. The paradox remained hidden until 1967, when

> the defeat announced the collapse of the project and revealed a problematic set of social relations which the text could neither absorb nor arrest. . . . The text failed to continue in its usual game of coopting reality by reducing it to symbols, conclusions, and totalizing representations. . . . Can the text break itself and open up its structure to the new possibilities? . . . The new reality of conflicts, wars, civil wars, and social destruction is an entirely new text. Ready-made models can no longer absorb the movement of the new reality. As we move to the center of conflict, the conflict assumes our image, the image of societies which have been broken by colonial relations and which try, by their own brokenness, to break those relations. (1982, 41–42)

Those colonial relations and their inadequate "text" have created the condition that Khoury describes as "lost memory"—memory being understood specifically here as the active capacity to confront the present based on a dynamic understanding of one's historical identity. Thus the Lebanese Civil War becomes for Khoury paradigmatic of Arab postcoloniality and of the destruction of its project: Western modernity as a model and the nation-state as its vehicle. The failure of this conception of modernity unmasked Arab society's cultural amnesia. Between the vain attempt to mimic the West and the nostalgic call for a "return" to tradition—that is, between the lure of an unattainable future and the weight of the past—the present is lost. This is the principal idea in *Bandarshah,* a text that to use Khoury's expressions, "breaks itself" and "assumes the image" of its society.

The situation of exile that Khoury describes and for which no script can be rehearsed calls for a "new writing" and a new, improvised "text": in the process of breaking colonial relations, Khoury explains,

> reality mingles with the text, and the new writing becomes a step beyond the conformance of modernity and a rush into the *unknown,* an acceptance of a project of new cultural configuration with no clear outlines. In it the text takes shape in the process of writing, levels [of experience and language] intermingle, and details alone become capable of building an incomplete world. It is a text which is open to change from inside and outside, which mixes signifiers and signifieds in search of new forms of signification. (1982, 42; emphasis added)

The uncertainty of this "unknown"—with the potential both for tragically devastating effects on the social and political levels, and for adventurous and experimental rejuvenation in art, letters, and intellectual life—has been perhaps one of the most distinguishing features of Arab culture and politics since the late 1960s. At best, the new text is free from the constraints of both imported and resurrected models, and born from experimentation and creative syncretism. At worst—and arguably the worst has come to pass since Khoury's pronouncement—the "text" as a metaphor for Arab reality remains broken and fragmented.

In response to Khoury, Nasr Abu Zayd argues that Arab cultural memory is not lost insofar as its vehicle, the Arabic language, was never eclipsed during the period of colonial domination, but was able to adapt and to absorb Western culture. Thus, as a medium for both cultural transmission and creative expression, the language has been able not only to survive but also to thrive (Abu Zayd 1983, 201). Both Khoury and Abu Zayd agree, however, that the rejection of Western modernity must go beyond fundamentalist notions of "returning" to the (religious) texts of the heritage: the new task must involve a critical reinterpretation of tradition in the light of present circumstances rather than the other way round. In words that seem to echo Salih's criticism of earlier Arab writers' "fascination with the West" (IM 1976b, 129)— especially Khoury's use of Salih's favorite word, *wahm*—as well as Salih's rejection of blind imitation of the Arab ancients (*RTS* 1997, 16), Khoury writes: "Here and now, we realize that the magic and mystery of the West is nothing but an illusion [*wahm*], and . . .

that the classical texts of the heritage offer no solution and cannot lead to a solution; that it is rather the solution that will rediscover them, penetrate them,
and control their signification" (1982, 20). Attempts along these lines have
been made in the fields of philosophy, religious thought, cultural criticism, and
literature. Progressive religious thinkers have attempted radically to reinterpret
the sources of the *shari'a*—the Qur'an and the Sunna—as well as Islamic history.[2] The results of these attempts include the execution in Sudan of Mahmoud
Muhammad Taha after a mock-trial on charges of apostasy (1988); the assassination in Egypt of Farag Foda by radical fundamentalists (1992); and legal pro-
ceedings, also in Egypt, on similar charges against Nasr Abu Zayd, who was
forced into exile (1994), and against Nawal al-Saadawi (2001), who was eventually acquitted. Such sensationally repressive measures on the part both of the
state and of fundamentalists (who, paradoxically, pose the greatest internal
threat to the state in countries like Egypt and Algeria) certainly arise from the
sensitivity of religious issues—especially critical discussions of those issues. Yet in
other areas of cultural discourse, similarly radical attempts have been made. In
the domain of literary and cultural criticism, the launching of the literary magazine *Mawaqif* (Positions) in Beirut in 1968 signaled the emergence of a new
sensibility. The avant-garde Syrian poet Adonis (Ali Ahmad Sa'id) wrote in
Mawaqif's first editorial:

> [*Mawaqif* speaks for] the generation that has experienced the disintegration
> and paralysis of contemporary Arab society; a generation determined to embark
> on a new search of discovery and rebuilding.
>   *Mawaqif* seeks to be in the forefront [of this movement]. But to be in the
> vanguard means to be inventive, original—that is to be on the offensive, willing
> and ready to destroy what is rejected and to replace it by what we wish to set up.
> Culture is creativity; it is not using tools, but inventing them. . . . It [should]
> symbolize the rejection of what we have inherited and what has come down to
> us, and what has been written for us and about us. (Quoted in Sharabi 1988,
> 104–5)

The literature of the period, especially the novel, became increasingly experimental, abandoning all the realism, symmetry, and structural economy of
Mahfouz's landmark achievements of the 1940s and 1950s. In fact, Mahfouz
himself embarked on a new style in the following decades with works such as *The
Thief and the Dogs* (1961), *Small Talk on the Nile* (1966), *Miramar* (1967),
Mirrors, (1972) and others. The works of major new novelists in the years following 1967, such as the Syrian Halim Barakat, the Palestinian Emile Habibi,

---

2. See, for example, the books by Nasr Abu Zayd, Muhammad Sa'id al-'Ashmawi, Farag Foda,
and Mahmoud Muhammad Taha listed in the References.

the Saudi 'Abd al-Rahman Munif, and the Lebanese Elias Khoury, defy all narrative conventions that imply the least sense of a stable reality.[3] Other novelists in Egypt—especially those known collectively as the "Sixties Generation" such as Sun'alla Ibrahim, Gamal al-Ghitani, Yusuf al-Qa'id, 'Abd al-Hakim Qasim, and Yahya al-Tahir 'Abdalla—have developed distinctive and experimental modes of storytelling and linguistic expression. Whatever the strongest characteristic of the literature of the late 1960s and 1970s may be—an overwhelming emphasis on the scene as a disjunctive narrative unit, according to Edward Said; the problematization of form, according to M. M. Badawi; the fervent attempts to reinvent language, form, and narration, according to Khoury; the prevalence of the ironic mode, according to Ceza Kassem—it is a literature that expresses a profoundly disturbed relation to the present and that attempts to articulate a new consciousness of that present.[4]

Tayeb Salih's *Bandarshah* fits squarely within Khoury's description of the "new writing" of the 1970s. The novel comprises a baffling string of dialogues, dreams, reveries, mystical visions, polyphonic mini-narratives, and historical accounts. The novel offers what may be the conclusion to Meheimeed's narrative, yet at the same time the other narratives within the novel unsettlingly stop *in medias res*. The proliferation of narrative points of view is more subtle in *Bandarshah* than in the earlier episodes of the Wad Hamid Cycle. Linear time all but disappears: past, present, and future merge indistinguishably in the uncertain spaces of memory, dream, hallucination, mystical experience, and intersubjectivity. Narrative techniques that in "Wedding" confirm the present and that in *Season* deny the fulfillment of the future envisioned by the *Nahda* become here the very articulations of a fragmented present, a shattered vision, a "lost memory." If "Wedding" is a narrative of fulfillment and catharsis, *Season* is a narrative of disappointment and anticlimax. *Bandarshah* lacks any such linear direction: it is an incomplete, episodic novel whose achievement lies precisely in the expression of discursive rupture. In that sense the unfinished novel may be seen in a larger cultural and historical context as the expression of ongoing, unresolved crisis.

Drawing on the full gamut of Arabic cultural and literary heritage, *Bandarshah* is a unique exercise in intertextuality that generates multiple levels of signification—symbolic, allegorical, mythical, psychological, mystical, and poetic. This is accomplished both through direct quotations from seminal texts and by drawing stylistically from a large pool of linguistic registers ranging from the poetic resources of classical Arabic to the majestic idiom of the Qur'an, the stylized

---

3. See Edward Said's Introduction to Trevor Le Gassick's translation of Halim Barakat's *Days of Dust,* and his Foreword to Maia Tabet's translation of Elias Khoury's *Little Mountain.*

4. See Badawi (1993, 158–238) and the special issue of *Fusul* 2:2 (January-March 1982), especially the roundtable discussion. See also Stefan Meyer's *The Experimental Arabic Novel.*

rhymed prose of medieval Arabic, Modern Standard Arabic, poetic prose, the highly fluid spoken dialect of the rural north Sudan, and even magical incantations and nonhuman, supralinguistic utterances. The novel engages dialogically and intertextually with various ancient and modern Arab poets such as Abu Nuwas and al-Fayturi, the Qur'an, *Kalila wa Dimna,* and *The Thousand and One Nights,* and contains (for the first time in Salih's fiction) explicit references to earlier episodes of the Wad Hamid Cycle. Radically different from the extensive and multilayered parodies of colonial discourse in *Season,* this stylistic fusion summons multiple levels of Arab cultural and historical memory, testifying to an effort to inventory Arab consciousness after the collapse of the nationalist project. Yet the novel proposes neither a simple "return" to the past nor a wholesale "rejection of the West"; rather, *Bandarshah* constitutes an attempt to reinvent the genre of the Arabic novel, which is a hybrid of European and Arabic narrative forms, and to create a distinctive narrative discourse, a "new writing."

The problem of authority discussed earlier in relation to "Wedding" lies at the heart of *Bandarshah* and informs its title. Salih explains, "I have chosen the name *Bandar Shah* because our problem is the search for the City (that is, the *bandar*), and also the search for a form of government that suits us—authority (*shah*).[5] The novel investigates those two things" (IM 1976b, 220). On another occasion, he has said that "we have two fundamental problems in the Arab world, which are building the City and [creating] the authority which governs it. This, in my opinion, is the core of civilization as discussed by Ibn Khaldun" (*RTS* 1997, 117). The "city" here is the equivalent of civilization, and the challenge identified by Salih lies in building its foundation. That the "city" is synonymous with "civilization" is justifiable in the context of Arab history, in which the rise of Islamic civilization transformed Arab society from nomadic to urban. Thus Islamic civilization became associated with cities like Damascus, Baghdad, Kufa, Basra, and Cairo. Even for the nomadic, tribal society of pre-Islamic Arabia, cities like Mecca, Yathrib, Ta'if, and San'a' were centers of culture.

This is a different conception of the city from the one found in patriarchal and colonial discourses critiqued in *Season,* where the city, identified with a presumed feminine essence, comes to signify both the object and the site of impe-

5. The Persian word *bandar* is used in provincial Egyptian and Sudanese Arabic to designate the city, especially the capital (and by extension, urban culture). Thus the word implies a distinction between "our" agrarian village life (with its positive and negative attributes of adherence to traditional values, authenticity, simplicity, spirituality, technological backwardness, lack of sophistication, and marginality to national politics), and that of the metropolis (with its attendant, equally ambivalent, characteristics of loss or weakening of traditional values, inauthenticity, complexity, materialism, refinement, luxury, and so on). *Shah* is Persian for "king." Salih's word rendered above as "authority" is *"sultan,"* which also carries implications of "absolute authority" (such as that of a sultan), but also, in its Qur'anic usage, "warrant" (53:23). Salih, therefore, is speaking of the search for a viable and legitimate form of government.

rial/masculinist hegemony. In *Bandarshah,* the city regains the significance it had for Arab Islamic as well as ancient civilizations—Egyptian, Mesopotamian, Greek—namely as the site of the fulfillment and refinement of culture, and the scene where civil society demonstrates the values of developed civilization. Thus the quest to articulate the city in *Bandarshah* is a quest for civilizational revival that must necessarily rearticulate gender. Significantly, this rearticulation of gender is the cornerstone of the intellectual projects of contemporary philosophers like Nasr Abu Zayd and religious reformers like Mahmoud Muhammad Taha, not to mention the life work of Nawal al-Saadawi. Along the same lines, Salih has said that Mustafa Sa'eed, who embodies the collusion of patriarchal and colonial violence in identifying cities with women, "represents a barbaric conquest of modern culture. . . . Violence against women is violence against civilization, and against life" (*TSS* 1982, 21). Both *Season* and *Bandarshah,* especially in *Meryoud,* propose that the social construction of gender is inseparable from the crisis of Arab society; both foreground that issue in relation to the concern for culture and authority.

Bandarshah tackles the subject of authority on the local scale of the village, and that of the city from the perspective of its dialectical opposite, the country. That does not indicate a return to the world of "The Doum Tree" and "Wedding," where the village was valorized at the city's expense. The village in *Bandarshah* is torn by conflicts that are no longer resolved peacefully through the benevolent agency of spiritual and secular leadership. Those authorities themselves become highly contested; generations and worldviews engage in a struggle that takes on not only cultural and historical but also mythical and metaphysical proportions. The struggle over village leadership results in the ousting of Mahjoub's gang, who ruled the village for two decades but are now perceived as tyrannical and self-interested, by "Bakri's boys," another "gang" led by Tureifi, Mahjoub's nephew and son-in-law, who was an unruly schoolboy in "Wedding" (*WZOS* 1969e, 31). Allegorically, this event represents the failure of democracy in most Arab and African nations. Dictatorships cling to power until removed by force, and typically the ousted regime is accused of "corruption, bribery, theft, nepotism, incompetence, dereliction of duty, and so on" (*B* 1996, 28), while the new regime promises "to extricate this village [or country] from the pit of backwardness and underdevelopment," to "keep up with progress" in an "age . . . of science and technology" (56). The empty rhetoric of Progress serves as transparent propaganda that betrays the bankruptcy of the new regime. Thus on the level of politics in Wad Hamid, as in many postcolonial states, the illusion of Western modernity lives on to supply each new revolution with a rallying cry, but does nothing to improve social, political, or economic conditions. In the meantime, some, like Abdul Hafeez, take refuge in fundamentalist fervor. Thus between the lure of an unattainable future and the pull of an ossified past, the villagers "lose their memory."

The balance shifts toward the city at the end of *Meryoud*, significantly in the closing speeches of the small girl Maryam, who decries traditional (village) patriarchy's oppression of women and sees the city as the place where her dreams of education and equal opportunity can be realized. That is, she sees the city as the site of modernity and a better future, with its schools, hospitals, electricity, automobiles, everything that the old man in "The Doum Tree" dismissed as signs of weakness and corruption. Maryam's aborted dream of going to the city represents the frustration of the dreams of *Nahda* intellectuals. In *Dau al-Beit*, Meheimeed, an aging member of the first generation of postcolonial Sudanese intellectuals, makes his final return to Wad Hamid after retiring from his government post in Khartoum; he is disillusioned, defeated, and nostalgic. He returns to Wad Hamid to search for his roots, relive his memories, and take stock of the past. He also returns as a historian, asking various people about their ancestors and collecting their tales of the past in order to write them down (*B* 1996, 91). Thus the *writing* of that oral history becomes more than an anthropological record of the past, as in "The Doum Tree"; it is also "a lesson to those who take heed" (100). In other words, writing becomes an effort to recover "lost memory" and to rearticulate the symbolic content of the city, which did not materialize within the postcolonial state.

Historical narration is, of course, central to ideology. *Bandarshah* problematizes historiography by positing two modes of representation—allegory and mythology—against realistic, linear narration. Meheimeed once believed in Progress; now he finds in the pervasiveness of the local myth of Bandarshah a cyclical conception of history that in part gives the novel its bewildering effect: the thrust of the Cycle as a whole leads progressively into the future, but that future seems always to reenact the past. The novel allegorizes this vicious circle through the peculiar relationship between grandfathers and grandchildren. According to Salih, "the premise in *Bandarshah* is that the past and the future are in constant conspiracy against the present—or that the grandfather and the grandson are always conspiring against the father" (IM 1976b, 220). The subtitle of *Dau al-Beit*—which does not appear in the English translation—describes the work as "A Tale of How a Father Becomes the Victim of His Father and His Son."

Sometimes grandfathers and grandchildren are mirror images of each other. For example, Bandarshah and Meryoud, and Hajj Ahmad and Meheimeed are "like twin brothers [who] had divided up between themselves the sum of their ages" (*B* 1996, 84). In this way, the past repeats itself in the future in countless reflections of the same image, a sort of eternal recurrence. At other times, characters' names rather than their physical likeness indicate their uncanny identification: for example, Mukhtar Wad Hasab ar-Rasul Wad Muktar Wad Hasab ar-Rasul, Hamad Wad Abdul Khalik Wad Hamad Wad Abdul Khalik, and al-Kashif Wad Rahmatallah Wad al-Kashif Wad Rahmatallah.[6] This pattern of names (ababab) seems to go on ad infinitum. As Salih puts it, "the name becomes a collective name which does not denote a particular individual," but a recurrent type (*TSS* 1982, 28).

The effect is a circular movement of time that perpetually enacts the Oedipal impulse to kill the father, as well as its reverse—the father's threat of violence that asserts his authority over the son. In *Totem and Taboo*, Freud explains the origin of the incest and parricide taboos in terms of this Oedipal conflict. Salih here is reworking Freud's account of the primal horde. Freud's theory of the Oedipal conflict is based on the nuclear family model, but in the extended family groups common in rural Sudan, the grandfather rules the household rather than the father, and thus the Oedipal conflict involves grandfather, father, and grandson. In *Bandarshah*, Salih refashions Freud's theory into an allegory in which the parricidal impulse of the grandson (Meryoud) conspires with the preemptive violence of the grandfather (Bandarshah), both of whose interests unite in killing the father (Bandarshah's eleven sons). This pattern prevails in the village: all grandfathers, including Hajj Ahmad, aspire to the condition of Bandarshah, and all grandsons, including Meheimeed, aspire to become like Meryoud. Grandfathers stand for an ossified but revered notion of tradition; the adherents to this tradition, be they religious fundamentalists or cultural nativists represented by the grandsons, want to extend it into the future. The cult of the past results in a failure to answer to the demands of the present. Khoury describes this situation in terms of "amnesia"; Salih describes it as conspiracy against the present/the father.

Throughout the Wad Hamid Cycle, Meheimeed's relationship with his grandfather is central to his sense of identity; in contrast, his father goes unnamed and largely marginalized. In "A Handful of Dates," Meheimeed says of his early childhood that "the strange thing is that I never used to go out with my father, rather it was my grandfather who would take me with him wherever he went" ("HD" 1969b, 23). In *Season*, Meheimeed rejects the present in favor of eternal continuity with an idealized past personified by his grandfather; he also represses the colonial legacy as represented by Mustafa Sa'eed (who is at one point mistaken for Meheimeed's father [*SMN* 1969c, 56]), and exhibits naïve

---

6. It is perhaps necessary here to say a word about Arabic names. Family names are not always used; instead, the first name is followed by the father's name (which usually takes the place of a middle name), then the grandfather's name, and then the great-grandfather's name (or family name if one is used). Furthermore, it is not unusual for a father to name his son after his own father, as exemplified by the names of such renowned writers as Mutran Khalil Mutran, Gibran Khalil Gibran, and Jabra Ibrahim Jabra. The highly unusual thing is for the alternation to continue beyond the third generation, as in *Bandarshah*.

optimism about the future. Meheimeed's first rebellion against Hajj Ahmad in "A Handful of Dates," then in the childhood episode of swimming to the whirlpool at the bend of the Nile related in *Meryoud* (*B* 1996, 88), and finally their disagreement in *Season* over the affair of Hosna, prepare the way in "The Cypriot Man" for accepting the father, who ransoms Meheimeed's soul with his own life. In the allegorical scheme of *Bandarshah,* it is not the father who comes to represent patriarchy and the Law, but the grandfather. As we shall see, the father in "The Cypriot Man" and in *Meryoud* comes to represent humbleness (he is a slave in *Meryoud*), asceticism, and saintly detachment from worldly concerns. This is not always true, of course, given the violence and authoritarianism of Hosna's father; however, this contradiction in the discourse of the Wad Hamid Cycle as a whole is resolved when we consider that in *Meryoud,* and subsequently in "A Blessed Day on the Coast of Umm Bab," love in all its forms (maternal, paternal, romantic, conjugal, fraternal, divine) breaks the vicious circle of patriarchal dominance.

The conspiracy against the present/father takes on a mythical dimension in the image of Bandarshah seated on his throne and delighting at the sight of his eleven sons chained like slaves and savagely whipped by his grandson Meryoud. Just as the ascetic Wad Hamid and his doum tree populated the dreams of an earlier generation of villagers, the sadistic torture scene recurs time and again in the dreams of many of *Bandarshah*'s characters. And unlike the world of "Wedding," where most of the villagers—even the nonreligious among them—perceive their existence as governed by mystical and metaphysical principles that only holy men can fathom, the world of *Bandarshah* seems dominated by manifestations of tyranny and by the struggle over worldly authority (*shah*). Thus within a single generation the myth of the doum tree and its protective saint has given way in the villagers' consciousness and in their dreams to the myth of the dictatorial rule of Bandarshah and Meryoud, which comes to enact the individual drama of each one of the villagers.

Salih has described his writing as myth making, as an attempt "to transform ordinary, regional Sudanese characters into mythical characters similar to those of the *Iliad,*" who are "artistic symbols representing several characters" (*TSS* 1982, 28). This notion of the mythic fits many of Salih's characters: the saints Wad Hamid and Haneen, Zein, Ni'ma, Mahjoub, Mustafa Sa'eed, Jean Morris, Hajj Ahmad, Wad Rayyes, Hosna Bint Mahmoud, Bint Majzoub, Dau al-Beit, Bandarshah, Meryoud, Bilal, Taher Wad Rawwasi, Maryam, and Asha 'l-Baytat. These characters are larger than life because each of them embodies cultural and historical forces and displays the contradictory traits that beset their societies. The unusual hearkening back to the epic in an era of defeat bespeaks the search for a heroic ideal. It is also a search for a new form and a "new writing"—a transformed novel that reflects a determined effort to recover cultural memory and to answer the Herculean challenges facing society. The task of the unfinished novel is to rewrite its genre, since no imported or prefabricated mold can possibly contain the restless, agitated movement of the present. *Bandarshah,* therefore, like *The Thousand and One Nights,* simply stops once it has constructed a new myth; with or without the arbitrary enclosure within the frame story of Scheherazade and Shahrayar (and Meheimeed's narrative provides a comparable frame story for the Wad Hamid Cycle), the inner narratives seem capable of proliferating endlessly. In fact, the challenge facing Salih's characters—mirrored in the fragmentary form of the novel—is to repossess that cultural and civilizational quality which Ferial Ghazoul identifies in the characters of *The Thousand and One Nights*:

> Humankind in *The Arabian Nights,* as represented by Scheherazade, fights destined end by continually being—by not ending—while humankind as represented by the hero in Greek tragedy tries to efface destiny once for all, and this is why the hero is a tragic figure. Humankind in *The Arabian Nights* is impotent in the face of the absolute, but is master of the relative. The most fundamental victory in *The Arabian Nights* is transformation of past and future into perpetual present. The tense of Scheherazade is the present indicative. (Ghazoul 1996, 96)

Salih's characters are similar in that they, too, submit to the absolute; but unlike Scheherazade, they are impotent vis-à-vis the relative, the present. The challenge facing them is to achieve her victory; yet unwittingly they lose the present to an idealized past and to a future that duplicates that past. Their historical amnesia perpetuates their entrapment in the condition expressed by the allegory of "conspiracy" and by the myth of Bandarshah and Meryoud.

Along with the problematization of form and the juxtaposition of historical, allegorical, and mythical modes in *Bandarshah* goes the fusion of languages (in Bakhtin's sense of different linguistic registers, discourses, and dialects). The emphasis on the local reintroduces the use of the Sudanese dialect in the dialogues between characters, which was a feature of "Wedding." In both texts, Modern Standard Arabic is used only by an unidentified third-person narrator. In "Wedding," the Sudanese dialect adds local color to characters and situations that are circumscribed by the relatively narrow confines of the village. The use of Modern Standard Arabic both in narration and in dialogues throughout *Season* can be seen as a function of the search for a pan-Arab identity in the face of external challenges, since Arab nationalism as an ideology emphasized common Arabism over the specificity of the local. Similarly, in *Bandarshah* the newly established modern schools have produced a generation of villagers who think differently from their elders. Voicing the opinion of the now marginalized elders, Sa'eed the Jurist muses: "Something strange had occurred of which we didn't know the beginning or the end. Our children were against us. We had opened schools with sweat and effort and with running about here and there, and the outcome was that we had children who'd mixed words with us. It seems that the village had got into a muddle right under our feet as we were sleeping the sleep of the just" (*B* 1996, 28). This younger generation uses a new language drawn from the discursive registers of Arab socialism of the 1960s (e.g., *B* 1996, 29, 38, and 99). Nevertheless, the return to spoken Sudanese in *Bandarshah* reclaims the specificity of local identity and underscores the "archaeological" character of the novel's investigation of the local (*TSS* 1982, 31).

Yet local identity still shares in the broader Arab cultural heritage that is the legacy of all Arabs. Thus the complex mixing of linguistic registers drawn from several distinct "languages" (classical, medieval, Modern Standard, and Sudanese varieties of Arabic) and discourses (Qur'anic, poetic, belle-lettristic, philosophical, folkloric, and so on) within the long history of that heritage indicates that the rediscovery of the local must occur *in the context of, not in isolation from* broader Arab Islamic identity. The result of this engagement is a layered, hybridized text that seeks to stretch the discursive capabilities of language to the point of the inexpressible: from the attempt to record the sound of primordial silence at the time when "speech had yet to be created" (*B* 1996, 30) to the transcription of the supralinguistic utterances of devils and supernatural forces— "hab, had, rab, dan, nad, nar, dar, ah, ha" (23–24).[7] At the same time, the array of linguistic registers represented between these two extremes fuses the full gamut of Arab, Islamic, and Sudanese consciousness and is part of an attempt to reconstruct cultural memory, which, as Abu Zayd points out (1983, 201), resides in language. This aspect of the novel calls for linguistic and semiotic analyses that lie beyond the scope of this discussion; therefore, I shall focus on the ideological significance of Salih's evocation of some of those registers.

Bandarshah is not, of course, the only novel by Salih containing references to the texts of the Arab Islamic heritage. The Qur'an is a subtext in his earliest works, even if only in spirit, as in "A Date Palm by the Stream." In "A Handful of Dates," the evocation of the Sura of "The Merciful" brings to Meheimeed's psychological conflict ethical and spiritual dimensions. In "Wedding," Ni'ma is defined by her love of the Suras of "Maryam," "The Merciful," and "The Stories." By the same token, in *Season*, Wad Rayyes characteristically misquotes the Qur'an. *Bandarshah* is infused with Qur'anic references, both through explicit, recurrent mentions of the Sura of "The Forenoon" and less explicitly in many places, in dialogue as much as in narration.[8] At other times, the style and

---

7. I have transcribed those syllables as they appear in the Arabic original. The English translation reads: "wailing and howling and shrieking and screaming unintelligible words" (12), and thus the sense of the stretching of language to its limits is lost in the translation.

8. Sura of the Forenoon, No. 93, is mentioned several times (*B* 1996, 34, 42, 72, 103), and the nonexistent Sura of Kaf Lam Mime once (*B* 1996, 22). Quotations and allusions to the Qur'an in-

rhythms of Qur'anic language infuse not just the speech of the characters, but also the discourse of the third-person narrator (*B* 1996, 74, 76–77). Many of those allusions serve to maintain a strong presence for Qur'anic discourse and for that reason are almost untranslatable. At other times, they evoke particular contexts that bear directly on the action. Some of these contexts will be discussed in the appropriate places below.

Evocations of classical literature are often equally direct. For instance, the passages concerning the characters' dreams of Bandarshah's palace evoke the atmosphere and language of *The Thousand and One Nights* (see below). Even more visible are the poetic epigraphs to each volume of the novel and the moral allegory from *Kalila wa Dimna* that prefaces *Meryoud*.[9] Those passages set the tone for the novel and situate it, for the Arab reader, within a specific field of cultural, intellectual, and linguistic signification. There is no evocation here of a vaguely abstract notion of "tradition"; rather, Salih is creating an epistemic field by balancing contrapuntal relations among clusters of associations. For example, the three passages cited at the beginning of *Dau al-Beit* are taken, respectively, from a poem by an anonymous Sudanese poet written in so regional a dialect as to be almost unintelligible to non-Sudanese Arabs; a philosophical poem by Abu Nuwas; and a Sufi poem by the contemporary Libyan-Sudanese-Egyptian modernist poet Muhammad al-Fayturi. Immediately one notices the combination of an anonymous regional poet, a preeminent eighth-century Abbasid poet, and a modern poet of multinational Arab background who is committed to pan-Arabism. Al-Fayturi is also a mystical poet who, in the manner of the Sufis, uses the language of lovers to speak of devotion to God in verses such as those used in annual celebrations of local saints (*mawalid*) in Sudan and Egypt:

> Ravaged by longing in the presence of my beloved,
> I stare without face and dance without feet.
> My banners and drums crowding the horizon,
> My love destroys my love, and my destruction is absorption.
> Your slave but the king of lovers I am.

---

clude the following: "Solomon chopping off legs and heads of horses" 38:33 (*B* 1996, 26); "close to him as his jugular vein" 50:16 (*B* 1996, 29); "the hour of doom seemed . . . imminent" 53:9 (*B* 1996, 46); "The Ababeel Birds" 105:3 (*B* 1996, 65); "like a structure that is tightly fitted together" 61:4 (*B* 1996, 69–70); "he had only to say 'Be' and it was" 2:117 (*B* 1996, 79); "the day when a father will not be compensated for by his son" 31:33 (*B* 1996, 102); "the hollow stumps . . . Aad and Thamud" 69:4–7 (*B* 1996, 112); "as particles of dust scattered by the wind on a day of desolation" 14:18 (*B* 1996, 112); "And not those that are astray. Amen" 1:7 (*B* 1996, 114); "You will not be able to keep up with me" 18:67 (*B* 1996, 121); "make for me a sign" 3:41 (*B* 1996, 121).

9. The four poetic passages are omitted in the English translation. The passage from *Kalila wa Dimna* appears in the Foreword to the whole novel, that is, before *Dau al-Beit*.

This certitude of faith is juxtaposed with the anxious impatience of the anonymous Sudanese poet who, returning near dawn from some business in the city, has missed a rendezvous and is urging his camel to move faster:

> The road extends endlessly, the Luse mountains grow taller [as I approach them],
> And the city's [*bandar*] burning torches have been extinguished.
> My camel, like ostrich chicks, runs this way and that:
> Quick, gallop! Night has fallen, and the appointment has been missed![10]

Also juxtaposed is Abu Nuwas's meditative, philosophical skepticism as he questions the time-honored convention of Arab poets of beginning an ode with weeping at the abandoned campsite of the beloved's tribe. The verses problematize the relationship between signifier (the remains) and signified (the beloved's tribe); they also express the poet's rejection of positivist meaning in favor of creativity and imagination, even at the expense of blurring the line between "knowledge" and "ignorance":

> Indeed I see no one, like me today, doubting the remains of a camp site,
> They fill my eyes with tears but my imagination [*wahmi*] denies them.
> Images of [other] things come between me and them,
> So that my ignorance becomes knowledge, and my knowledge ignorance.

Abu Nuwas (c. 755–c. 813 C.E.) was of mixed Arab and Persian ancestry and was notorious for his wine and homosexual love poetry. He is the greatest of all Arab-Islamic rebel poets—certainly more profound, subtle, and philosophical than the Persian Omar Khayyam, who is better known in the West. This passage and the one that follows clash with al-Fayturi's devotional verse and with the pervasive presence of the Qur'an throughout the two parts of the novel; furthermore, in their preoccupation with *"wahm"* (illusion), these same passages lie thematically at the heart of the novel and the Wad Hamid Cycle as a whole. This one is quoted at the beginning of *Meryoud*: "Yet I lend voice to my imagination, disbelieving my eyes, / And constrain myself to compose something, one in expression, multiple in signification, / Wrapped in illusion [*wahm*], so that to it seek you grope in the dark."

Abu Nuwas's evocation in *Season* is directly related to the exotic appeal of his wine poetry, as when Mustafa delivers a lecture on him at Oxford. In *Bandarshah,* however, Abu Nuwas's remarkably modern philosophical and psycho-

---

10. I am indebted to Tayeb Salih for kindly explaining to me the regional Sudanese verses, which I have rendered in English as literally as possible. My translation of Abu Nuwas's verses, which bear more than one interpretation, is also based on my conversation with Tayeb Salih.

logical preoccupation with the sign ties in with the novel's attempt to create a "new writing." The remains of a campsite have no clear meaning for Abu Nuwas, as they do for his predecessors; rather, the remains become a sign that calls for but eludes interpretation, like an ancient hieroglyph. It is important here to recall Salih's statement, quoted at the beginning of chapter 1, about his rejection of the convention of weeping at campsites—a rejection that echoes Abu Nuwas. This stance indicates a refusal to follow a fetishized tradition, which is the fundamentalist or nativist stance. Instead, Salih agrees with Abu Nuwas that tradition must be critically reinterpreted anew in every age. In the second passage the sign ostensibly becomes a "symbol," something "one in expression, multiple in signification." The sign in both cases is the site of contestation between, on the one hand, the positivistic impulse to recover "true" meaning and, on the other hand, the free play of signification that deconstructs positivist interpretation. The first passage identifies *wahm* (which in classical Arabic means "thought" or "mind," in addition to "illusion"), a keyword in Abu Nuwas's poetry and Salih's fiction, as an obstacle to true knowledge. The semantic association in *wahm* between "thought/mind" and "illusion," the play of images and associations, is the source of the conflict between "ignorance" and "knowledge," or (to bring Abu Nuwas's concern to bear on the predicament of Arab culture and discourse on the heritage), creative reinterpretation and slavish repetition. Yet the poet is painfully aware that "illusion" is the condition of all knowledge. In the second passage he is more assertive of the creative power of illusion that enables him to produce symbols—and of course poetry—even though he remains conscious of the reality to which creative illusion must ultimately answer.

Psychologically, *wahm* is shorthand for desire—which according to Lacan, always expresses a lack. As we saw in the preceding chapter, Salih deploys the notion of *wahm* as a function of the desire for the cultural and racial Other. Moving beyond the colonial context, the textual return of Abu Nuwas in *Bandarshah* recasts the desire-as-lack in terms of *écriture*—writing. As a way of Being-in-the-World (Abu Nuwas was aware of this and Salih seems to concur) writing is the constant, anguished production of signifiers of lack. Salih describes his own writing as myth making in the same way that he sees Abu Nuwas engaged in symbol making (*RTS* 1997, 121); at one point Salih uses *"ramz"* (symbol) and *"ustura"* (myth) more or less interchangeably (*TSS* 1982, 28). The symbol—"one in expression, multiple in signification"—belongs to the domain of the ternary, of language, of writing, and of creativity, but also to the domain of uncertainty ("blindness" for Abu Nuwas) and the unknown. Thus, for a poet who experienced his entire existence as crisis, writing as a symbol-making process is an act of creating a reality. For intellectuals like Khoury and Salih who sense the historical experience of their societies as crisis, writing becomes the creation of a new memory and a step into the unknown.

The final epigraph defines writing as a search for a moral way of life. That is the theme of such literary works of moral philosophy as the Indian *Panchatantra,* freely translated into Arabic (from a Persian translation of the Sanskrit original) by the Persian-Arab writer 'Abdullah ibn al-Muqaffa' (724–59 C.E.) as *Kitab Kalila wa Dimna* (750, *The Book of Kalila and Dimna*), the first Arabic work of prose fiction. *Meryoud* is prefaced with an important passage from *Kalila wa Dimna* in which the human condition is allegorized as essentially one of brief sensual enjoyment spent in *forgetfulness* of death and the afterlife. The passage was written by Ibn al-Muqaffa' in his adaptive translation of the *Panchatantra,* which he advertises as a compendium of wisdom intended for the moral instruction of kings; thus the theme is the wise conduct of both individual life and of government, *shah.* The passage begins thus: "Searching for an allegory about man, I found that he is like someone who has escaped from the danger of an enraged elephant into a well." He clings to two branches that two rats, one white and one black, are gnawing. Below him he sees an open-mouthed dragon at the bottom of the well; from holes in the walls of the well, four snakes emerge. Then he sees a beehive, and as he busies himself with eating the delicious honey, he puts of out his mind all thoughts of escape. Barzawaih, the narrator, then explains that the well stands for life with its evils and perils, the snakes represent the four humors, the dragon represents fate, and the honey is sensual pleasure. The rats probably represent night and day, hence the passage of time that brings us closer to death.

The atemporal religious lesson of the parable with which Barzawaih illustrates the human condition ends with a powerful affirmation of the present and of the function of writing. Speaking of the moral purpose of his stay in India to copy the *Panchatantra* and other books, Barzawaih writes that he "became content with my lot and with improving what I could of my endeavors that perchance I might encounter, during the remainder of my days, a time when I would attain a guide to put me on the path, control over myself, and meaning to my existence. I have abided in this state and have transcribed many books, and I departed from the lands of India having copied out this book" (*B* 1996, ix-x; *Kalila wa Dimna,* 111–12). Barzawaih expresses his philosophy of life in an allegory that, unlike Abu Nuwas's symbols, is one in expression, one in signification. This unidirectional character of allegory, which makes it suitable for a moral tale, imbues writing with a *transferential* rather than *creative* function: like Abu Nuwas, Barzawaih is searching for meaning, but he discovers rather than invents it. He does not indicate whether the allegory is of his own creation or if he has found it in one of the books he has *copied out.* Barzawaih is no *author*; authority for him is invested not in himself, but in the wisdom of the ancients, which shall school him until the "time when I would attain a guide to put me on the path." Thus from Abu Nuwas's creative secularism we turn a page in *Meryoud* to find Barzawaih's mystical conception of knowledge as divine gift selectively transmitted to the mortal seeking enlightenment through a Sufi guide or guru. In *Bandarshah,* story and characters are trapped in this tug of war between opposing ideological worldviews and systems of signification; this reflects the tension in the Arab Islamic world today between the advocates of theocracy and those of democracy, fundamentalists and secularists.

The significance of Salih's strategic placement of his novel in so direct a relationship to the prenovelistic prose fiction of the Arabs, which begins with *Kalila wa Dimna,* is great. This liminal work is born of a fruitful cultural and civilizational encounter with Persia and India. If the Arabs imported the novelistic genre from Europe, then *Bandarshah* situates itself positively in relation both to the prenovelistic narrative tradition of the Arab and a collective Asian culture. With its Persian title, the bicultural background of Abu Nuwas and Ibn al-Muqaffa', the pan-Arab background of al-Fayturi, and the Arab-Persian-Indian lineage of *Kalila wa Dimna* and *The Thousand and One Nights, Bandarshah* brings the Arabic novel full circle by reclaiming for itself the cultural hybridization that gave rise to Arab Islamic civilization—hybridization that preceded the dislocations of the colonial and postcolonial eras. The immensely ambitious project of *Bandarshah* as a civilizational text makes it the Arabic hybrid novel *par excellence,* and a paradigmatic embodiment of Bakhtin's conception of the novel.

In the Name of the Grandfather

In *Bandarshah,* little happens in the present besides recollections of the past. Narrative time seems to encompass just a few days after Meheimeed's return to the village, while story time stretches all the way back to the earliest episode of the Wad Hamid Cycle: the arrival of Dau al-Beit to the village in the mid-nineteenth century. Meheimeed is still the central narrator, but he seems incapable here of organizing either his memories or those of the villagers into a coherent narrative of village history. Ironically, this occurs at a time when Meheimeed returns to Wad Hamid not only to spend his retirement but also to research and write the history of the village (*B* 1996, 91, 99–100). Meheimeed's unreliability as a historian is not surprising, given his problematic conception of history as revealed in *Season.* He nonetheless acts as a catalyst for the excavation of the villagers' collective memory: Taher Wad Rawwasi tells him, "there is something about you which encourages one to say things to you that one wouldn't ordinarily say to a soul" (*B* 1996, 99). Meheimeed's first-person narration is balanced by a third-person narrator who takes turns with Meheimeed and who introduces other narrators as well: the "reliable historian" Ibrahim Wad Taha (who himself does not appear in the novel), and less "reliable" narrators like Mukhtar Wad Hasab ar-Rasoul, Mukhtar Wad Haleema, Sa'eed the Jurist, and Sa'eed Asha 'l-Baytat, whose stories are infused with the supernatural.

Add to that Meheimeed's own memories, experiences, and dream visions, which are reported by himself and by the third-person narrator, and which also mix fact with fantasy and mystical experience. In "The Doum Tree" the old man controls and organizes his tales in such a way as to present a coherent picture of the village and to convey the specific message he wishes to communicate to his young companion; in *Bandarshah,* however, the plurality of narrative voices and modes gives the complex organization of the text a sense of fragmentation of consciousness that yields no coherent narrative of the past, and thus no clear understanding of the present.

In this way, amnesia as a cultural and historical condition is enacted in narration. Amnesia also finds in the novel a concrete characterization in the figure of Dau al-Beit. He arrives around the early 1860s, nearly ninety years before Mustafa Sa'eed. Like Mustafa, Dau al-Beit comes from the river and disappears into it, and is accepted by the Wad Hamidians without any knowledge of his past. Yet while Mustafa is a Sudanese, Dau al-Beit is a complete stranger. He has fair skin, blond hair, green eyes, and a foreign accent. To the villagers who see such a creature for the first time, he may even be a devil. He wears what seems to be a Turkish military uniform, but other than broken Arabic, he utters Persian words. When asked about his name, he lists Persian names: " 'I certainly had a name,' said the man. 'Bahloul. Bahdour. Shah. Khan. Mirza. Mihran—I don't know' " (*B* 1996, 63). He also seems to come from Persia or its surrounding areas: " 'Caucas, Ahwaz, Khorassan, Azerbaijan, Isphahan, Samarkand, Tashkent. I don't know. From some faraway place' " (63). Yet unlike Muslim Turks and Persians, he is uncircumcised. In other words, he is an amalgamation of Eastern and Western, European and Asian, a symbol of foreignness who has come—as evidenced by his attire and his life-threatening wound—as an invader. Probably he is a soldier in the multiethnic army of the Turko-Egyptian government of Sudan (1820–83). His strange appearance and the rhyming, incantatory sounds of the foreign names and places he utters ("names of jinn . . . not sanctified by God" [63]) do not prevent the simple, untraveled farmers from recognizing him, eventually, as a human being who is "tired, hungry and ill" (63). After falling into a month-long coma during which they care for him, he awakens only to discover that he has completely lost his memory. His symbolic death/rebirth humanizes him in the eyes of the villagers, who accept him in their midst and offer him a new identity: the auspicious name of Dau al-Beit (literally, "Light of the House"), a religion, a piece of land to farm, and eventually a wife.

Chronologically, Dau al-Beit's episode is the earliest in the Wad Hamid Cycle. And as the story of Dau al-Beit becomes mythicized and passes into the collective memory of Wad Hamid, merging with the myth of Bandarshah and Meryoud, so are the values of the society and its conflicting tendencies confirmed—its nobility, dignity, tolerance, and generosity, as well as its patriarchy and masculinist ethos. The three chapters concerning Dau al-Beit (12, 13, and 14) create an atmosphere of peace and tolerance that prevails so long as the villagers' world is not threatened by the kinds of dislocations and ruptures depicted in *Season* and in the first eleven chapters of *Dau al-Beit*.[11] Mahmoud, the village elder at that time, explains the villagers' values and worldview to the stranger in one of the most moving passages in all of Salih's fiction; these are the same values according to which the Wad Hamidians of a century later accept Mustafa Saʿeed in their midst:

> O servant of God . . . we live, as you can see, under the protection of the Almighty. Our life is one of toil and austerity, but our hearts are filled with contentment and we accept the share that God has given us. We perform the prayers as laid down, we safeguard our honor, and we stand up to the vicissitudes of time and the batterings of fate. Having much does not make us arrogant; having little does not make us uneasy. The path that our life takes is drawn and known from cradle to grave. The little that we have we have achieved by the strength of our muscles; we have not violated the rights of any man or eaten from usury or ill-gotten gains. Peaceful people in times of peace, angry people in times of anger. Those who don't know us think we're weak, that a breath of wind would carry us off, yet in actual fact we are like the haraz trees that grow in the fields. And you, O servant of God, have come to us from we know not where; like God's ordinance and destiny the waves have cast you up at our doors, and we don't know who you are or where you're bound for, someone bent on good or bent on evil. At any event, we have accepted you in our midst in the same way as we accept the heat and the cold, death and life. You can live with us, having what we have and taking upon yourself what we take; if you're good, you'll find all goodness with us, and if you're evil, then God will be our protector and guardian. (*B* 1996, 66)

The conversion of Dau al-Beit takes place in the same spirit of tolerance:

> Dau al Beit, we are Muslims, but we are not fanatical on the question of religion. Every soul has what it has gained and God is He who chooses amongst His servants. If we had known you had a faith, we would have left you in your faith. However, since you do not know what religion you are, what do you

---

11. Chapter numbers are used only in the English translation; in the original Arabic version of *Dau al-Beit* there are no chapter divisions, but instead fourteen unnumbered sections separated with asterisks. In the original of *Meryoud* there are four numbered chapters, while the English translation has five: the long chapter 3 in the Arabic corresponds to chapters 3 and 4 in the English. This division makes, perhaps, for more a symmetrical text, but may obscure the fact that the content of chapter 4 is narrated by Taher Wad Rawwasi, who is the focus of Meheimeed's narration in chapter 3. The transition from Meheimeed's to Taher's narration in the Arabic version is seamless. For convenience, I shall refer to the chapter numbers in the English translation.

think about us taking you with us into the faith of Islam? We shall earn merit
and you will escape from God's wrath, also it will help you in your dealings with
the people of the village if you want to get married and settle down. (*B* 1996,
67)

Dau al-Beit's full integration with the people whose country he has come to in-
vade becomes possible through his amnesia. In contrast, Mustafa Sa'eed hides
the past and lives the doubleness of his identity among the villagers as a lie. Even
though the past haunts Dau al-Beit in his dreams, he dies before he recovers it or
before it claims him.

Without the memory of violence and conquest, the Wad Hamidians and
Dau al-Beit enrich one another's lives materially and spiritually. Like Mustafa,
whose ideas help the villagers organize the agricultural project and avert the exploitation of the merchants, Dau al-Beit "brought date seedlings of every sort
and kind . . . and he taught the earth to grow tobacco and he taught us to grow
oranges and bananas. . . . He grew in stature and we with him, as though the
Lord, may He be glorified, had sent him to us to invigorate our lives, and then
go on his way" (*B* 1996, 80). Moreover, he is a catalyst that brings out the best
in them. When they honor his request—the stranger with an unknown past—to
marry one of them, they feel themselves transformed into something new: "We
were seized by a frenzy of yearning, an ecstasy of love, as though we were at
some Sufi gathering for the invocation of the Lord's name, while Dau al-Beit the
stranger sat in the middle, connected with all that was taking place" (71). He becomes part of the living memory, lore, and identity of the village: a story of the
good that comes out of tolerance, humanity, generosity, and reciprocity. Like
Zein's wedding a century later, Dau al-Beit's is "a memorable marriage . . . attended by all the neighborhoods of Wad Hamid" (73). Dau al-Beit's wedding is
depicted in one of those untranslatably rhythmic passages characteristic of *Bandarshah,* one that relies on mystical and Sufi symbolism, poetic and Qur'anic
diction, rhymed prose, contrast, and parallelism, as well as on evocations of both
the sacred and the profane, the carnival and the pilgrimage to Mecca. The guests

> arrive by ones and twos, thin and emaciated, every back bowed, every shoulder
> weighed down by the burdens of life and death, and the great concourse takes
> them over so that each one becomes himself and something more. Today the
> wise man will behave foolishly, the religious man will get drunk, and the sober
> will dance; a man will look at his wife in the circle of dancers as though he is see-
> ing her for the first time . . . They come like grains of wheat in a heap of wheat,
> each grain autonomous, holding within itself a great secret. . . . They come all
> of them poor to varying degrees, and are encompassed by a harmonious orbit
> rotating round its axis at a predestined rate. They come weak and return strong,
> needy and return rich, astray and find right guidance. Today the parts will be
> united and each one will become the one. (74)

As the festivities continue through the night, however, the beatific harmony of this mystical union gradually turns into a frenzy: the "harmonious orbit" becomes a chaotic, violent scene the center of which is also Dau al-Beit. Such catalyzing moments carry the potential for creation and destruction. In "Wedding," that moment is sanitized; the novella ends just at the point when Zein "assumes his place at the heart of the circle, like the mast of a ship" (*WZOS* 1969e, 120), the center of order and guarantor of unity and strength. Here, the scene continues until order suddenly turns into chaos, bringing forth the destructive potential of patriarchal and masculinist values, repressed in "Wedding": Dau al-Beit was

> standing in the center of the circle brandishing a whip of hippopotamus hide above the women dancers, while the men sprang one after another into the circle to vie with one another, and he would strike about him as he pleased. Abdul Khalek Wad Hamad, the dauntless champion, entered the circle, bared his back and stood firm to receive the lashes. At once Hasab al-Rasoul Wad Mukhtar, his rival and peer, came to join him, and Dau al-Beit began wielding his whip, bringing it once on Abdel Khalek's back and once on Hasab al-Rasoul's. As each whiplash landed, the women let out trilling cries of joy and the men shouted happily. The roaring of the drums grew louder, breaking up and reassembling round Dau al-Beit as he stood at the center of the [chaos], his whip raised above everybody, appearing and disappearing among the crush, as though there and yet not there.[12] (*B* 1996, 76–77)

Dau al-Beit's position at the center of the circle of dancers, whip in hand, is identical to Zein's at his wedding. The function of the whip is not explained in "Wedding" but is revealed here. The bloody contest of *al-butana* dramatizes notions of violent masculinity and illustrates the "chaos" that inevitably sets in with the gory ritual. To emphasize this point, *al-butana* scene in chapter 13 is parodied in chapter 4 (which, significantly, precedes it in the order of narration but follows it in chronology), where the namesake offspring of those seemingly eternal rivals, Abdul Khalek Wad Hamad and Hasab ar-Rasoul Wad Mukhtar, play at being grown-up men, but their enactment of the violent whipping contest almost costs them their lives. And there, too, it is Dau al-Beit's son, Isa, nicknamed Bandarshah after the legendary tyrant, who controls those present. Moreover, the incident occurs because Mukhtar Wad Hasab ar-Rasoul, the bully, gives Hamad Wad Abdul Khalek, the weakling boy, the nickname "Wad Haleema," which plagues him for the rest of life. It is a derogatory title because

12. *Al-butana*, the whipping contest, used to be a feature of wedding celebrations in Sudan. It is a contest in endurance and valor: the groom lashes the male contestants with a whip made of hippopotamus or crocodile skin, and the winner is he who withstands the most whipping without the slightest show of pain.

it assigns Hamad's parentage to his mother, Haleema, instead of to his father, implying that Hamad is effeminate. To prove his manhood, Hamad devours a pound of hot pepper to numb his senses, then challenges his tormentor to a whipping contest. The painkiller supplies the necessary manliness that leads the two boys to enact a travesty of the macho ideal that nearly kills them. Significantly, the end of the blood bath comes not through renunciation of that ideal, but through its affirmation by young Isa/Bandarshah, who ends the contest by force: " 'If Wad Haleema thinks he's a man, there's a better one than him.' All of a sudden I [Hamad] felt a blow to the stomach from Bandarshah, after which I don't know what happened" (23).

The myth of Bandarshah and Meryoud, with which Isa and his grandson Meryoud become identified, dominates the first eleven chapters of *Dau al-Beit*. The myth is repeatedly enacted and remembered in *Dau al-Beit*, yet it is not until chapter 4 of *Meryoud* that any attempt is made to historicize it. In that chapter, the third-person narrator lists various contending accounts of who Bandarshah "really" was: an ancient Christian king of Nubia north of Wad Hamid, a pagan king from the south, an Abyssinian prince from the east, a white slave trader from the west. This lack of certainty indicates that the story, like all myths, has no verifiable origin. In all versions, however, Bandarshah is foreign, wealthy, extravagant, and ruthless. He comes to Wad Hamid, builds a magnificent palace on a nearby hill, and rules over his sons or slaves, according to different versions, with an iron fist. This rule is epitomized by one scene that recurs three times in *Dau al-Beit*: Bandarshah sits on his throne in his legendary hall, his grandson Meryoud sits beside him, naked slave women dance, then Bandarshah orders Meryoud to whip the eleven sons or slaves, while Bandarshah sadistically enjoys the sight. Eventually, the eleven sons or slaves rebel and kill Bandarshah and Meryoud (*B* 1996, 46–47).

The effect of this rebellion on the villagers is described in chapters 2 and 9 of *Dau al-Beit*. In chapter 2, Meheimeed begins by leading the reader to assume that he is referring to the violent deaths of Wad Rayyes and Hosna Bint Mahmoud in *Season*:

> If things appeared to me as I have recounted to you on that journey, then it maybe pleaded in my defense that I didn't mean to deceive you. My grandfather was as I told you, and my relationship with my grandfather used to appear to me at that time, and for a long time afterwards, as I told you on that journey. Then befell that catastrophe that defies description, be it in a single journey or in several, or even in a whole lifetime. Suddenly the harmony in the universe had been disrupted. And so, between night and morning, we found ourselves not knowing who we were or what our situation was in terms of time and place. (*B* 1996, 9).

The language of "catastrophe," "disruption," chaos, and disorientation is also used to describe the murder-suicide in *Season*. A little later, however, it becomes clear that Meheimeed is speaking of the murder of Isa/Bandarshah and Meryoud. This deliberate ambiguity links together two crimes that profoundly shake the villagers' sense of who they are. It also becomes clear that this crime, like Hosna's, is a revolution against tyranny and injustice.

But as long as the villagers do not know of what goes on within the walls of Bandarshah's castle, they hold Bandarshah and Meryoud in great esteem. The castle walls, like Mustafa Sa'eed's locked library, enclose a "horror" that the villagers would rather know nothing about; but following the law of the return of the repressed, that horror eventually disrupts their illusion of harmony and order. Before that happens, Bandarshah and his offspring "glittered in people's eyes and were the pride of the village. . . . They're people our Lord is pleased with" (*B* 1996, 10). Even the fifteen-year-old Meryoud's "self-confidence that bordered on insolence" vis-à-vis the village elders wins him their awe and admiration. When Meryoud, an adolescent, treats Hajj Ahmad (who is his grandfather's age) as his equal, the timid and well-behaved fourteen-year-old Meheimeed is astounded that his "grandfather was happy at that abnormal event. I saw Mukhtar Wad Hasab ar-Rasoul's narrow eyes growing wider with unreserved reverence. Hamad Wad Haleema gazed at Meryoud, as he left guffawing with laughter, as a human created of clay might gaze at an angel that has descended from above. . . . At that moment I felt that I had been witnessing a miracle. Had someone told me that the Fates had chosen Meryoud to effect a reconciliation between the past and the future, I would have believed it" (11). What makes this "abnormality" so admirable to the grandfathers is that Meryoud represents the grandson they would like to have. As the mirror image and extension of his grandfather—a "reconciliation" between past and future—Meryoud is the embodiment of the elders' desire for continuity, free from the threat of their sons' Oedipal impulses. In violation of "natural order," each of them will strive to transform his own grandson into his image; the monotonous pattern of names confirms that desire, and the authoritarianism with which Hajj Ahmad charts Meheimeed's future—regardless of the boy's wishes and those of his father—enacts that selfish desire. Meheimeed's personal tragedy lies in his failure to resist his grandfather: "he should have fought with his own weapon but he fought with that of his grandfather and was defeated" (86–87).

When the inevitable revolt takes place and the eleven sons murder Bandarshah and Meryoud, the apocalypse seems to have arrived:

> what a momentous thing occurred that forenoon. The winds were coming from faraway caverns shrieking [of evil and fire]; the [demons] were leaping down from the roofs of houses and branches of trees, from the fields and sand-dunes and mountain passes, from under the hooves of cattle, from the bends of

alleyways, wailing [hab, had, rab, dan, nad, nar, dar, ah, ha]. Then the hubbub manifested itself in one single word: Bandarshah. Despite that great distance of time, I cannot now recall that forenoon without a shiver. It was as if the village had been torn out from its roots by some fearsome bird, which had then carried it in its claws, had circled around with it, and then cast it down from on high. . . . All the images were like specks of dust that no sooner settled in the mind than they disintegrated into fragments—and with them the universe and life. . . . Then [rad, rash, shab, shan, shar, ba, bah, yad, na, da, da], the images are welded together, mingle and form a tangible shape, that of Bandarshah in the form of Meryoud; or Meryoud in the form of Bandarshah, and it is as though he is sitting on the throne of that hubbub, gripping the threads of chaos in both hands, amidst it and above it at one and the same time, like a resplendent and destructive ray. (*B* 1996, 11–12)

The revolutionary disruption of social order is described as a catastrophe of cosmic proportions. Chaos that defies reason, sanity, and even human language prevails. Nightmare, confusion, and demonic forces produce uncertain "signs" that leave the beholder in no sense wiser than before, but "paralyzed" and disoriented. The confusion is described in apocalyptic images, recalling Qur'anic descriptions of the Day of Judgment: "When Earth is shaken with her (final) earthquake/And the Earth yieldeth up her burdens,/And man saith: What aileth her?" (Sura 99: 1–3/Pickthall 447); "The Calamity!/What is the Calamity?/Ah, what will convey unto thee what the Calamity is!/A day wherein mankind will be as thickly-scattered moths/And the mountains will become as carded wool/ . . . Ah, what will convey unto thee what she is!—/Raging fire" (Sura 101/Pickthall 448). These verses communicate, among other things, the inability of language to describe the full scale of the "Calamity," just as Salih's language breaks up into incomprehensible utterances and fragmented syllables as it attempts to describe the cataclysmic "chaos."

The revolt of the eleven sons or slaves devastates the elders especially (*B* 1996, 46). These are, of course, the same elders who count Wad Rayyes as one of their number in *Season,* and who are devastated by his death more than a decade later (in the chronological scheme of the Cycle). And typically, after each miracle or catastrophe, strange things happen: after Haneen miraculously saves Seif ad-Din's life in "Wedding," the village is showered with blessings; conversely, after the murder of Bandarshah and Meryoud,

Al-Kashif Wad Rahmatallah, despite being well-advanced in years, suddenly decided to leave the village; the imam refused to take the people in prayer and said they were doomed and that neither prayer nor admonition would avail them, after which he took himself to Mecca to die there. Bakri's wife, after fifty years of marriage [*satr*[13]], left her husband's house with head bared, swearing not to return. Those who weren't rebellious rebelled, and those who weren't quarrelsome quarreled, and people said that devils had begun to walk in the squares and streets, openly in broad daylight. (46)

Allegorically, the incident is a social, political, and cultural revolution, the meaning of which becomes complete with the image of the state suppressing the insurgents and confronting the rebellious masses: "On the fringes of that nightmare, bareheaded women, their faces covered in dust, were grasping at men whose hands were fettered and tied with a thick rope to a camel's saddle; on the camel, a [soldier] carrying a gun, with tens of men barring his way. . . . On that forenoon the past and the future were murdered and no one was there to bury their corpses or mourn them" (*B* 1996, 12). This image fuses together the repressiveness of patriarchal and political authority with regimes of thought that cling to a cult of the past.

The dream visions in which the villagers see themselves confronted with Bandarshah reflect their position within the network of social and political affiliations in the village, and express their individual fantasies, desires, and traumas. Two such dreams are narrated, those of Meheimeed and Asha 'l-Baytat; a third, Tureifi Wad Bakri's, is mentioned in passing but not recounted. The dreams are almost identical, and all occur on the same night as though a spell has been cast on the entire village. It is the night following the burial of Maryam, who is sister to Mahjoub, the former village leader, and mother to Tureifi, the current leader. The villagers gather at the funeral, and then the men congregate for a dawn prayer in the mosque that will be remembered long afterward. Some of those men have never entered the mosque before. Maryam funeral provides the village with an occasion for emotional and spiritual unification. Weddings and funerals, otherwise commonplace social occasions, become more than what they are when they revolve around an important and unusual figure. Here, Maryam's funeral becomes the catalyst for a collective, mystical experience.

Yet Maryam's full significance is not revealed until later on in *Meryoud*. She is Meheimeed's childhood sweetheart, and his dream on that particular night sums up his entire life: summoned by his grandfather's voice to Bandarshah's castle, he is puzzled to discover that Bandarshah speaks with Hajj Ahmad's

---

13. Literally "hiding" or "veiling," *satr* is proverbially used to signify "protection" of a woman through marriage, the implication being that marriage guards a woman's honor, which is understood in terms of sexual conduct. The "veil" here is both literal and metaphoric; thus the rebellion of the wife consists of both baring her head and leaving her husband's house for good.

voice: "the very voice that had guided me there, the voice, that of my grandfather—there was no doubt about it—the face of Bandarshah. How strange!" (*B* 1996, 30). Meheimeed watches Meryoud (the projection of his own ideal self) savagely whip his father and uncles until they lose consciousness. He then watches the naked slave girls dance before the intoxicated Bandarshah and Meryoud. Not understanding the import of all this, he "wanted Bandarshah to explain . . . but he said nothing and I finally realized that the voice had called me solely that I might be a witness" (32). Meheimeed's incomprehension is very much in character. He has always been a passive agent and an impotent, albeit indignant, observer of injustice. As a child, in "A Handful of Dates," he rebels against his grandfather's ruthlessness and greed, sympathizing with Masood; but he also understands that the handful of dates his grandfather has given him from Masood's crop has made him an accomplice in the metaphoric "slaughtering" of Masood. Meheimeed reminisces about this episode in *Dau al-Beit* while recalling the incident of Meryoud's extraordinary transaction with Hajj Ahmad (12–13): a boy his age, Meryoud is everything Meheimeed is not—confident to the point of insolence, assertive, even manipulative—whereas Meheimeed is "tucked away in a corner, only speaking when . . . asked something and then doing so with no more than a sentence or two" (10–11). Meheimeed is deeply disturbed by Meryoud, his double, because the latter, like Mustafa a decade later, displays what Meheimeed fears and/or desires but strives to repress. At that early stage in his life, Meheimeed himself is becoming the image of Hajj Ahmad; this becomes clear in chapter 1 of *Meryoud,* where Meheimeed merges with Meryoud and Hajj Ahmad with Bandarshah, so that the "Meryoud" of the title is unequivocally Meheimeed. The language and images describing the uncanny physical and mental likeness between Meheimeed and Hajj Ahmad are identical to those describing Bandarshah and Meryoud (84–5 and 10). However, unlike Meryoud the grandson of Isa Wad Dau al-Beit, Meheimeed is a reluctant replica of his grandfather. The alliance between past (Hajj Ahmad) and future (Meheimeed) is half-hearted and ambivalent.

Despite himself, Meheimeed wants to be Meryoud, and he plays at being Meryoud when a year after he witnesses Meryoud's business transaction with Hajj Ahmad, Meheimeed insults and comes to blows with his uncle, who according to social codes has the status of a father. In a society in which respect for parents is sacred, "beating one's father" violates divine command [14]:

Abdul Kareem had come with the news of his divorce and remarriage. Speaking on behalf of his grandfather, he [Meheimeed] had said to his uncle that he was

14. This is emphasized repeatedly in many passages in the Qur'an. See, for example, 6: 152, 17: 23–4, 29: 8, 31: 14–5, and 46: 15–7.

a useless man—all he was interested in was running after women. He had been less than fifteen and his uncle in his forties. They quarreled violently, while the grandfather lay stretched out on his bed saying nothing, and the son nearly [beat] his own [father [15]], who left after that and did not return. All of them broke away one by one. When the father [i.e., Hajj Ahmad] died not one of his sons was with him. (*B* 1996, 85)

Meheimeed in this scene emulates Meryoud, and Hajj Ahmad is satisfied that Meheimeed is becoming an extension of himself—that he, Hajj Ahmad, is finally becoming Bandarshah. As a result, Hajj Ahmad estranges his sons and dies alone.

Sometimes, however, Meheimeed is revolted to discover Hajj Ahmad's selfish motives. For example, he throws the seven-year-old Meheimeed into the river and makes him swim across a dangerous whirlpool at the bend of the Nile and then boasts to his friends that "Meheimeed is the exact replica of me, the splitting image" (89). As the nickname of the whirlpool ("the cosmic") suggests, Hajj Ahmad exposes his grandson not only to death by drowning, but symbolically to spiritual destruction as well; the "cosmic" whirlpool is "the very center of chaos." At that moment, what saves the boy is the voice of Maryam calling him (89). He emerges from the water after traversing the river from south to north, which prefigures his later journey to England. Maryam's voice guides him to safety, and her image is the first thing he sees on reaching the river's northern bank; at that point he feels hatred for his grandfather. Next, Hajj Ahmad refuses to allow Meheimeed to become a farmer, as the boy and his father wish; he also refuses to allow Meheimeed and Maryam to marry, thus breaking their hearts. Meheimeed gives in without a show of resistance. Then his grandfather starts him on the actual journey to the north, from which he returns at the beginning of *Season*. During his exile in England he characteristically forgets the reason for his exile and idealizes his grandfather and the entire village in the manner discussed in the previous chapter.

The violent disruption of Meheimeed's illusion of wholeness in *Season* leads him to a lifetime of soul searching that never results in a satisfactory reconciliation with the world. In "The Cypriot Man" he learns to accept his father and the simple life of modesty and integrity he exemplifies, and to reject the selfish and ruthless ambition of characters like Hajj Ahmad, Mustafa Sa'eed, the Cypriot

---

15. "*Abahu*" (his father) is rendered in the translation as "his uncle." There is no semantic ambiguity in the Arabic between "father" (*abb*) and "uncle" (*'amm*), so the substitution in the translation seems to have been meant as a correction of a perceived error in the original. I believe, however, that the word "*abahu*" is used deliberately to magnify the violation of family codes that gives an uncle the status of the father, and to emphasize the Oedipal pattern in the novel.

Man, Bandarshah, Meryoud, Mahjoub, and Tureifi Wad Bakri. Returning to Wad Hamid as an old man, Meheimeed admits that his error all his life has been to comply with and submit to authority:

> One has to say no from the very beginning. I was happy in Wad Hamid [as a boy]. By day I'd cultivate the land and at night I'd serenade the girls. I'd snare birds and splutter around in the Nile like a hippo. One's heart was free and at peace. I became an effendi because my grandfather wanted me to. When I became an effendi I wanted to become a doctor. Instead I became a teacher. When I was teaching, I told them I'd like to work in Merowe, so they told me to work in Khartoum. In Khartoum, I told them I'd like to teach boys, but they told me to teach girls. In the girls' school I told them I'd like to teach history, so they told me to teach geography. In geography I told them I'd like to teach Africa, so they told me to teach Europe. And so on and so forth. (*B* 1996, 51)

His official post reflects the chaotic, haphazard policies of the postcolonial state, which dash the great hopes Meheimeed entertains on his return from England, hopes centered around rebuilding an independent nation. Through his compliance and complicity, he is "defeated by the days and defeated by the government" (25).

Meheimeed's final return at the beginning of *Dau al-Beit* is depicted in a scene that powerfully evokes and contrasts with the opening scene in *Season*. Gone are the overwhelming nostalgia and sense of stability found in the scene in *Season*; instead, *Dau al-Beit* opens on a resonant, mournful note. Time and change have asserted themselves; gone is the familiar Wad Hamid; it has been replaced by a Brave New World dominated by struggles over *shah*—authority. The book opens with a description of Mahjoub's gang as old, defeated, and ravaged by time: "Mahjoub was like an old tiger, seated as in former times, despite the years and ill health, as though ever ready to spring . . . In the eyes there was nothing but anger. . . . Taher Wad Rawwasi laughed in the way he used to laugh in the old days. . . . Abdul Hafeez had previously been the most tolerant of them, in the days when he had been able to look at things from both sides. But now, having defined his position, [he spoke in] a quarrelsome voice devoid of affection" (*B* 1996, 3). Taher Wad Rawwasi and Abdul Hafeez have more than changed—they have become the opposite of what they were in "Wedding." The former, who used to have the quickest temper among the group, has now become the most serene and the least attached to power and status; the latter has lost his tolerance since "discover[ing] the road to the mosque" (28). Other people in the village are likewise radically changed: "Seeing that Abdul Kareem Wad Ahmad's [Meheimeed's uncle] become a mystic, and Zein's become one of the leading personalities, and Seif ad-Din's about to become a Member of Parliament, what's so strange about Sa'eed the Owl being known as Sa'eed Asha 'l-Baytat?[16] . . . Do you think Wad Hamid's the same Wad Hamid you used to know?" (4). For Meheimeed, who yearns for stability and abhors change (*SMN* 1969c, 2), these transformations accentuate his nostalgia for a world that has disappeared. By the end of the novel he is submerged in the bitter regret that old age casts over the memory of missed opportunities and lost love.

As for Asha 'l-Baytat, who represents an enterprising younger generation, his dream of Bandarshah points out to him the choices he has still to make, not (as for Meheimeed) the irrevocable ones that have sealed his fate. For Asha 'l-Baytat, the call summoning him at night to Bandarshah's palace is clear and unmistakable; it is the holy man Haneen himself who appears to him in a dream vision to give him instructions. Haneen identifies Bandarshah as "[o]ne of the sultans of olden times. . . . He had one son and eleven slaves. . . . Do not greet them. Do not talk to them. Do not turn right or left. . . . Go in, take what they give you and go. Be very careful not to say a single word: you would enter the abode of destruction and he who looks for you would not find you. The thing kept in trust is wealth. It is your inheritance by right. Bandarshah thought of himself as inheriting the earth and all that was on it. The earth [belongs to you and to] the meek after you" (*B* 1996, 40–41). Thus Asha 'l-Baytat believes that he has divine guidance and a birthright, and his dream fits the religious archetype of the test consisting of a choice between good and evil, with reward following the right choice. The story of the Prophet's *isra'* and *mi'raj,* or Night Journey, exemplifies that pattern: escorted by the angel Jibril (Gabriel) to Jerusalem, Muhammad is given the choice between wine (sin) and milk (*fitra,* literally, natural disposition toward righteousness enjoyed by newborn infants who are still pure); on that choice depends the fate of his *umma,* except that the beverages are not assigned any explicit value up front. Only after he has made the correct choice is he told what each represents; thus, what is being tested is his innate (or mystical) ability to discern the hidden nature of things (Ibn Kathyr 1969, vol. 3, 4). Asha 'l-Baytat's own night journey (which he insists was not a dream or a vision but an actual event) involves a similar choice between what he can rightfully claim for himself (an inheritance) and mortal temptation. That temptation, in masculinist imaginary and its attendant theological metaphysics, is woman, the primordial Eve. Asha 'l-Baytat's description of his temptation occurs in another

---

16. Unlike its positive association with "wisdom" in the West, the owl, in various parts of the Middle East and Asia, is considered a bad omen and associated with death, the reason being that it is a nocturnal bird believed to inhabit deserted areas, ruins, and cemeteries. "The Owl," therefore, is hardly a flattering nickname. "Asha 'l-Baytat" literally means "one who provides food and shelter for women away from home," hence one who is generous and chivalrous. It should be understood that this is the younger of the two Sa'eeds; the older one, nicknamed the "Jurist," is the shop owner who belongs to Mahjoub's gang.

one of those untranslatable passages full of rhythmical and rhymed phrases, in which Classical and Sudanese Arabic diction combine to form a semicolloquial idiom that evokes the medieval prose of the *maqama* and the exotic, sensual atmosphere of *The Thousand and One Nights.* Asha 'l-Baytat says that after obeying Haneen's instruction not to return Bandarshah's greeting,

> A young girl like a houri came in. Her breasts had only just begun to grow and were the size of the berries of the laloub tree; stark naked she was, swaying about. Her buttocks were as smooth as lizard skin, her belly like the orchards of Shaygiyya. She grasped me by my thing and said, "Come to me, I'm ready for you." She lay down and opened her thighs and I saw what she had and what she could give. She said to me, "Come, light of my eyes, and lie between my thighs. There you'll attain the heights of joy." Ah, brothers, what fires were raging in me! With my two eyes I saw the path to salvation and the path to perdition. Had it not been for God's providence I would have fallen into the direst of calamities, and I wouldn't have cared. (*B* 1996, 41–42)

This representation of woman as temptress is subverted later on in *Meryoud,* but here Asha 'l-Baytat uses it to legitimize his rise in the world as one of the village leaders, and to explain away the source of the new wealth he has acquired since becoming the treasurer of the Cooperative: it is a birthright and a divine reward for his prophetlike righteousness.

Asha 'l-Baytat's dream/journey/fabrication is immediately followed by his call for the memorable dawn prayer. His voice is not known for its charm, and his call for prayer often sounds "like a lorry that had stuck in the sand" (*B* 1996, 26). That night, however,

> the voice did not come out as my own. It was a voice full of sorrows. I gave the call over the housetops; I called to the water-wheels and the trees; I called to the sand-dunes and to the graves; to those present and to those absent; I called to those that are astray and to the defeated, to the broken, to the sober and to the drunk. I called to the Christians and the Muslims. . . . I heard with my own ears the winds of Amsheer echoing my call to prayer, as though I the miserable, puny Sa'eed was the Bandarshah of my time, saying to the people of this world and the next "Come to perdition. Come to success. Come to error. Come to salvation." [17] . . . I had the feeling that the angels and the devils were saying with one voice, "Amen. Amen." I came down to find the mosque filled with people—Mahmoud and Masood, Khair ad-din and Seif ad-Din, Mahjoub and Alloub, Meheimeed and Abu 'l-Waleed, Wad Hasab ar-Rasoul, Wad Bakri, Wad

---

17. This is a distortion of two verses in the Call for Prayer, which say, "Come to prayer. Come to Prayer. Come to salvation. Come to salvation."

Rahmatallah and Wad Miftah al-Khazna—people who'd never been inside the mosque before. It was as though the whole village had gathered together . . . because they had heard the voice. The person calling had called them with my tongue. . . . The imam recited the Chapter of the Forenoon . . . [A]ll those praying were weeping warm tears that dawn . . . At the left-hand window was a stranger who had some connection with all that had taken place, disappearing and reappearing until the people said, "Peace be upon you." He vanished without a trace and poor Meheimeed was shouting at the top of his voice saying, "Where's the person who was here gone to?" (42–43)

Asha 'l-Baytat would have them believe (and Taher Wad Rawwasi and Ahmad Isma'il ridicule him for it) that passing the test qualifies him for prophecy, for transmitting a message from the beyond. That message is addressed to all mankind regardless of their differences, and shows them the way to "error" and "perdition" on the one hand, and to "salvation" and "success" on the other. The entire village responds (as indicated by the pairing of rhyming names [18]), and all of those present experience a mystical communion. He is, properly speaking, "the pivot [*qutb*]" (36)—the center of the attention not only in every gathering (e.g., in chapter 8 of *Dau al-Beit* and chapter 2 of *Meryoud*), but also in the Sufi sense of "pole." Asha 'l-Baytat, therefore, is paired with Bandarshah at the dawn prayer: Bandarshah, the ruler over chaos, is sitting on the (left) margin of the congregation, appearing and disappearing like a phantom, and finally fleeing like the devil once the words of peace are uttered by the worshippers. In that position, he represents the path of error and perdition. His presence is felt most strongly by Meheimeed, the chronicler of change in the village and its most alienated and confused member.

Asha 'l-Baytat's story is one of social mobility and protean identity—an extraordinary transformation from "Sa'eed the Owl," servant and handyman, to "Asha 'l-Baytat," the well-to-do treasurer of the Cooperative, son-in-law of the school's headmaster, and one of the village leaders. This change occurs in the context of the dramatic change in village leadership, which shifts from Mahjoub's gang—virtual rulers of the village in "Wedding" and *Season*—to a gang of a younger generation, Bakri's sons. In that other context, Asha 'l-Baytat is a highly ambiguous figure. His role remains unclear; he may simply be an embezzler and a crafty opportunist who knows how to manipulate others' feelings

---

18. Ferial Ghazoul points out that in *The Thousand and One Nights* as well as in legends and myths, names of paired characters tend to carry "phonetic duplication"—for example, Shahrazad (also spelled Scheherazade) and Dinazad, Shahrayar and Shahzaman, Shahrayar and Shahrazad, Sindbad the Porter and Sindbad the Sailor, Gog and Magog, Harut and Marut, Qahtan and 'Adnan. This "confirms and accentuates parallelism on the semiotic level" and denotes the "coupling" of complementary opposites "like the yin-yang principles in Chinese cosmology" (Ghazoul 1996, 22–3).

and religious beliefs. His newly acquired wealth and the way he manipulates the headmaster (*B* 1996, 15–19), betraying his friends, Mahjoub's gang, and single-handedly changing the outcome of the Cooperative meeting in which they are removed from power (39–40), speak volumes about his Machiavellian shrewdness. His dream of Bandarshah may well be a clever story to tell the village; that said, the pivotal role he plays in the dawn prayer following Maryam's funeral helps unite the village. Asha 'l-Baytat has gained his new status partly through women—by marrying the headmaster's daughter and by buying Fattouma's panegyric (14–15)—yet he is at a loss how best to spend his money to acquire even more prestige: Should he purchase a new donkey? Should he take another wife? Should he make a pilgrimage to Mecca so as to acquire the title of "hajj" (93)? He is a highly ambivalent character, "a man of his time and his star was in the ascendant" (39), who represents the crisis of ideology and leadership in the Arab world.

So is the case with Bakri's sons, the new rulers in Wad Hamid. They have the potential to make positive changes; for example, their generation promises greater equality between the sexes, and their revolution against Mahjoub's gang is joined by young, educated women. In contrast, Mahjoub asserts his sexism in rebuking the only woman who comes to his defense, his sister Maryam (*B* 1996, 28). Yet all signs indicate that the new gang is no better than the old one, that "Bakri's son Tureifi is trying to make himself into a Bandarshah" (26), that village politics is no different from national politics (25–26). In a significant departure from the prevailing discourse in "The Doum Tree" and "Wedding," the village is, as it turns out, no more virtuous or righteous than the city.

Meheimeed, who has lost his belief in Progress, sees the affinity between the old and new regimes as inscribed on Tureifi's body: "I was struck by the similarity between him and Mahjoub: the way of standing and of sitting, the laughter, the expression in the eyes, the gestures. He had nothing of his mother" (*B* 1996, 58–59). Mahjoub is Tureifi's maternal uncle (and thus his honorary father), so Tureifi's dream of Bandarshah, which is never reported, is likely to have been a parricidal one, a prefiguration or justification of his coup against Mahjoub. Tureifi admits to Meheimeed that he had a vision of Bandarshah on the night of the memorable dawn prayer, but he refuses to disclose that vision (59). Tureifi himself is a complex character, and he is not fully developed in the novel as it stands; he combines the leadership qualities of independence, reliability, and strong social responsibility (which sometimes prompts him to perform heroic acts) with the ambition, self-aggrandizement, and Machiavellian cunning of a tyrant (54–57). He has a soft and sensitive side, which he reveals at his mother's funeral, yet at all other times he projects an image of impassivity and masculine aggressiveness. As Bandarshah holds the "threads of chaos in both hands" (12), so the new leaders, Bakri's sons and Asha 'l-Baytat, hold the key to an uncertain future.

Alternative Vision

Meryoud, subtitled "The Second Part of *Bandarshah*" in the Arabic original, contrasts in important ways with *Dau al-Beit,* the first part. *Dau al-Beit* revolves around the problem of authority (*shah*); the sequel centers around the question of how to lead a moral life. Prefaced by Abu Nuwas's verses, which thematize writing as a means of organizing experience, and by the religious allegory from *Kalila wa Dimna, Meryoud* is concerned with the meaning of experience. *Dau al-Beit* depicts a predominantly masculine world of violence, struggle, ambition, and betrayal; in *Meryoud,* femininity, mystical detachment, nature, and love represent a countervailing current.

There are fewer female than male characters in Salih's fiction—a reflection of the power structure in the male-dominated society it depicts. However, strong female characters populate the narratives and succeed in carving out a space for themselves. In "Wedding," Ni'ma imposes her will on her parents. In *Season,* there are Bint Majzoub, Jean Morris, Hosna Bint Mahmoud, and Mrs. Robinson. A function of her age, wealth, and strong personality, Bint Majzoub is practically an honorary man; she joins the village elders as one of their number, exchanging bawdy jokes with them, smoking cigarettes (an exclusively masculine habit in conservative sectors of the society), and often uttering the oath of divorce, technically a male prerogative. However, like Jean Morris, who has already been discussed at length, Bint Majzoub has appropriated patriarchal ideology wholesale and has become an enforcer of it rather than a subverter, as her reaction to Hosna's revolt demonstrates. Contrary to that, Hosna Bint Mahmoud revolts against the strictures and injustices of male hegemony, and suffers grave consequences. As for Mrs. Robinson, her strength lies in her integrity, in the fact that she is practically the only character who seems capable of maintaining an unclouded vision of human relations amidst the novel's heady atmosphere of cultural and racial misconceptions. In *Dau al-Beit,* one minor female character plays an important role: Fatima Bint Jabr ad-Dar is a girl "worth ten men" (*B* 1996, 64) who nurses Dau al-Beit back to health, teaches him the Qur'an, and finally marries him. Another, Maryam, publicly denounces her sons for undermining their uncle, her brother Mahjoub, only to be gruffly told by the latter, "Go home, woman" (28). Defeated by other men, Mahjoub asserts whatever authority is left to him on the woman who dares support him, to the further humiliation of his masculine pride. Other female characters are faceless and nameless: the young, educated women who vote against Mahjoub, and the naked slave girls who dance in Bandarshah's palace, including the "houri" who plays the archetypal temptress in Asha 'l-Baytat's dream.

In *Dau al-Beit,* those contradictory roles occupy the troubled space of the present; mythic, archetypal, traditional, and modern sensibilities contest one another for control over the social construction of gender identity and its representation. The decenteredness of the narrative privileges none of those points of view; in the masculine imaginary that prevails in *Dau al-Beit,* they coexist as discrete constructions of Otherness. It thus becomes possible for Asha 'l-Baytat, for example, to express both his admiration for the educated young women of the village and at the same time to maintain his conception of woman as eternal temptress. Each of the two contradictory female types serves a separate function within the masculine psychic economy. Salih's use of multiple first-person narrators enables him to represent these contradictory patriarchal attitudes toward women.

In contrast, *Meryoud* presents a critique of patriarchy. It counters *Dau al-Beit's* paradigm of patriarchal tyranny and violence with a mystical one based on love—romantic, conjugal, maternal, paternal, and fraternal. Thus each of the novel's two parts depicts a distinct approach to social and human relations. Meheimeed is caught between these two approaches. While there is a clear parallel between him and the mythical Meryoud in *Dau al-Beit,* in the second part of the novel Meheimeed becomes one with Meryoud. However, this is an ambivalent variation on the mythic character, for besides being Meryoud the grandson and duplicate copy of his grandfather, Meheimeed is the *meryoud* (literally, "the beloved") of Maryam. The two sides of this identity are irreconcilable; each appeals to him and contradicts the other. Ultimately, Meheimeed is torn between the two distinct ways of being Meryoud—the grandfather's and Maryam's. He chooses his grandfather's way and lives to regret it.

The two ways of being Meryoud also formally frame *Meryoud,* the one occupying the first chapter, the other the last, respectively. The three intermediate chapters counterbalance the myth of Bandarshah with that of Bilal; the path of violence and power with that of mysticism and spirituality; and woman as temptress with woman as savior. The first chapter adds the episode of the "cosmic" whirlpool to the story of Meheimeed's relationship with his grandfather. This is followed by a final, brief glimpse at Asha 'l-Baytat. His ambiguous characterization in *Dau al-Beit* as a crafty politician and possibly a spiritual force of unification now gives way to an image of a greedy, evil-eyed, yet ridiculous embodiment of vanity as he proudly rides his bedecked donkey looking "like a goose sitting on a camel's hump" (*B* 1996, 91). A shift follows those two short chapters with the lengthy chapter on Taher Wad Rawwasi, which complements his portrayal in "The Cypriot Man." Taher tells Meheimeed the story of his remarkable father Bilal, whose life represents a radically different ideal from that of Hajj Ahmad, Mahjoub, and Asha 'l-Baytat. The final chapter depicts Maryam from childhood to her posthumous transformation into a prophetic, redemptive force. In that process, the spell of the pervasive myth of Bandarshah is broken, and Meheimeed's transition from the embodiment of the mythical Meryoud to Maryam's *meryoud* is complete. Having discussed the whirlpool episode earlier, I shall focus here on the narratives of Taher Wad Rawwasi and Maryam, and then conclude by discussing how "The Cypriot Man," written in the interval between the publication of the two parts of *Bandarshah,* sheds light on *Meryoud.*

Al-Taher (literally, "the Pure") Wad Rawwasi, appears in "Wedding" and "The Cypriot Man," but not in *Season.* Meheimeed's closest friend from childhood and Mahjoub's most attached companion among the "gang," Taher is the only unembittered old man in *Bandarshah.* His excellent health, the subject of the group's admiration and wonder (*B* 1996, 5–6; "CM" 1981a, 11), is attributed to his Sufi detachment from the passions of the world, a detachment which he expresses in his habitual refrain, "Time comes and Time goes" (*B* 1996, 6; *WZOS* 1969e, 106). Because of that detachment, his insights into the hypocrisy of religious and political institutions are often the clearest expression of popular disillusionment in the novel (*B* 1996, 7 and 99). Despite his deeply religious outlook, Taher never prays or goes to the mosque, even though he labored harder than any one else in its construction (7–8). He contends that his wife "has been praying all her life—her prayers will do for both of us" (96). If not from the observance of religious ritual, Taher derives his inner peace from the love inspired by human relations and nature: "[L]ife, Meheimeed, is there anything more to it than two things, friendship and love? Don't talk to me about good birth and family background, position and wealth. If a son of Adam leaves the world and has the confidence of one person, he has won. The Lord, may He be glorified, was very kind to me. Instead of one blessing He conferred on me two—He gave me the friendship of Mahjoub and the love of Fatima Bint Jabr ad-Dar" (98). In "The Cypriot Man," he further explains his lifestyle, which has its own quasi-religious rhythm:

> "I go to sleep . . . early or late, on condition that I wake up when the muezzin first calls out . . . for the dawn prayer."
>
> "But you don't pray?"
>
> "I say [the proclamation of faith] and ask for forgiveness [of God] . . . I make the tea and wake Fatima. She performs the morning prayer. We drink tea. I step out to face the sun over the surface of the Nile and I say to God's morning: 'Greetings and welcome.' I return to find the breakfast ready. We sit, Fatima and I, and anyone of God's worshippers that fate brings to us. For more than fifty years, it has been like this." ("CM" 1981a, 11)

His excellent health, unchanging routine, and the sense of stability and peace he inspires recall Meheimeed's description of Hajj Ahmad at the beginning of *Season.* Also like Hajj Ahmad, Taher has his fixed ideas, such as his belief that "even in fishes a woman's a woman and a man's a man" (*B* 1996, 95). That side of him does not escape ridicule in the novel. His fantastic tales about his eternal enemies among the fish and their genealogy take away from his credibility even among his own superstitious companions (95–97). Taher remains otherwise a highly sympathetic character and a counterweight to the cruelty of Bandarshah and Meryoud, yet the satirical treatment of his essentialist notions of gender reasserts Salih's uncompromisingly critical stance toward patriarchal ideology.

Taher is the only character in *Bandarshah* to escape the sinister conspiracy of past and future against the present. In contrast to other, parricidally inclined characters, Taher has always cherished both his father and his mother. According to the logic of the allegory, Taher thus affirms the present. Like Meheimeed's scarcely mentioned father, Taher's father Bilal is neither rich nor powerful; in fact, he was a slave. Meheimeed's grandfather was distinguished and wealthy; similarly, Taher's grandfather was the formidable Isa Wad Dau al-Beit himself, the Bandarshah of his day. The persistence of slavery in some parts of Sudan and East Africa, and the social stigma attached to former slaves, are critiqued in "Wedding," and in "The Doum Tree," the eponymous patron saint of the village was himself a former slave. Taher's father is another such figure. Hassan by name (literally, "beautiful and good"), he was nicknamed Rawwasi ("boatman") because he was believed to ferry angels in human form across the Nile at dawn— hence the epithet "boatman of the boats of Omnipotence" (*B* 1996, 102). However, he was better known as Bilal, a name given him by the holy man Nasrullah Wad Habib. As in "Wedding," there is a sharp distinction between the orthodox and the mystics, the latter being favored, although that distinction disappears in the story of Bilal and Nasrullah Wad Habib, who are great Sufis and also a muezzin and an imam, respectively. The name "Bilal" clearly evokes another former slave, the great early Abyssinian Muslim who was the Prophet's close companion, first muezzin, treasurer, and deputy imam.[19] Bilal of the novel also occupies those positions under Nasrullah Wad Habib, and retires from them on Wad Habib's death, just as the early Bilal retires from the post of muezzin on the Prophet's death. The manner of the fictional Bilal's death indicates that he has attained a high spiritual rank usually reserved for saints and prophets (103–4). Indeed, like the story of the holy man Wad Hamid, Bilal's story—as told by his son Taher and remembered by the village—belongs to the genre of hagiography.

Hassan/Rawwasi/Bilal is cast out by his eleven half-brothers for being born of a slave mother. The stigma of slavery erases all but Bilal's nickname from the name of his son (who is known simply as Taher Wad Rawwasi rather than Taher Wad Hassan Wad Isa Wad Dau al-Beit); as a result, his lineage becomes subject to conflicting accounts (*B* 1996, 104–8). Unlike other grandsons in the novel, Taher resembles his grandfather neither in appearance nor in character. Instead, Taher lives by the memory of both his father and his mother (98); thus Taher seems to be the only character in the novel who is reconciled to the present.

19. See note 11 to chapter 1.

Apart from Mustafa Sa'eed's mother, whose significance lies in her cold detachment and her absence (*SMN* 1969c, 19), Taher's mother Hawwa is the only mother of note in the masculine, patriarchal world of the Wad Hamid Cycle. There are, of course, some minor characters who are mothers (e.g., Zein's and Ni'ma's), but Hawwa is the only one who seems to have had a remarkable impact on the son she raises single-handedly, since he is the best adjusted and most at home in the world among his peers. Taher is the only son not caught in the vicious circle of Oedipal conspiracy that prevails in *Dau al-Beit*; his peace with the world derives from Hawwa, not from religious or other institutional codes:

> I have not seen love like that of this mother; I have not seen tenderness like hers. She filled my heart with love until I became like an inexhaustible spring. On the Day of Reckoning, when mankind stands before the Glorious, the Magnificent, bearing their prayers and their almsgiving, their pilgrimage and their fastings, their night vigils in prayer and their worship, I shall say, "Owner of Majesty and Might, Your wretched servant, Taher Wad Bilal, the son of Hawwa Bint Oreibi, stands before You empty-handed, devoid of merit, having nothing to place in the scales of Your justice but love." (*B* 1996, 113)

Though possessing the qualities of the temptress—"of stunning beauty . . . exceedingly intelligent and bold with a degree of coquetry and obscenity in her speech" (112)—she comes to possess the "devotion known only to single-minded Sufis" (113). She becomes, in other words, the saintly figure whose archetypes are Mary Magdalene and Rabi'a al-'Adawiyya. Moreover, Hawwa (Arabic for Eve) becomes less the embodiment of the archetypal temptress responsible for the Fall, and more like Dante's Beatrice, the heavenly guide and savior. This transformation of Hawwa/Eve carries a deinscription of the biblical representation of humankind's primal mother, which has for millennia furnished patriarchy and misogyny with a theological justification.[20]

20. Although the biblical account of the Fall is well known to Muslims through the biblical tradition, the Qur'an does not blame Eve for tempting Adam to eat from the forbidden tree. In two accounts the blame falls equally on Adam and Eve (Suras 2: 36; 7: 20–2), and in another the Qur'an suggests that Eve may have followed Adam's example in eating from the tree (20: 115–21). The biblical version is often cited, however, to supplement the Qur'an's sketchy narrative, as in al-Tabari's *Jami' al-bayan 'an ta'wil al-Qur'an*, vol. 1, 335. In other words, Salih's Arab readers would be quite aware of the discursive shift involved in the characterization of Hawwa/Eve, yet also understand that Salih is not contradicting the Qur'an, but rather calling into question a narrative extraneous to it. In fact, in *Al-mar'ah fi khitab al-azmah* (Woman in the discourse of crisis), Nasr Abu Zayd is able to deconstruct the biblical story of the Fall and the role it plays in the discourse of gender in contemporary Egypt while at the same time demonstrating that the Qur'an itself negates the premises of that discourse.

Taher's narrative offers an ethical and moral alternative to the nightmarish world of *Bandarshah* and "The Cypriot Man." This narrative is populated by Bilal, the saintly Sufi; Hawwa, the reinvented Eve; and Sheikh Nasrullah Wad Habib, the Sufi Pole who disdained worldly authority (*shah*) by daring to refuse the Mahdi and to rebuff his Khalifa (*B* 1996, 111). In the time of those saintly figures, as popular belief in the village has it, "[t]he doors of heaven were . . . opened, as they say." That, however, is a by-gone time, and those who remember it believe that since the death of Nasrullah and Bilal, "the shadows of mercy were rolled up and the doors of sovereignty were locked, right up to this very day" (102). The "strangers" who used to fill the mosque each dawn for the prayer and whom Bilal was seen ferrying across the river are the angels believed to gather around with the believers whose faith is pure; those angels are no longer seen in Wad Hamid. While "Wedding" constructs a utopia that sanitizes the present, *Meryoud* presents an idealized past that serves as a moral and ethical standard to foil the corruption of the present. The characterization of Bilal sets off vanity, ambition, and materialism; that of Nasrullah Wad Habib unmasks the pride of rulers and politicians' lust for power; and that of Hawwa debunks the negative attitudes toward women that patriarchy claims derive from religion.

Taher's tale about his saintly mother triggers in Meheimeed a reverie made up of "the dust of unfulfilled dreams." It is a dream about the memorable night of the dawn prayer after Maryam's burial. In this dream, Maryam is resurrected as an ethereal being who sums up Meheimeed's life in a refrain: "Meryoud. Meryoud. You are nobody. You are nothing, Meryoud" (*B* 1996,114). As he carries Maryam to her grave, he remembers her as a child who defied social convention and who set an example that he failed to follow. The passages describing young Maryam's challenge to socially constructed gender roles are marked by an intense and infectious optimism unmatched anywhere else in the Wad Hamid Cycle. Here is a child who intuitively understands the injustice of a patriarchal system that would curb her intense desire for personal growth. For three years she disguises herself as a boy in order to attend school, at a time when there was only one school for boys (86, 117–19). At that young age "when all the possibilities were open" (87), before patriarchal ideology claims Meheimeed and Mahjoub, the intensity of Maryam's determination made them sense the excitement and the revolutionary simplicity of her question, "Why not?" It made them question, for a brief moment, the gender roles that patriarchy represents as natural and intuitive, and immediately they saw gender differences disappear into biological "nonsense" (118). At that moment they could all envision a different future: "As though we were a chorus welcoming in a dawn that had begun to appear, the three of us said in one voice, 'That's right, why not?' " (119).

Maryam's rebellion against patriarchy further articulates itself as a rejection of the village and a desire for the *bandar,* the city. This desire embodies a strong wish not only to acquire modern things, but also to be released from the constraints that traditional patriarchal society threatens to impose on her as she grows into a woman. For young Maryam, Wad Hamid is synonymous with old customs, while the *bandar* represents a modern utopia: "We'll live in the city. Do you hear? Water from the tap and light by electricity, and travel by train. Got it? Cars and all the latest inventions. Hospitals and schools and this and that. In the city. Got it? God curse Wad Hamid. It's a heap of ashes. It gives nothing but disease, death and headaches. All our children will become effendis. Got it? No more farming" (114). Modern technology tantalizes the younger generation of villagers, including young Maryam, yet in the passages spoken by her, it is education that is the persistent theme. For her the schools are the gateway to another way of life, that of the educated effendis she wants her future children, both male and female, to be—teachers, lawyers, engineers, doctors (115). Eventually Meheimeed leaves his own sons and daughters in the city, "a gift . . . to the age of freedom, civilization, and democracy" (53); however, his own experience as someone who became an "effendi by mistake" (53) and who has lived through the failures of modernization counterbalances the nine-year-old Maryam's idealized notion of the *bandar.*

Fundamentally, however, her dream of living in the city is about gender equality, and in that sense the city becomes a metaphor for the ideal society. Interestingly, the first words spoken by Taher in *Dau al Beit* describe Wad Hamid as a "wretched village" (*B* 1996, 3; see also 53); this reverses the hierarchy of values established by the old narrator in "The Doum Tree." This dialectical view of village and city reveals a desire—never realized in the Wad Hamid Cycle—for, as Salih puts it, "a village in the form of a city, or a city in the form of a village" (UIWH 2002)—that is, a synthesis of the positive aspects of both.[21] This formulation rearticulates the unfulfilled project of the *Nahda,* which reasserts itself as a cultural-civilizational necessity in the aftermath of the failure of official projects undertaken by postcolonial Arab regimes. The incompleteness of the novel becomes all the more significant in this regard when we remember that it stops shortly after the point where young Maryam vehemently denounces Wad Hamid in favor of its dialectical opposite, the *bandar* (city). Recall here that the word designating "city" in Ibn Khaldun (*al-hadar*) is etymologically related in Arabic to the word for "civilization" (*hadara*); and civilization for Ibn Khaldun develops within a viable form of political organization. In *Bandarshah,* all forms of political and social authority are in crisis; thus the *bandar* remains no more than the embodiment of the tyranny of power (*shah*). This situation accurately describes sociopolitical life in the contemporary neopatriarchal Arab world— nearly three decades after the publication of *Meryoud.*

21. See note 5 to chapter 4.

Maryam's dream of going to the city never comes true. Patriarchal coercion triumphs, and she marries Bakri against her will. This can be attributed not only to patriarchy's hold on the lives of the young, but also to the complicity of the young themselves. Consider the conspiracy between grandfather and grandson, as Meheimeed submits to Hajj Ahmad's will and his own desire to be like Meryoud, abandons Maryam, and goes to the north. Maryam's death at the end of *Meryoud* is the death of a dream for a better future that Meheimeed and Mahjoub were able to glimpse. Meheimeed's final return to witness her death and carry her to her grave represents the climax of his narrative, such as it stands in the incomplete novel. In a sense, he buries his own dream together with the woman who once embodied it.

What is left for him is the bitterness expressed in the final scene, which depicts a reverie, daydream, or vision that resembles the first "relief after distress" dream in "The Doum Tree."[22] Lost in the desert and exhausted from walking, Meheimeed is met by Maryam, now transformed into an angel. Yet unlike the saints in other such dreams who relieve the faithful, she cannot offer Meheimeed any relief in this life—a life that he wasted because he "hesitated" (*B* 1996, 121). Instead, her incantatory words, which seem to be "coming down from the sky and surrounding me from all directions" (122), sum up once and for all the respective merits of son, father, and grandfather:

> "O Meryoud. You are nothing. . . . You have chosen your grandfather and your grandfather has chosen you because the two of you are most weighty in the scales of the people of the world. And your father is greater than both of you in the scales of Justice. He loved without growing weary, he gave without hope of any reward, and he sipped as a bird sips, and he lived as though continually about to travel, and he departed in a hurry. He dreamt the dreams of the meek, and he partook of the provisions of the poor; he was tempted by glory but he restrained himself, and when life called him—when life called him—"
>
> I said yes. I said yes. I said yes. But the way back was harder because I had *forgotten*. (122; emphasis added)

Unlike the faithful who are cured by the Prophet or a holy man through dream visions, Meheimeed cannot be saved until he "remembers"—but that event does not occur in *Meryoud*. The last word in the text, "forgotten," confirms the condition of amnesia from which he and his society continue to suffer.

---

22. The scene also alludes to the story of Moses and the prophet al-Khidr in the Qur'an (18: 61–83); see note 4 to chapter 2. Meheimeed's inability to follow Maryam because of his personal inadequacy parallels Moses' deficient knowledge and his failure to obey the instructions of al-Khidr, which disqualifies Moses as al-Khidr's companion and disciple. Maryam's statement, "You will not be able to keep up with me" (cf. Sura 18: 67) and the reference to "water" (*B* 1996, 121) are obvious allusions to the Qur'anic story.

"The Cypriot Man"

The composition of "The Cypriot Man" (originally published as "Al-rajul al-qubursi" in 1973 and revised in 1976) coincided at least with the writing of *Meryoud*, if not also that of *Dau al-Beit*, and is likely to have been intended as an episode in *Bandarshah*. The story displays the full development of the techniques that distinguish *Bandarshah* from Salih's previous works. All distinctions between dream, reality, and reverie disappear in "The Cypriot Man." Time and space, history and geography become reflections of psychic states, and characters become indistinguishable from their Others, who become the projection of their fears and desires. Nevertheless, in its fusion of the local with the international and the cosmic the story also represents a departure from *Bandarshah*. The short story refocuses on the contemporary reality of the Arab world in an international context. Here is found the only direct reference in Salih's fiction to Palestinian refugees and the 1967 Six Day War, and the most explicit statements on the convergence of racism, colonialism, religious prejudice, and misogyny. "The Cypriot Man" condenses those themes in the characterization of the titular character, a nightmare figure who is an amalgam of several literary and allegorical characters—Bandarshah, Mustafa Sa'eed, Mephistopheles, Death.

The story can be read as one of Meheimeed's frequent dream recollections in *Bandarshah*, but Meheimeed is younger, his career still unfolding. Meheimeed sees himself in the dream as Bandarshah, for he tells Taher Wad Rawwasi (with whom he has almost the same conversations reported in *Bandarshah*) that he was the man appearing and disappearing by the window in the mosque during the dawn prayer on the night of Maryam's burial. Furthermore, Meheimeed is tempted also by the Cypriot Man to become like Mustafa Sa'eed, a manipulator of racist stereotypes of Africans to seduce two American girls who, according to the Cypriot Man, would find Meheimeed's color "delight[ful]" ("CM" 1981a, 13). In the dream, Meheimeed recognizes such temptations as desires and unfulfilled potentials within himself that could cost him his soul (15). The battle between the armies of good and evil that Meheimeed perceives in the interplay of light and darkness on the surface of the water (13), and the horrible pains he suffers in his hotel room afterwards give symbolic expression to his anxiety about his *place* in the social, historical, and moral scheme of things.

That place is determined by, among other things, the setting: Nicosia, Beirut, and Wad Hamid. The outlying cities of London, Damascus, and Khartoum are not part of the setting but are mentioned as geopolitical reference points. The unnamed site of "the great tragedy" ("CM" 1981a, 14), Palestine, also looms large on the scene, which now encompasses four continents: Europe, Africa, Asia, and North America. Here, Meheimeed's identity is defined along a historical and geopolitical trajectory that spans the four points of the compass, with Nicosia as the middle point between North and South, East and West. This setting is significant both for its symbolic geography and for the fact that in 1972, the year before the first publication of the story, Cyprus was the scene of fighting between Muslim Turkey and Christian Greece. Meheimeed's presence in Nicosia reenacts the closing scene in *Season* when he swims across the bend of the Nile (the "center of chaos" as it is called in *Meryoud* [*B* 1996, 89]), in order presumably to clear his mind after he leaves Mustafa Sa'eed's library. It should be clear by now that middle points seem to have both a fascination all their own and a destabilizing effect on him. They are places where he confronts the "destructive forces" that echo within himself (*SMN* 1969c, 168), and reassess his position, his alliances, and his identity. It is there that he must overcome the chaos and find stability and peace. Since Meheimeed's rejection of Hajj Ahmad, Taher Wad Rawwasi comes to symbolize those things. It is for that reason that in his dream Meheimeed incongruously goes to meet Taher (who has never left Wad Hamid) in Nicosia. Taher "refused to visit me in London [the north]. And meeting him in Beirut [the east] exhausted me" ("CM" 1981a, 13). As shown earlier, Meheimeed consciously gravitates toward Wad Hamid (the South) and is willing to negate the importance of both his own experience in England and colonial history in general. Even in *Bandarshah,* he still hopes to find answers *only* in Wad Hamid, hence the novel's emphasis on "excavating" the village and its memory. Unconsciously, however, he is tormented by those realities which he represses and tries to "forget"; they return to assume horrific forms in his dreams. Note that the "return of the repressed" and "forgetting" are psychic operations that define the characterization of Meheimeed in *Season* and *Bandarshah,* respectively.

The Cypriot Man is thus called for no other reason except that he allegorizes those psychic forces and represents their projection onto symbolic geography. He is analogous to—perhaps a dream representation of—the deadly whirlpool at the bend of the Nile, where Meheimeed has almost drowned twice. Apart from that, there is nothing "Cypriot" about him; he defies all appearances (e.g., his age), assumes different shapes (like the Devil), and speaks with an all-Western accent: "Occasionally his voice was English with a sort of German accent. And at times he seemed to be French, and he used American words. . . . 'Some consider me Italian, others consider me Russian, and some, German, or Spanish' " ("CM" 1981a, 13). Reminiscent of Joseph Conrad's Kurtz, all of Europe and America contributed to the making of the Cypriot Man, who embodies all the racism and misogyny that have informed Western discourses on Africans, Arabs, Jews, and women. He thinks of women as a commodity for which he sets the price. He "loathes Jews" because "they play skillfully . . . [t]he game of death." Next in the degree of his hatred come African Americans, to whom he feels that he "must pay more attention." Then come the Arabs, who only "provoke laughter or pity. They submit easily, at least these days. It is not gratifying to play with them because it's one-sided." His hatred matches the degree of their defiance, and the more he hates a group, the more he enjoys their women (10). He seems, moreover, to have the supernatural power of the "evil eye," which destroys whatever he covets (11).

The Cypriot Man, like Mustafa Sa'eed and Bandarshah, embodies forms of evil to which Meheimeed has turned a blind eye—colonial, racist, and misogynist. Meheimeed also meets their victims: in "The Cypriot Man" these are the happy English family by the pool who share their joy with him, and the Palestinian woman who knocks on his door in Beirut and reminds him of "the great tragedy." He readily identifies with the English family; however, he is reluctant to hear the Palestinian refugee, and he soon becomes "occupied with his own personal tragedy" ("CM" 1981a, 14). The Palestinian woman has lost her eldest daughter to the conflict and is now dispossessed and homeless. She is nursing her baby and trying to tell him a story which he, usually an avid and attentive listener, does not want to hear and thus cannot report. In this way he participates in the conspiracy of silence against Palestinians; as Edward Said writes, "they are named, it is true, but are no more substantial than a phrase" (1980, 63).

The silenced narrative of the Palestinian woman (part of "the great tragedy") is substituted by the story of the father's death (Meheimeed's "personal tragedy"). To read "The Cypriot Man" in the context of, or as an episode in, *Bandarshah* is to interpret the death of the father allegorically as the loss of memory and of the sense of one's place in history. (Note that the Cypriot Man mocks Meheimeed by saying, "You, Your Excellency, realize your position in time and place" ["CM" 1981a, 13].) As such, the loss of the father and the loss of Palestine, which is the content of the Palestinian woman's untold narrative, are one and the same event, experienced on two levels. Throughout his life, Meheimeed has refused to recognize the connectedness of these levels. The Palestinian woman's "personal tragedy" (dispossession, exile, daughter's death) is causally linked to the "great tragedy" (the Six Day War). Her words may be erased within Meheimeed's narrative of his own personal tragedy (father's death), but they will nourish her baby (the future). Like Hawwa's in *Meryoud*, the Palestinian woman's motherhood holds the key to recovered memory.

In this way the allegorical scheme of *Bandarshah* fulfills itself: it is only through this alliance between "fathers" and "mothers" that the "conspiracy" of past and future against the present can be effectively broken. The allegory spells itself out on several levels. Socially, it signifies a critique of patriarchal hegemony and of masculinist construction of gender; only a society restructured along lines of equality and justice can face up to the challenges of the outside world. Ideologically, the allegory as restated in "The Cypriot Man" indicates that the local cannot be divorced from the pan-Arab, which in turn articulates itself in a transnational and cross-cultural context; while one form of nationalism has de-emphasized the particularity of the local, the latter in turn cannot be allowed to lead to regionalism and isolationism. Morally, the message is summed up in verses by al-Fayturi, which serve as an epigraph to the story:

> [The] world is not owned by those who own it,
> The richer of its inhabitants are her masters, the poor.
> The wise man is one who takes what it shyly gives,
> The heedless man is one who thinks things are merely things. ("CM" 1981a, 9)

The contrast between the father's simplicity and honesty and the mother's love on the one hand, and the various forms of corruption which the Cypriot Man lists in his closing speech—lust for power, vanity, and pride—underscore al-Fayturi's moral lesson. Most importantly, all of those aspects are connected in ways that should not be overlooked, so that any viable reform must necessarily be comprehensive.

F I V E

The Latest Writings

IN 1978, two years after the publication of *Meryoud,* Salih described the unfulfilled project of *Bandarshah* in a way that can bring the foregoing discussion to
a tentative conclusion:

> *Bandarshah* is an act of discovering a place over long periods of time. . . . The
> method here is that of an archaeologist. . . . As a writer, I had not understood
> *Bandarshah* clearly until work on *Meryoud* advanced. . . . Among the conclu-
> sions I have reached is that events recur in the one place. Generations lived and
> overcame, by different means, the circumstances of environment. But from a
> psychic point of view, it seems things will never change completely because "the
> place" has its own melody, charisma and tone. It is impossible to make a crack
> within this cosmic harmony which has its own compelling rules. To quote from
> *Bandarshah*: "The dead shall be buried without crying. And change will hap-
> pen as the seasons change in a temperate place." And there is a reference to a
> Qur'anic verse: ["It is not for the sun to overtake the moon, nor doth the night
> outstrip the day. They float each in an orbit" [36:39; Pickthall 316]. There is a
> system. The nearer you are to the system the more you understand it. Societies
> at certain periods of time think they are capable of reorganizing this system or
> initiating a new alternative. But it seems to me this is not [possible]. (*TSS* 1982,
> 31–32)

The peculiar thing in this passage is the extent to which the locale seems to take
precedence over all else—even the human element—so that protean things like
culture and ideology seem to be governed by the regularity of a cosmological
system that assigns a particular "melody" to each "place." If this borders on de-
terminism, it does not necessarily eliminate revolutionary change (for example,
Hosna Bint Mahmoud's revolt and the rebellion of Bandarshah's eleven
sons/slaves), insofar as change is part of the cosmic system. Yet change, not just
seasonal or natural but also sociopolitical and cultural, remains governed by
local conditions, which are cast now in positive terms of "melody," "charisma,"
and "cosmic harmony" instead of a sinister "conspiracy" of past and future
against the present. This seems to have been the shift in Salih's understanding of
the novel during the composition of its second part: a radical break with the past

173

is neither possible nor indeed desirable, and this law is as much sociological and historical as it is cosmological or mystical. It remains to be seen how Salih can re-assess Arab modernity from this perspective in the parts of the novel still to come.

This new vision, perhaps already discernible in embryonic form in "The Doum Tree of Wad Hamid," implies that no one can control the direction or outcome of social change. Intuitive as this may be, it refutes the paternalistic, hypocritical claims made by colonial administrations, postcolonial regimes, and neocolonial institutions (such as the World Bank/IMF) and structures of domi-nation (foreign aid, military coercion, and so on) that they know and do what is best for the "natives." In the Arab world since the *Nahda,* various traditionalist ideologies (conservative, reformist, fundamentalist), as well as secularist ones (liberal, nationalist, socialist), have adopted the same attitude toward the masses in an attempt to create new societies.

Still other questions arise from the novel's unfulfilled design and from Salih's comments on it. At what point does the archaeological excavation of the past and the search for the "melody" and "charisma" of the place turn into a form of nativism that makes the "conspiracy" between past and future against the present a self-fulfilling prophecy? Where should the line be drawn between critical investigation of, and paralyzing fixation on, tradition? How can the re-discovery of the heritage be prevented from turning imperceptibly into another form of fundamentalism? Fundamentalism, in the allegorical scheme of the novel, is one form of Arab postcoloniality that fosters tyranny and dictatorship; it is rejected in favor of a mystical conception of love (divine, paternal, maternal, fraternal, romantic, conjugal, philanthropic). It is possible to embrace this ethos (in Sufi fashion) on the individual level; however, it is simply too abstract a solu-tion to entrenched social, political, and economic problems. Might this not, in effect, signal to us that the "new writing" is unable to articulate a progressive ideology that can stem the rising tide of fundamentalism, dictatorship, and neo-colonial hegemony?

This perhaps partly explains Salih's switch from literature to journalism. In January 1989, after a decade of silence, he began contributing a regular column to London's Arabic-language weekly magazine, *Al-Majalla.* A few months later, on 30 June, when a military coup toppled Sudan's democratically elected government and brought the National Islamic Front to power, Salih emerged as one of the strongest voices denouncing the new regime (*RTS* 1997, 79–82). In one of the many articles he wrote on the subject over the following years, he stated forcefully that "a military coup against an elected government, however ill one may think of it, is no different from opening fire on worshippers in a mosque" (*Al-Majalla* 733 [27 Feb.-5 March 1994]: 94). (Here he was alluding to the massacre by Baruch Goldstein, an American-born West Bank settler, of twenty-nine Palestinian worshippers in the Abrahamic Sanctuary in Hebron on

25 February 1994.) Journalistic writing, with its directness and immediacy, is more effective for dealing with such events than allegory, symbolism, or myth making.

Is this, then, the end of the project of the "new writing"—at least for one of the most original and gifted contemporary writers, the "genius of the Arabic novel"? Has the ongoing and deepening crisis aborted the recovery of memory? In Sudan and elsewhere in the Arab world, have political repression, civil war, neocolonial intervention, the loss of social freedom, and the ravages of occupation, dispossession, massacres, and exile—the chaos that characters like Bandarshah, Meryoud, and the Cypriot Man allegorizes—rendered literature an unaffordable, bourgeois luxury? Perhaps, for Salih at least, the grand intellectual project of recovering memory cannot proceed at a time of social destruction; perhaps writing alone cannot change the material conditions of society; rather, to overcome amnesia the patient must first, like Dau al-Beit, awake from a coma.

All of this is, of course, highly controversial in itself, but this reading of what seems to be Salih's abandonment of literature is supported by various statements that his characters have made and that he himself has made in interviews. For example, in *Season*, Meheimeed, still a fresh Ph.D. in literature, becomes "furious" when Mustafa Sa'eed says to him, "We have no need of poetry here. It would have been better if you'd studied agriculture, engineering, or medicine" (*SMN* 1969c, 9). (Note that Mustafa reveals his hidden past by reciting English poetry and on several occasions recites and composes Arabic poetry.) As Amyuni observes, what Mustafa says to Meheimeed about poetry is "an exact replica of what Salih said at AUB about his own experience, twenty years later" (1985, 17), which was to express his "intimate feeling that the writer [is] somehow superfluous in our world" (16). Salih himself studied agriculture, then international relations; he could not bring himself to study literature, even though that is what he loved and what his professors at the university advised him to do (*RTS* 1997, 44–45), because he "grew up in the thirties and forties when [his] country had no need for writers, although there is a tradition of scholarship in Sudan. It rather needed doctors, engineers and teachers" (LAUB 1980a, 14). And even though he has showered praise on poets and devoted many of his weekly articles in *Al-Majalla* to commenting on al-Mutanabbi, al-Jahiz, Yusuf Idris, Hamid al-Khawwad, Jorge Amado, René Depestre, Ghazi al-Qusaibi, and others, the value Salih sets on his own literary achievement is far less than what modesty calls for (back cover of *RTS*). He has even made statements about his aversion to the writing process itself (IM 207, 218; *RTS* 111–17).

In addition to political commentary and literary criticism, his articles in *Al-Majallah* have also focused on topics like colonial history in Africa (including, obviously, Sudan), Asia, and Australia (a series of articles on the conditions and mythology of the Aborigines); the Sudanese civil war; the slave trade; socioeconomic conditions in East Asia (for example, prostitution in Bangkok); literacy in the Arab world; and the perennial anti-Arab racism of the Western media. Many of these topics are intimately related to the themes of his fiction. His choice of journalism as a medium is perhaps comparable to Naguib Mahfouz's and Ousmane Sembene's use of the cinema to reach those who cannot or do not read their novels.

Yet in 1993 Salih agreed, at the request of Egypt's Al-Ahram Center for Translation and Publishing, to write a short story for the collection *Mukhtarat min al-qisas al-qasira fi 18 baladan 'arabiyyan* (A selection of short stories from 18 Arab countries). The resulting story, "Yawm mubarak 'ala shati' Umm Bab" (A blessed day on the coast of Umm Bab), was Salih's first published work of fiction in seventeen years. It does not seem to be part of the Wad Hamid Cycle, at least in its present form: set in a coastal area of the Qatari desert and the city of al-Madina in Saudi Arabia, the story is populated by characters whose national origin is unspecified. It is significant, after the exclusive regional focus of *Bandarshah,* that Salih was coming out of his novelist's retirement, so to speak, in order to take part of a pan-Arab literary project, and that his contribution to it focused exclusively—for the first time ever in Salih's fiction—on Arab countries other than Sudan. Yet the story retains the cross-cultural, intercontinental frame of reference that prevails in *Season* and "The Cypriot Man," once again situating Arab history in relation to Africa, Asia, and Europe.

The story focuses on the young girl Rabab, the only character given a name. Two narrators take turns: Rabab's father, who speaks in the first person, and an unidentified third-person narrator. The events take place during a family picnic on a beach on the Persian Gulf coast called Umm Bab, a few hours' drive from Doha; a flashback describes the highly unusual meeting and immediate marriage, ten years earlier, of Rabab's parents in al-Madina, the city where the Prophet Muhammad settled after he fled Mecca, and the first capital of the nascent Islamic state, where his shrine is located. "Al-Madina" is also an Arabic term for "the city" (for which the Persian word is *bandar*); thus the birthplace of the Islamic state and of Islamic civilization merges both semantically and metaphorically with the city as conceptualized in *Bandarshah.* In this way the choice of setting ties cultural revival as the goal of Arabs since the *Nahda* to the holy site that witnessed the birth of their civilization.

In al-Madina, where they visit the Prophet's mosque after completing the rites of 'umra, or minor pilgrimage, Rabab's parents meet for the first time following the dawn prayer, and immediately recognize one another as soul mates. They are married by evening, and the wife gives birth to Rabab seven months later (note the mystical symbolism of the number seven), also in al-Madina. This surreal encounter sets the tone for Rabab's life, and for a story that begins to take on the aura of a dream. Born in a holy place as the product of love, the child seems divinely guided: she "came complete, wearing her own name like a gown: Rabab, like a cloud within a cloud [*rabab* is Arabic for white

clouds]. And she brought us new names [i.e., Abu Rabab and Umm Rabab].
. . . When we brought her to that place [the Prophet's shrine], her strange eyes
gleamed, and she listened to a voice that called to her alone" ("BDCUB" 1993,
161). The motifs of the dawn prayer, dream/vision, the mystical/divine voice
heard by a chosen individual, and the theme of peace and harmony with all
creation, all establish an unmistakable link between "A Blessed Day" and *Bandarshah,* notwithstanding the differences in setting and character. Such themes
and motifs seem no longer to embody the "melody" of a single place. They
characterize a mode of Being-in-the-World—a world with a spiritual center,
al-Madina.

Nine years later and in another setting, the same mood of beatitude prevails
on the "blessed day" when the family goes for a picnic to the coast of Umm
Bab. The story opens with the father questioning Rabab about the source of
pieces of wood drifting to shore. The precocious child's answers, as she identifies the places where the wood came from, reveal knowledge far beyond her
years ("She learned as though she was remembering things she had already
known before" ["BDCUB" 1993, 161]); furthermore, they recall a network of
historical trade relations—Qatar, Sweden, Oman, Bahrain, Zanzibar—that establish an international frame of reference that recalls the symbolic geography
of "The Cypriot Man." The two stories, in a sense, mirror each other structurally and thematically: a conversation between a first-person narrator and an
interlocutor who seems to be endowed with supernatural powers (the Cypriot
Man and Rabab) frames the narrator's own spiritual state in a Manichean world
(confusion and loss in the earlier story, certainty and serenity in the later one).
The narrator's state of mind reflects the dominant force embodied by the central character. Here, Rabab's unusual birth in a union based on love and spirituality and her uncanny, intuitive wisdom (a "Babylonian priestess" who speaks in
tongues [162] and quotes medieval Muslim Sufis [164]) set her up as the
Cypriot Man's moral counterpart. And just as the Cypriot Man seems to possess
an evil power that destroys whatever he touches, so does Rabab galvanize her
surroundings into a mystical force field that harmonizes with the order of the
universe. As she speaks of her desire to go on pilgrimage and to pray in the holy
places, a large camel descends from a nearby hill and wades into the sea, followed by a herd of camels. She explains that the camels are performing ablutions, and when they emerge from the water and sit still on the shore, that they
are praying (165). Moments after the camels leave, a group of women appear,
perform their ablutions in the sea, then line up to pray in the same spot the
camels had just occupied.

These mystical, dreamlike events counterpoint the nightmarish world of the
Cypriot Man and confirm the belief in a divine order that governs the universe.
This is the message of the Qur'anic verse that Salih quotes in the above-cited in-
terview. The divine system governs nature and is intuited by all living things, ex-

cept for the majority of human beings who have not reached the state of spiritual purity that allows them to perceive it.

But an element of chaos intrudes for a moment on the harmonious world of "A Blessed Day." Reminiscent of the metaphysical conflict between Good and Evil thematized in "The Cypriot Man" through the structural contrast between the nightmarish title character and the quasi-saintly figure of Taher Wad Rawwasi, here also is a contrast between mystical harmony—which extends to include all of nature—and the forces of destruction, though much diminished. If "The Cypriot Man" depicted a Manichean world in which Meheimeed's soul was at stake, "A Blessed Day" portrays a world where Good has succeeded in keeping Evil at bay. The representative of chaos and disruption, the counterpart to Rabab, is a young man on a jet ski who appears on the horizon at the moment when the camels are about to descend toward the sea for their "ablutions":

> [T]he camel did not move, for at that moment a loud sputtering like that of heavy artillery exploded, and a young man riding a metal horse with a tail-like stream of water gushing from its backside appeared. His hair disheveled and his face glowering, he looked like a demon. "God protect us," said Rabab. The young man turned his jet ski sharply around, causing it to capsize. He fell in the water and, not knowing how to swim, he kept sinking and popping up. We fetched him and his ski out, and he put it in his car and disappeared. The calm returned, the sky smiled, and the light brightened on the horizon. ("BDCUB" 1993, 163)

The description of the young man's appearance recalls "The Wedding of Zein," in which Seif ad-Din functioned as Zein's antagonist before his "conversion" or spiritual rebirth at the hands of Haneen. Likewise in "A Blessed Day," the young man is Rabab's counterpart, both in his effect on his surroundings—obnoxious, disruptive, disturbing—and in his inability to swim, which functions here and elsewhere in Salih's fiction as a metaphor for spiritual loss. In contrast, Rabab's body "glides over the surface of the water like a ray of light reflected on crystal" as she swims for more than a mile offshore, and on her return she protests laughingly to her worried father, "Were you afraid I might drown? Does water drown in water?" ("BDCUB" 1993, 162). By the same token, being rescued from drowning, as Meheimeed is at the end of *Season* and the young man is in "A Blessed Day," signifies being given another chance.

In the final scene of "A Blessed Day," husband, wife, and daughter enter the water together and swim into the twilight until "they nearly ascended into the heavens" ("BDCUB" 1993, 166). This impressionistic image recalls Dau al-Beit as last seen by Mahmoud and Hasab ar-Rasoul, "suspended between sky and earth, surrounded by a green glow. . . . in the heart of the red dusk" (*B* 1996, 80). Dau al-Beit drowns after saving his two companions, but his self-sacrifice makes him a martyr and ushers him literally into the heavens. In "A Blessed Day," the happy family also nearly enter the heavens at the same time of day—just before sunset. It should be clear now that this is an uncertain time of day; the Cypriot Man tempts Meheimeed to his diabolic world as "darkness and light were struggling around the pool and on the surface of the water" ("CM" 13). Thus in "A Blessed Day" the danger of spiritual loss once more presents itself, as the father gradually drifts off by himself, leaving wife and daughter behind. At that moment he is in danger of drowning. As wife and daughter call him back (the way Maryam calls Meheimeed), the large camel, who seems to have been keeping a watchful eye on the family, begins to descend the hill once more, heading toward the sea as if to save the man. The father's momentary confusion results from his mistaking the source of a mysterious voice that seemed to call him toward the horizon (hence toward death), "then as though he woke up, he realized that the summoning voice came from behind. He *remembered* the woman and the child, so he turned around and swam with his full force. He was like a garment pulled in opposite directions between the sea and the shore. The voices of the woman and the child came to him as one voice that sang to him the song of lasting purity in the time of migration." When he returns to shore and his wife expresses her fear that he might have drowned, Rabab declares, "No, he had to come back. Our call comes from another place, in another time. Come on, let's return to *the city*" ("BDCUB" 1993, 166—emphasis added). The father is in danger once he "forgets" his wife and daughter; at that point, he loses direction and heads toward perdition. But the wife and daughter help him "remember" and guide him back to safety and to "the city," and so the story ends with the attainment—by "blessed" individuals on a "blessed day"—of the symbolic object of quest in *Bandarshah*.

The story presents a vision valorizing love, faith, and harmony—the predominant values in *Meryoud*—over ruthless ambition, conflict, and masculine violence—which prevail in *Dau al-Beit* and "The Cypriot Man." The prized values in *Meryoud* and "A Blessed Day" are voiced by, or embodied in, young visionary girls (Maryam, Rabab) and saintly women (Hawwa, Umm Rabab, the women praying by the sea), who guide the male characters they associate with (Taher Wad Rawwasi, Abu Rabab) to a state of inner peace that makes them at home in the world—except for those, like Meheimeed, who fail to heed their lesson. This sums up Salih's unrelenting critique, throughout his work, of male-dominated society and of patriarchal ideology. The characterization of Maryam and Rabab also valorizes the optimism and potential of youth (recall that in *Season,* Meheimeed's daughter is called Hope), something that accords well with Salih's acute sense (echoed in "The Doum Tree," *Season,* and *Bandarshah*) that the intellectuals of his own and the following generation have failed their country in profound ways (*RTS* 1997, 116).

Salih's latest story offers the consolation of mysticism in return for a retreat from the irredeemably fallen world of materiality, of history. This classic stance toward the world, which is common to all mystical traditions, proposes an alternative form of religiosity to fundamentalism, whose pitfalls were dramatized in *Bandarshah,* as well as an ethical alternative to the radical secularism that, for many progressive Muslim intellectuals in the 1990s, lies at the root of Western imperialism:

> Secularism is not the separation of religion and the state, as propagated in both western and Arab writing. Rather, it is the removal of absolute values—epistemological and ethical—from the world such that the entire world—humanity and nature alike—becomes merely a utilitarian object to be utilized and subjugated. From this standpoint, we can see the structural similarity between the secular epistemological vision and the imperialist epistemological vision. We also realize that imperialism is no more than the exporting of a secular epistemological paradigm from the western world, where it first emerged, to the rest of the world. (Elmessiri 1994, 403)

This view opens the way for a critique of Arab modernity that dissolves the old debates, deadlocked since the *Nahda,* over the supposedly possible choice between "tradition" and "modernity."[1] It represents a new, progressive trend in Arab-Islamic thought during the 1990s that is able to look beyond the violent clash between radical fundamentalism and Western imperialism that threatens to dominate the twenty-first century.

As for Salih's own work, the mystical retreat proposed in "A Blessed Day" should be read dialectically in the context of his twin careers as a novelist and a columnist who can intervene directly in the sphere of politics. To the extent that his fiction seems to withdraw from the material world of history and politics, Salih seems to withdraw from fiction. It remains to be seen how this dialectical tension might be resolved.

---

1. Elmessiri has elaborated this reading in a number of books; see, for example, *Ishkaliyyat al-tahayyuz, Al-lugha wa al-majaz,* and especially *Al-ʿilmaniyya al-juzʾiyya wa al-shamila.* In *Unveiling Traditions,* Anouar Majid uses Elmessiri's critique of secularism as a point of departure for a critical reading of postcolonial theory's secularist foundation, which renders it "inattentive to the question of Islam in the global economy [and] exposes its failure to incorporate different regimes of truth into a genuinely multicultural global vision" (Majid 2000, 19). See also my review of Majid's book (Hassan 2001).

Appendix
References
Index

Appendix

Chronology of the Wad Hamid Cycle

ALTHOUGH IT IS FIRMLY ANCHORED in modern Arab history, few dates are mentioned in Salih's fiction. In preparing this cumulative chronology of the entire Wad Hamid Cycle, I have revised Raja' Ni'ma's chronology of *Season* while accounting more fully for all the historical and narrative clues found in Salih's novels and short stories. Many of the dates are approximate, but I believe they give a good sense of the temporal frame of Salih's fiction. One must note, however, that some contradictory clues make the assignment of dates to events almost impossible, and that many of those clues are found in characters' reminiscences about the past and may, therefore, be subject to their imperfect memory. For example, Mustafa Sa'eed says that he spent thirty years in England, and that he left London while Europe was preparing itself for unprecedented violence. We know for certain that he arrived there at the age of fifteen, and that he was born in 1898, which means he went to England in 1913. If he is correct in saying that he spent thirty years there, he must have left in 1943, less than two years before the end of World War II, not before the war started. Ni'ma estimates that he left in 1933, immediately after his release from prison, but that does not fit with his count of thirty years, nor with his other statement that Europe was preparing for war when he left. Therefore, I suggest that he left toward the end of 1941 or the beginning of 1942, around the time of the Arcadia Conference (December 22, 1941-January 14, 1942) in which twenty-six countries pledged to fight the Axis until victory and signed the United Nations Declaration. This estimate best reconciles Mustafa's statements: at that time he would have spent twenty-eight or twenty-nine years in England, and left when the Allies were pulling their forces together before the final years of the war. This suggests that he did not leave England until seven or eight years after his release from prison; this period of time, like the seven years he spent traveling around the world, does not form part of his narration and is not accounted for elsewhere in the novel.

Bandarshah presents a more challenging case. The fusion of history, myth, and allegory, and the repetition of character names from generation to generation, pose problems for the chronologist. Other difficulties arise from contradictory accounts; for example, Meheimeed says in *Meryoud* that his grandfather is fifty years older than himself, even though in *Season* his own calculation indicates that the age difference is sixty-three years. In *Dau al-Beit* it is established that Isa Wad Dau al-Beit and Hajj Ahmad are of equal age, that Meryoud is a year older than Meheimeed, and that sixty years separate the births of Isa and his grandson. This implies that sixty-one years is also the age difference between Meheimeed and Hajj Ahmad, despite what Meheimeed says in *Meryoud,* and close enough to what he says in *Season.* Many of the dates assigned here are therefore approximate. Those difficulties notwithstanding, the following chronology will, I hope, allow the reader to situate the events of the Cycle within their historical context.

1860s	(early)	Dau al-Beit arrives in Wad Hamid.
1865		Dan al-Beit dies.
		His son Isa is born three months after the death of Dau al-Beit.
		Hajj Ahmad, Meheimeed's grandfather, is born.
1870s	(early)	Isa Wad Dau al-Beit is given the nickname "Bandarshah."
1898	(June)	Battle of Atbara occurs.
	(August 16)	Mustafa Sa'eed is born.
	(September)	Battle of Umm Durman and conquest of Sudan occur.
1907		Mustafa (age nine) goes to school.
1910		Mustafa (age twelve) goes to Cairo.
1913		Mustafa (age fifteen) goes to England.
1916		The Arab Revolt takes place.
		Britain and France sign the Sykes-Picot Agreement to divide the Arab world.
1917		The Balfour Declaration is announced.
1922		Mustafa (age twenty-four) is appointed lecturer in economics at London University.
		The League of Nations grants a mandate to Britain and France.
1922 (October)– 1923 (February)		Mustafa calls himself by five different names and lives with five women simultaneously, promising to marry each of them.
1923		Mustafa (age twenty-five) meets Jean Morris.
1926		Mustafa (age twenty-eight) marries Jean.
1927		Meryoud, grandson of Isa Wad Dau al-Beit, is born.

1928	Mustafa becomes president of the Society for the Struggle for African Freedom. Mustafa kills Jean and goes to prison. Meheimeed is born.
1935	Mustafa is released from prison. Events in "A Handful of Dates" take place.
1941 or 1942	Mustafa leaves England to roam Europe and Asia before returning to Sudan.
1942	Meryoud negotiates calf sale with Hajj Ahmad. Bandarshah and Meryoud are murdered.
1946	Meheimeed (age eighteen) goes to England.
1948	Mustafa (age fifty) settles in Wad Hamid. State of Israel is established; first Arab-Israeli war occurs.
1953	Sudanese Parliament is formed. Meheimeed (age twenty-five) returns from England. Mustafa (age fifty-five) disappears seven months later.
1953–55	Meheimeed marries a Sudanese woman and has a daughter, Amal (Hope).
1956	Sudan gains its independence. Suez Crisis occurs. Hosna is forced to marry Wad Rayyes, kills him, and commits suicide. Narrative time of *Season* ends.
1956–58	Events in "The Doum Tree of Wad Hamid" take place.
1950s (late)	Zein's wedding takes place.
1967 (June 5–11)	Arab-Israeli War occurs and Israel occupies the West Bank and Gaza Strip.
1967-early 1970s	Events in "The Cypriot Man" take place.
1973 (October)	Arab Israeli War occurs.
1970s (early to mid)	Bakri's sons overthrow Mahjoub's gang. Meheimeed retires early and returns to Wad Hamid. Narrative time of *Bandarshah* begins.

References

Abbas, Ali Abdallah. 1985. "The Father of Lies: The Role of Mustafa Sa'eed as Second Self in *Season of Migration to the North.*" In *Tayeb Salih's* Season of Migration to the North: *A Casebook,* edited by Mona Takieddine Amyuni. Beirut: American Univ. of Beirut Press.

'Abdalla, Muhammed Khalafalla. 1999. "Mustafa's Migration from the Sa'id: An Odyssey in Search of Identity." *Edebiyt* 10, no.1:43–61.

Abu-Zayd, Nasr. 1983. "Al-dhakira al-mafqudah wa al-bahth 'an al-nass." *Fusul* 4, no.1 (October-December):199–205.

———. 1990. *Mafhum al-nass: Dirasa fi 'ulum al-qur'an.* Cairo: Al-hay'a al-misriyya al-'ama lil-kitab.

———. 1994. *Al-mar'a fi khitab al-azma.* Cairo: Dar Nusus.

———. 1995. *Al-Nass, al-sulta, al-haqiqa.* Casablanca: Al-Markaz al-thaqafi al-'arabi.

Accad, Evelyne. 1985. "Sexual Politics: Women in Tayeb Salih's *Season of Migration to the North.*" In *Tayeb Salih's* Season of Migration to the North: *A Casebook,* edited by Mona Takieddine Amyuni. Beirut: American Univ. of Beirut Press.

Ahmad, Aijaz. 1992. *In Theory: Classes, Nations, Literatures.* London: Verso.

Ahmad, 'Uthman Hassan. 1976. "Al-qaryah fi '*Urs al-Zayn* hiya al-sudan bi qaba'ilihi al-mutanafira." In *Al-Tayyib Salih: 'abqari al-riwaya al-'arabiyya,* edited by Ahmad Sa'eed Muhammadiyya et al. Beirut: Dar al-'awda.

Ahmed, Leila. 1992. *Women and Gender in Islam.* New Haven: Yale Univ. Press.

al-Afghani, Jamal al-Din. 1883. "L'islamisme et la science." *Journale des débats* 18 May.

———. 1903. *Al-Rad 'ala al-dhahiriyyin.* Cairo: n.p.

Ali, Abbas Ibrahim. 1972. *The British, the Slave Trade and Slavery in the Sudan, 1820–1881.* Khartoum: Khartoum Univ. Press.

Allam, Mahdy, Anwar Luqa, and Ahmad Badawi, eds. 1958. "Muqaddimah" to al-Tahtawi, *Takhlis al-ibriz fi talkhis bariz.*

Allen, Roger. 1995. *The Arabic Novel: An Historical and Critical Introduction.* 2nd ed. Syracuse: Syracuse Univ. Press.

Amin, Qasim. 1894. *Les Égyptiens: Réponse à M. le duc d'Harcourt.* Paris: n.p.

———. [1899] 1992. *The Liberation of Women.* Translated by Samiha Sidhom Peterson. Cairo: The American Univ. in Cairo Press.

Amyuni, Mona Takieddine, ed. 1985. *Tayeb Salih's* Season of Migration to the North: *A Casebook.* Beirut: American Univ. of Beirut Press.

Ashcroft, Bill, Gareth Griffiths, and Helen Tiffin. 1989. *The Empire Writes Back: Theory and Practice in Post-Colonial Literatures.* London: Routledge.

al-'Ashmawi, Muhammad Sa'id. 1979. *Usul al-shari'a al-isalamiyya.* Cairo: Dar Sina.

―――. 1987. *Al-islam al-siyasi.* Cairo: Dar Sina.

―――. 1990. *Al-khilafa al-islamiyya.* Cairo: Dar Sina.

Badawi, M. M. 1970. *"The Lamp of Umm Hashim*: The Egyptian Intellectual Between East and West." *Journal of Arabic Literature* 1:145–61.

―――. 1993. *A Short History of Modern Arabic Literature.* Oxford: Clarendon Press.

Bakhtin, Mikhail. 1981. *The Dialogic Imagination: Four Essays.* Translated by Caryl Emerson and Michael Holquist. Austin: Univ. of Texas Press.

―――. 1984. *Problems in Dostoevsky's Poetics.* Translated by Caryl Emerson. Minneapolis: Univ. of Minnesota Press.

―――. 1984. *Rabelais and His World.* Translated by Helene Iswolsky. Bloomington: Indiana Univ. Press.

Barakat, Halim. 1969. *'Awdat al-ta'ir ila al-bahr.* Beirut: Dar al-Nahar. In English, *Days of Dust.* 1983. Trans. Trevor Le Gassick. Washington, D.C.: Three Continents Press.

Berkley, Constance E. 1979. "The Roots of Consciousness Molding the Art of Tayeb Salih: A Contemporary Sudanese Writer." Diss., New York Univ.

Bloom, Harold. 1973. *The Anxiety of Influence.* New York: Oxford Univ. Press.

Boullata, Issa. 1980. "Encounter between East and West: A Theme in Contemporary Arabic Novels." In *Critical Perspectives on Modern Arabic Literature,* edited by Issa Boullata. Washington, D.C.: Three Continents Press.

Burton, Richard. [1885] 1934. "Terminal Essay." *The Book of a Thousand and One Nights.* Vol. 3. Translated by Richard Burton. New York: Heritage Press.

Cartelli, Thomas. 1999. *Repositioning Shakespeare: National Formations, Postcolonial Appropriations.* London: Routledge.

Cleaver, Eldridge. 1968. *Soul on Ice.* New York: Dell.

Conrad, Joseph. 1988. *Heart of Darkness.* 3rd ed. Edited by Robert Kimbrough. New York: Norton.

Eagleton, Terry. 1991. *Ideology: An Introduction.* London: Verso.

Elmessiri, Abdelwahab. 1994. "The Secular Epistemological Vision," *American Journal of Islamic Social Scientists* 11 (fall): 403.

―――. 1998. *Ishkaliyyat al-tahayyuz: Ru'ya ma'rifiyya wa da'wa lil-ijtihad. Al-muqadimma: Fiqh al-tahayyuz.* 3rd ed. Herndon, Virginia: International Institute of Islamic Thought.

―――. 2002. *Al-lugha wa al-majaz: Bayn al-tawhid wa wihdat al-wujud.* Cairo: Dar al-shuruq.

―――. 2002. *Al-'ilmaniyya al-juz'iyya wa al-shamila: Namudhaj tafsiri jadid.* Cairo: Dar al-shuruq.

Fanon, Frantz. 1967. *Black Skin, White Masks.* Translated by Charles Lam Markmann. New York: Grove Press.

Foda, Farag. 1985. *Qabl al-suqut.* Cairo: n.p.

Freud, Sigmund. 1953–74. *The Standard Edition of the Complete Psychological Works of Sigmund Freud.* 24 vols. Edited and translated by James Strachey and Anna Freud. London: Hogarth Press.

Gates, Henry Louis, Jr. 1988. *The Signifying Monkey: A Theory of African-American Literary Criticism.* New York: Oxford Univ. Press.

Ghattas-Soliman, Sonia. 1991. "The Two-Sided Image of Women in *Season of Migration to the North.*" In *Faces of Islam in African Literature,* edited by Kenneth W. Harrow. Portsmouth, NH: Heinemann.

Ghazoul, Ferial. 1996. *Nocturnal Poetics:* The Arabian Nights *in Comparative Context.* Cairo: The American Univ. in Cairo Press.

Ghazoul, Ferial, and Barbara Harlow, eds. 1994. *The View from Within: Writers and Critics on Contemporary Arabic Literature. A Selection from* Alif: Journal of Comparative Poetics. Cairo: American Univ. in Cairo Press.

al-Haggagi, Ahmad Shams al-Din. (1983) 1994. "The Mythmaker: Tayeb Salih." In *The View from Within: Writers and Critics on Contemporary Arabic Literature. A Selection from* Alif: Journal of Comparative Poetics, edited by Ferial Ghazoul and Barbara Harlow. Cairo: American Univ. in Cairo Press.

al-Hakim, Tawfiq. 1939. *'Usfur min al-sharq.* Cairo: Maktabat Misr.

Haqqi, Yahya. 1944. *Qindil Umm Hashim.* Cairo: Dar al-Ma'arif. In English, *The Saint's Lamp and Other Stories.* 1973. Translated by M. M. Badawi. Leiden: E. J. Brill.

Harb, Ahmad Musa. 1986. "Half-Way Between North and South: An Archetypal Analysis of the Fiction of Tayeb Salih." Diss., Univ. of Iowa.

Harlow, Barbara. 1979. "Othello's Season of Migration." *Edebiyt* 4, no. 2:157–75.

Hassan, Waïl S. 2001. "Alternatives to Secular Modernity: A Review of Anouar Majid's *Unveiling Traditions: Postcolonial Islam in a Polycentric World.*" *Jouvert: A Journal of Postcolonial Studies* 6 (Fall):1–2. http://social.chass.ncsu.edu/jouvert/v6i1–2/con61.htm

———. 2002. "Postcolonial Theory and Modern Arabic Literature: Horizons of Application." *Journal of Arabic Literature* 33, no.1:45–64.

Hourani, Albert. 1970. *Arabic Thought in the Liberal Age, 1789–1939.* Reprint. London: Oxford Univ. Press.

Husayn, Taha. 1938. *Mustaqbal al-thaqafa fi misr.* Cairo: Matba'at al-ma'arif.

Ibn al-Athir, 'Aziz al-Din. 1970. *Usd al-ghaba fi ma'rifat al-sahaba.* Cairo: Maktabat al-sha'b.

Ibn Kathyr, Isma'il. 1969. *Tafsir al-Qur'an al-'adhim* 4 vols. Beirut: Dar al-turath al-'arabi.

———. 1980. *Al-bidaya wa al-nihaya* 14 vols. Beirut: Maktabat al-ma'arif.

Ibn al-Muqaffa', 'Abdullah. 1965. *Kitab Kalila wa Dimna.* Beirut: Dar maktabat al-hayah.

Ibn Sirin. n.d. *Muntakhab al-kalam fi tafsir al-ahlam.* Cairo: 'Isa al-Babi al-Halabi.

Idris, Suhayl. 1954. *Al-hayy al-latini.* Beirut: Dar al-adab.

Idris, Yusuf. 1961. "Shaykh Shaykha." In *Akhir al-dunya.* Cairo: Maktabat Misr. In English, "The Freak." In *"The Cheapest Nights" and Other Stories.* Translated by Wadida Wassef. London: Heinemann, 1978.

Khairallah, As'ad. 1985. "The Travelling Theater or the Art of Entertaining a Doomed Caravan with Amusing Stories." In *Tayeb Salih's* Season of Migration to the North: *A Casebook,* edited by Mona Takieddine Amyuni. Beirut: American Univ. of Beirut Press.

al-Khanji, 'Abd al-Rahman. 1982. "Al-lugha, al-zaman, da'irat al-fawda." *Fusul* 2, no.2 (January–March): 261–65.

Khouri, Elias. 1982. *Al-dhakira al-mafquda.* Beirut: Mu'assasat al-abhath al-'arabiyya.

Krishnan, R. S. 1996. "Reinscribing Conrad: Tayeb Salih's *Season of Migration to the North.*" *The International Fiction Review* 23 nos. 1–2:7–15.

Kristeva, Julia. 1982. *Powers of Horror: An Essay on Abjection.* Translated by Leon Roudiez. New York: Columbia Univ. Press.

———. 1991. *Strangers to Ourselves.* Translated by Leon Roudiez. New York: Columbia Univ. Press.

Lacan, Jacques. 1977. *Écrits: A Selection.* Translated by Alan Sheridan. New York: Norton.

Laroui, Abdallah. 1976. *The Crisis of the Arab Intellectual: Traditionalism or Historicism?* Translated by Diarmid Cammell. Berkeley and Los Angeles: Univ. of California Press.

Macaulay, Thomas Babington. 1952. "Indian Education: Minute of the 2nd of February, 1835." In *Macaulay: Prose and Poetry,* edited by G. M. Young. London: Rupert Hart-Davis.

Majid, Anouar. 2000. *Unveiling Traditions: Postcolonial Islam in a Polycentric World.* Durham: Duke Univ. Press.

Mahfouz, Naguib. 1947. *Zuqaq al-midaq.* Cairo: Maktabat Misr. In English, *Midaq Alley.* Translated by Trevor Le Gassick. New York: Anchor Books, 1992.

Makdisi, Saree S. 1992. "The Empire Renarrated: *Season of Migration to the North* and the Reinvention of the Present." *Critical Inquiry* 18, no.4 (summer):804–20.

———. 1995. " 'Postcolonial' Literature in a Neocolonial World: Modern Arabic Culture and the End of Modernity." *boundary 2* 22, no.1 (spring):85–115.

Malti-Douglas, Fedwa. 1982. "Al-'aniasir al-turathiyya fi al-adab al-'arabi al-hadith: Al-ahlam fi thalath qisas." *Fusul* 2, no.2 (January–March):21–29.

Meyer, Stefan. 2001. *The Experimental Arabic Novel: Postcolonial Literary Modernism in the Levant.* Albany: SUNY Press.

Muhammadiyya, Ahmad Sa'eed, et al., eds. 1976. *Al-Tayyib Salih: 'abqari al-riwaya al-'arabiyya.* Beirut: Dar al-'awda.

al-Nabulsi, 'Abd al-Ghani Ibn Isma'il. n.d. *Ta'tir al-anam fi ta'bir al-manam.* Cairo: 'Isa al-Babi al-Halabi.

Naqd, Muhammad Ibrahim. 1995. *'Alaqat al-riq fi al-mujtama' al-sudani.* Cairo: Dar al-thaqafa al-jadida.

Nasr, Ahmad A. 1980. "Popular Islam in al-Tayyib Salih." *Journal of Arabic Literature* 11:88–104.

Nazareth, Peter. 1982. "Out of Darkness: Conrad and Other Third World Writers." *Conradiana* 14 (December):173–87.

Nerval, Gérard de. 1980. *Voyage en Orient.* 2 vols. Paris: Garnier-Flammarion.

Ni'ma, Raja'. 1986. *Sira' al-maqhur ma'a al-sulta: Dirasa fi al-tahlil al-nafsi li-riwayat al-Tayyib Salih* Mawsim al-hijra ila al-shamal. Beirut: R. Ni'ma.

Peters, Barbara Diane. 1989. *Power Relations and Conflict in Selected Works of Tayeb Salih: Implications for a New History.* Diss., Univ. of Wisconsin-Madison.

Pickthall, Mohammed Marmaduke. 1930. *The Meaning of the Glorious Koran*. New York: Mentor.

al-Qur'an al-karim. Cairo: Matba'at al-Halabi.

al-Ra'i, Ali. 1976. "Zaghruda tawila li al-hayah." In *Al-Tayyib Salih: 'abqari al-riwaya al-'arabiyya*, edited by Ahmad Sa'eed Muhammadiyya et al. Beirut: Dar al-'awda.

Said, Edward. 1978. *Orientalism*. London: Penguin Books.

———. 1980. *The Question of Palestine*. New York: Vintage.

———. 1983. "Introduction." Haleem Barakat, *Days of Dust*. Translated by Trevor Le Gassick. Washington, D.C.: Three Continents Press.

———. 1989. Foreword to *Little Mountain,* by Elias Khoury. Translated by Maia Tabet. Minneapolis: Univ. of Minnesota Press.

———. 1993. *Culture and Imperialism*. New York: Knopf.

Salih, Tayeb. [1968] 1969a. "The Doum Tree of Wad Hamid." In *The Wedding of Zein and Other Stories*. Translated by Denys Johnson-Davies. London: Heineman. Originally published in Arabic as "Dawmat Wad Hamid."

———. 1969b. "A Handful of Dates." In *The Wedding of Zein and Other Stories*. Translated by Denys Johnson-Davies. London: Heineman. Originally published in Arabic as "Hafnat tamr."

———. 1969c. *Season of Migration to the North*. Translated by Denys Johnson-Davies. Boulder, Colo.: Lynne Rienner, 1997. Originally published in Arabic as *Mawsim al-hijrah ila al-shamal*.

———. 1969d. "The Wedding of Zein." In *The Wedding of Zein and Other Stories*. Translated by Denys Johnson-Davies. Boulder, Colo.: Lynne Rienner, 1997. Originally published in Arabic as "'Urs al-Zayn."

———. [1968] 1969e. *The Wedding of Zein and Other Stories*. Translated by Denys Johnson-Davies. Boulder, Colo.: Lynne Rienner, 1999. Contains the novella "The Wedding of Zein" (originally published in Arabic as "'Urs al-Zayn"); "The Doum Tree of Wad Hamid" (originally published in Arabic as "Dawmat Wad Hamid"); and "A Handful of Dates" (originally published in Arabic as "Hafnat tamr").

———. [1960] 1970a. "Dawmat Wad Hamid" (The doum tree of Wad Hamid). In *Dawmat Wad Hamid: sab' qisas*. 3rd printing. Beirut: Dar al-'Awda.

———. 1970b. *Dawmat Wad Hamid: sab' qisas* (The doum tree of Wad Hamid: Seven short stories). 3rd printing. Beirut: Dar al-'Awda. Contains "Muqadimat" (Preliminaries); "Risala ila Eileen" (A letter to Eileen); "Hakadha ya sadati" (So it was, gentlemen); "Idha ja'at" (If she comes); "Nakhla 'ala al-jadwal" (A date palm by the stream); "Hafnat tamr" (A handful of dates); and "Dawmat Wad Hamid" (The doum tree of Wad Hamid).

———. [1957] 1970c. "Hafnat tamr" (A handful of dates). In *Dawmat Wad Hamid: sab' qisas*. 3rd printing. Beirut: Dar al-'Awda.

———. [1961] 1970d. "Hakadha ya sadati" (So it was, gentlemen). In *Dawmat Wad Hamid: sab' qisas*. 3rd printing. Beirut: Dar al-'Awda.

———. [1961] 1970e. "Idha ja'at" (If she comes). In *Dawmat Wad Hamid: sab' qisas*. 3rd printing. Beirut: Dar al-'Awda.

———. [1962] 1970f. "Muqaddimat" (Preliminaries). In *Dawmat Wad Hamid: Sab' qisas.* 2nd ed. Beirut: Dar al-'Awda. Includes five sketches: "Al-ikhtibar" (The test); "Ughniyat hubb" (Love song); "Susan wa 'Ali" (Susan and Ali); "Laki hatta al-mamat" (Yours till death); and "Khutwa ila al-amam" (A step forward).

———. [1953] 1970g. "Nakhla 'ala al-jadwal" (A date palm by the stream). In *Dawmat Wad Hamid: sab' qisas.* 3rd printing. Beirut: Dar al-'Awda.

———. [1960] 1970h. "Risala ila Eileen" (A letter to Eileen). In *Dawmat Wad Hamid: sab' qisas.* 3rd printing. Beirut: Dar al-'Awda.

———. [1962] 1970i. "'Urs al-Zayn" (The wedding of Zein). 3rd printing. Beirut: Dar al-'Awda.

———. 1971a. *Bandar Shah: Dau al-Bayt* (Bandarshah: Dau al-Beit). Beirut: Dar al-'Awda.

———. [1969] 1971b. *Mawsim al-hijrah ila al-shamal* (Season of migration to the north). Reprint. Beirut: Dar al-'Awda.

———. [1973] 1976a. "Al-rajul al-qubrusi" (The Cypriot man). *Majallat al-Dawha.* January: 105–8.

———. 1976b. Interviews in *Al-Tayyib Salih: 'abqari al-riwaya al-'arabiyya,* edited by Ahmad Sa'eed Muhammadiyya et al. Beirut: Dar al-'awda.

———. [1976] 1978. *Maryud: al-juz' al-thani min Bandar Shah* (Meryoud: The second part of Bandar Shah). 2nd printing. Beirut: Dar al-'Awda.

———. 1980a. Lecture delivered at the American University in Beirut on May 19, 1980. In *Tayeb Salih's Season of Migration to the North: A Casebook,* edited by Mona Takieddine Amyuni. Beirut: American University of Beirut Press, 14–16.

———. 1980b. "A Letter to Eileen." Translated by N. S. Doniach. *Journal of Arabic Literature* 11:76–79. Originally published in Arabic as "Risala ila Eileen."

———. 1981a. "The Cypriot Man." Translated by Constance E. Berkley. In *Sixteen Sudanese Short Stories,* edited by Ossman Hassan Ahmed. Washington, D.C.: Office of the Cultural Counselor, Embassy of the Democratic Republic of Sudan. Originally published in Arabic as "Al-rajul al-qubrusi."

———. 1981b. "A Date Palm by the Stream." Translated by Denys Johnson Davies. *Azure: The Review of Arabic Literature, Arts and Culture* 8:21–24. Originally published in Arabic as "Nakhla 'ala al-jadwal."

———. 1982. *Tayeb Salih Speaks: Four Interviews with the Sudanese Novelist.* Translated and edited by Constance E. Berkley and Osman Hassan Ahmed. Washington, D.C.: Office of the Cultural Counselor, Embassy of the Democratic Republic of Sudan.

———. 1993. "Yawm mubarak 'ala shati' Umm Bab" (A blessed day on the coast of Umm Bab). In *Mukhtarat min al-qisas al-qasira fi 18 baladan 'arabiyyan* (A selection of short stories from 18 Arab countries). Edited by al-Tahir Ahmad Makki. Cairo: Markaz al-Ahram li al-tarjama wa al-nashr.

———. 1996. *Bandarshah* (Bandar Shah). Translated by Denys Johnson-Davies. London: Kegan Paul International. Composed of two parts, *Dau al-Beit* and *Meryoud,* originally published separately in Arabic as *Bandar Shah: Dau al-Beit* (Bandarshah: Dau al-Beit) and *Maryud: al-juz' al-thani min Bandar Shah* (Meryoud: The second part of Bandar Shah).

———. 2002. Interview by author. July.

Salih, Tayeb, and Talha Jibril. 1997. *'Ala al-darb ma'a al-Tayyib Salih: Malamih min sira dhatiyya* (On the road with Tayeb Salih: Outline of an autobiography). Rabat: Tub lil-istithmar wa al-khadamat.

Shaheen, Mohammad. 1985. "Tayeb Salih and Conrad." *Comparative Literature Studies* 22, no.1:156–71.

Shakespeare, William. 1974. *Othello.* In *The Riverside Shakespeare.* Boston: Houghton Mifflin.

———. *The Tempest.* In *The Riverside Shakespeare.* Boston: Houghton Mifflin.

———. *Hamlet.* In *The Riverside Shakespeare.* Boston: Houghton Mifflin.

Sharabi, Hisham. 1988. *Neopatriarchy: A Theory of Distorted Change in Arab Society.* New York: Oxford Univ. Press.

Sidahmed, Abdel Salam. 1996. *Politics and Islam in Contemporary Sudan.* New York: St. Martin's Press.

Siddiq, Muhammad. 1978. "The Process of Individuation in Al-Tayyib Salih's Novel *Season of Migration to the North.*" *Journal of Arabic Literature* 9:67–104.

———. 1986. " 'Deconstructing' *The Saint's Lamp.*" *Journal of Arabic Literature* 17:126–45.

Subhi, Muhyyiddin. 1976. "Aqasis al-Tayyib Salih." In *Al-Tayyib Salih: 'abqari al-riwaya al-'arabiyya,* edited by Ahmad Sa'eed Muhammadiyya et al. Beirut: Dar al-'awda.

Spurr, David. 1993. *The Rhetoric of Empire: Colonial Discourse in Journalism, Travel Writing, and Imperial Administration.* Durham: Duke Univ. Press.

al-Tabari, Abu-Ja'far Muhammad. 1984. *Jami' al-bayan 'an ta'wil al-Qur'an.* Beirut: Dar al-fikr.

Taha, Mahmoud Muhammad. 1996. *Al-risala al-thaniyya min al-islam.* Reprint. London: Sudanese Human Rights Organization.

al-Tahtawi, Rifa'a. 1993. *Takhlis al-ibriz fi talkhis bariz.* Reprint. Cairo: Al-hay'a al-misriyya al-'amma lil-kitab.

al-Tarabishi, George. 1977. *Sharq wa gharb, rujula wa unutha: Dirasat fi azmat al-jins wa al-hadara fi al-riwayya al-'arabiyya.* Beirut: Dar al-Tali'a.

Torgovnick, Marianne. 1990. *Gone Primitive: Savage Intellects, Modern Lives.* Chicago: Univ. of Chicago Press.

Trimingham, J. Spencer. 1965. *Islam in the Sudan.* London: Frank Cass & Co.

'Uthman, 'Abd al-Fattah. 1990. *Al-sira' al-hadari fi al-riwaya al-'arabiyya: ru'ya tahliliyya naqdiyya.* Cairo: Dar al-'Adala.

West, Cornel. 1993. *Race Matters.* Boston: Beacon Press.

Young, Robert. 1995. *Colonial Desire: Hybridity in Theory, Culture and Race.* London: Routledge.

Žižek, Slavoj. 1989. *The Sublime Object of Ideology.* London: Verso.

———. ed. 1994. *Mapping Ideology.* London: Verso.

Index

Abbas, Ali Abdallah, 116
'Abdalla, Muhammed Khalafalla, 91
'Abdalla, Yahya al-Tahir, 133
'Abd al-Rahman, Omar, 8
'Abd al-Raziq, 'Ali, 5
'Abd al-Wahab, Muhammad, 5
'Abduh, Muhammad, 3–4
Abu Nuwas: exoticization of, 96; his poetry,
    111, 134, 141, 142–43, 144, 161; and
    Omar Khayyam, 77, 142; translation of,
    142n. 10
Abu Zayd, Nasr: context of his work, 4,
    132n. 2; on gender, 135, 165n. 20; on
    language, 131; his methodology 8–9; on
    the *Nahda*, 4–5, 15, 51; persecution of, 8,
    132
Accad, Evelyne, 92
Achebe, Chinua, 38, 87
Adonis (Ali Ahmad Sa'id), 132
al-Afghani, Jamal al-Din, 4, 50
Ahmad, Aijaz, 9–10
Ahmed, Leila, 114n. 15
Ahmed, Osman Hassan, 55–56, 77
Ali, Abbas Ibrahim, 77n. 7
Ali, Muhammad, 1
Allam, Mahdy, 1n. 2
Allen, Roger, 12n. 5
Allenby, Edmund, 96, 110
Althusser, Louis, 9
Amin, Qasim, 4, 50n. 1
Amyuni, Mona Takieddine, 16, 118,
    175
Antun, Farah, 5
Arabism. *See* Arab nationalism
Arab-Israeli wars, x, xi, xii, 7, 88, 116, 129,
    130, 169, 171, 174–75

Arab nationalism, x, xi, xii, 3, 5, 6–7,
    171–72, 174. *See also* under *Bandarshah*
    and *Season of Migration to the North*
al-'Araoui, Abdallah. *See* Laroui, Abdallah
Arnold, Matthew, 9
Ashcroft, Bill, 82n. 1
al-'Ashmawi, Muhammad Sa'id, 8, 132n. 2
al-Azhar, 1, 8, 69

Badawi, M. M., 85, 112n. 14, 133
Bakhtin, Mikhail: on discourse 35, 45, 51,
    82–83, 90, 139; on the novel, 9, 10–13,
    145
Balfour Declaration, 92
Bandarshah (Tayeb Salih), xii, 129–72;
    allegory in, 135, 136–38, 139, 141,
    144–45, 153, 161, 164, 171, 175;
    amnesia in, 44, 130–34, 137, 145–48,
    168, 171, 179; and Arabic narrative
    discourse, 12, 145; and Arab nationalism,
    129–31, 134, 139–40, 141;
    characterization in, 32n. 4, 44, 58–59,
    61, 67, 68, 70, 75; and colonialism,
    130–31, 137, 145; and "The Cypriot
    Man," 171; dreams in, 153–60; and
    fundamentalism, 180; gender in, 21, 64,
    134–35, 153n. 13, 157–58, 160, 161–68,
    179; imagery and symbolism in, 26, 42n.
    10, 57, 73, 143, 178–79; incompleteness
    of, 129, 173–75; Meheimeed as narrator
    in, 15, 33, 34, 36, 52, 116, 118, 124,
    125, 126, 127, 128, 136, 137–38,
    145–46, 150–51, 154, 169, 170;
    modernity in, 130–34, 161–62;
    motherhood in, 149–50, 164–65;